Global
Fracture

Global Fracture

The New International Economic Order

New Edition

Michael Hudson

Pluto Press

LONDON • ANN ARBOR, MI

First published in 1977 by HarperCollins Publishers

This new edition first published 2005 by Pluto Press
345 Archway Road, London N6 5AA
and 839 Greene Street, Ann Arbor, MI 48106

www.plutobooks.com

British Library Cataloguing in Publication Data
A catalogue record for this book is available from the British Library

ISBN   0 7453 2395 2 hardback
ISBN   0 7453 2394 4 paperback

Library of Congress Cataloging in Publication Data applied for

10   9   8   7   6   5   4   3   2   1

Produced for Pluto Press by
Chase Publishing Services, Fortescue, Sidmouth, EX10 9QG, England
Printed and bound in Canada by Transcontinental Printing

Contents

CONTENTS

III. THE NEW INTERNATIONAL ECONOMIC ORDER

Preface

This book is a successor to *Super Imperialism: The Economic Strategy of American Empire* (1972), which analyzed the evolving methods by which the United States has dominated its Free World allies economically, politically and militarily. As the Cold War pushed America's balance of payments into massive deficit, forced it off gold, and indebted it to foreign governments beyond its willingness to repay, the United States enacted increasingly protectionist trade and investment policies while continuing to inflate the world economy with excess dollars. These tactics finally led other industrial nations and Third World countries to press for a new international economic order. Europe's closing of its foreign exchange markets in 1973, its repudiation of Kissinger's proposed New Atlantic Charter, the Middle East War and the subsequent quadrupling of oil prices, followed by foreign moves to achieve economic self-sufficiency in place of their previous dependency, all represent attempts to break America's hold on the world economy. A North-South conflict has been superimposed on the growing tensions among the leading industrial nations. Europe, Japan and America, each in their own way, are jockeying for position vis-à-vis each other and the newly self-assertive Third World. The resulting diplomacy reflects new values and implies new seats of economic power, characterized by regional alliances that may leave the United States isolated within its own hemisphere.

Whatever the resolution of the forces that have recently been set in motion, they connote an ending of the postwar world order that enabled the United States to tap foreign wealth with almost no constraint. For better or worse America is finding itself thrown back upon its own relatively high-cost resources in the face of inadequate domestic savings and reduced ability to secure from abroad the wealth it is no longer producing at home. The present book describes the principles underlying this global fracture and outlines its most probable economic and political consequences.

Introduction to the New Edition

Global Fracture (1977), the sequel to *Super Imperialism* (1972), describes how debtor countries and raw-materials exporters sought to create a New International Economic Order (NIEO) in the 1970s. A program more of nationalist regimes than of the political left, the NIEO advocated a non-Communist New Deal to improve the terms of trade for raw materials and build up agricultural and industrial self-sufficiency so as to avoid trade dependency and the foreign debt trap.

This program today has become a forgotten interlude. Its optimism has been replaced by the financial austerity and privatizations imposed by the World Bank and International Monetary Fund (IMF) since the 1980s, after Margaret Thatcher was elected Prime Minister of Britain in 1979 and Ronald Reagan won the American presidential election a year later. Over the past two decades foreign countries have been stripped of the public enterprise whose development had been a central plank of the NIEO. Rather than seeking an alternative to the Washington Consensus and its U.S.-centered pattern of global development, even Europe has embraced a monetarist austerity hitherto adopted only by hapless debtor countries.

The term Washington Consensus was coined in 1989 by a World Bank economist, John Williams, to signify America's policy response to the collapse in the prices of Third World bonds and bank loans after Mexico's default in 1982 triggered the Latin American "debt bomb." The hallmark of this neoliberal (that is, pro-creditor and pro-monopoly) program was a monetary drain that has obliged debtor countries to sell off their public domain on credit to insiders (crony capitalism) and foreign buyers, while "freeing capital flows," that is, permitting capital flight without limit. As one economic reporter recently observed in the *Financial Times*: "Mixed with mismanagement and corrupt governance, the Washington Consensus managed to undermine a dozen economies in a decade. Countries like Argentina and Indonesia found that the speed and greed of modern finance was a pipeline for every sort of instability."[1]

Already in the 1970s American diplomats sought to impose a division of labor in which other countries were to import U.S. high-technology, high-wage and high-profit goods and services in exchange for raw materials and consumer goods made with low-wage labor, and to become dependent on American farm surpluses rather than feeding themselves.

The 1980s saw the World Bank and IMF use their creditor leverage to impose an era of privatization that dismantled and sold off public enterprises and social infrastructure, leaving economies much further indebted and more foreign-owned than anyone imagined in the 1970s. Soviet Communism was vanquished with the accession of Boris Yeltsin in Russia in 1991. Countries not obeying the Washington Consensus faced the prospect of being isolated as international pariahs, subject to sanctions such as those imposed on Cuba, Libya and North Korea. Meanwhile, the United States has retained its agricultural and industrial protectionism but opposed such policies abroad. This double standard has thwarted the drive by other countries to achieve their own national self-determination in industry, agriculture and trade.

No General de Gaulle or comparable European or Third World leader emerged to challenge the U.S.-centered global order. Labour Parties in New Zealand, Australia and Britain (and most recently Brazil under Lula) have imposed neoliberal policies that no non-labor government could have enforced without being thrown out of office. (What are labor parties for in today's world, after all, if not to betray their constituencies?) Even Russia was persuaded to adopt the Washington Consensus by the mid-1990s, dollarizing its economy as its central bank followed IMF dictates and refrained from paying public employees. Only the United States has inflated its economy by running twin government budget deficits and balance-of-payments deficits, obtaining a free ride beyond the expectations of anyone in the 1970s.

Nobody had speculated on what it would mean for other countries not to promote a more equitable and symmetrical alternative to the American-centered order, or what it would mean specifically for economies to recycle their foreign-exchange earnings to finance the U.S. Government's federal budget deficit, as much of Asia and Europe have done. The natural expectation is that a nation cannot get something for nothing, as the exploited parties will soon catch onto the game. But as the modern science of advertising has demonstrated, people can be convinced that what is bad for them actually is good. It is all a question of how to frame their decision-making process.

In Japan, the nation that at one point loomed as the major potential economic rival to the United States, politicians sandbagged their economy by agreeing to the Plaza and Louvre Accords of 1985 and 1986. These agreements committed Japan and Germany to lower their interest rates and create financial bubbles, for no better reason than to facilitate low interest rates so as to promote U.S. financial expansion that followed the 1981 tax cuts that made real-estate speculation and junk-bond takeovers effectively exempt from income taxation. The takeover movement helped inflate a financial bubble, coupled with an unprecedented credit creation to finance asset-price inflation in the 1990s.

The dollar standard had arisen without much forethought. American diplomats insisted on veto power in any international organization they joined, so as to protect their nation against policies that might impinge on its interests. After the gold-exchange standard ended in 1971, the United States used this go-it-alone power to turn its balance-of-payments deficit into a tax on the rest of the world, obtaining its imports for paper promises to pay at some future date, at low rates of interest.

Chapter 2 of *Global Fracture* describes the dilemma with which America confronted the central banks of Europe to Japan and China. Whereas America was the world's major creditor nation in 1945, it is now the world's largest debtor. Yet unlike other debtors, it has not had to forfeit its autonomy. Rather, other countries have had to adjust their economies to the U.S. payments deficit. If they refuse to lend their trade surpluses to the U.S. Government, their currencies will rise and the dollar will fall, threatening to price their exports out of world markets. Powerless to use their economic strength for anything more than to become the major buyers of Treasury bonds to finance the U.S. federal budget deficit, foreign central banks have enabled America to cut its own tax rates (at least for the wealthy), freeing savings to be invested in the stock market and property boom.

How the world's economic philosophy has been inverted since 1945

On the deepest economic plane the U.S. Government has come to represent the interests of finance capital. Its economic dominance can be traced to its emergence during World War I as the world's major creditor. The government subsequently has used its influence—and veto power in any international organization it joins—to move the heady ideals voiced in the aftermath of World War II away from a regime of currency stability to sinking exchange rates for debtor countries (including in recent decades the United States itself); from full-employment objectives to financial austerity; from using budget deficits to fuel economic expansion to fiscal surpluses, at least for countries outside the United States; from a symmetrical spirit of international law and trade agreements to a double standard favoring the United States; from currency values being determined mainly by foreign trade and investment to currency speculation creating sharp and rapid fluctuations in exchange rates; from government regulation to creditor planning and control over economies; from the Cold War isolation of Russia to co-opting its leaders through neoliberalism; and ultimately from the Cold War into an international class war waged by industrialists against labor, and even more by creditors against debtors.

Probably it was inevitable that finance would have come to rule the modern world, regardless of what nation was in the lead. Although the early power of finance was nurtured by government, the financial sector's growing strength has led it to unseat its parent. The primary mode of accumulation has become financial, enabling investment bankers to replace government planners and wrest control from landed property and industrial capital.

This shift has been accompanied by a neoliberal ethic that opposes traditional social values, above all the long-held hope that governments would lead the way toward more egalitarian societies via public regulation, progressive taxation and infrastructure spending. As President Reagan expressed neoliberal philosophy: "Government is not the solution to our problems; government is the problem." Although this philosophy portrays itself as resting on the Enlightenment values of individualism and equality of opportunity, it places unprecedented power in the hands of a financial class whose philosophy is anything but democratic and progressive. This helps explain why it was first introduced by the Chicago Boys in Chile under General Pinochet after 1974.

For centuries the idea of economic progress depicted rising productivity as enhancing living standards. Economic theory focused on how profits made on producing consumer goods would be spent on capital goods to produce yet more output. But today's austerity programs imposed by the IMF and World Bank have shrunk domestic markets and dislodged exchange rates. Debtor countries have been forced to relinquish control over their fiscal and financial policy, permitting foreign investors to rush in like vultures to appropriate their assets at distress prices as their currencies collapse.

The Achilles' heel of proposals to create a better economic order was the inability to cope with the twists that modern finance has taken. Rather than funding new productive powers, bankers lend mainly against property and public monopolies already in place, headed by real estate and corporate stocks and bonds. The richest lode of new assets since 1980 has been the public domain, whose privatization has turned government enterprises into financial vehicles to generate interest, dividends and capital gains.

What is remarkable is that while the United States has acted as a creditor nation toward the Third World, it has used quite a different economic diplomacy toward Europe and Asia. Having become the world's largest debtor nation, America itself refuses to follow what the Washington Consensus dictates to other debtor countries. It supports its own employment and growth, by running federal budget deficits, inflating its capital markets, reducing its interest rates and trying to lower its exchange rate to make its producers more competitive.

When the dollar's value fell against the euro, sterling and the yen after the 1985 Plaza Accords, European and Asian central banks holding these dollars suffered a twofold loss. In addition to a lower value of the U.S. Treasury's dollar bonds in terms of their own currencies, these securities yielded only about 4 or 5 percent—a far cry from the 45 percent rate that deficit countries such as Argentina and Brazil had to pay by the end of the decade.

These losses suffered by foreign central banks on their dollar holdings serve as a measure of modern international financial exploitation. It is the cost of the failure of creditor nations and others to develop an alternative to the Treasury-bill standard. Meanwhile, freed from having to finance their own government deficit, U.S. investors put their money into the bubbling stock and real estate markets.

If economic models and geopolitical game theory accurately described countries as acting in their own self-interest, a New International Economic Order would have emerged in one form or another as a system of negotiated checks and balances in the 1970s. There was widespread hope that low-income countries might catch up with the world's industrial creditor nations. A parallel belief was that world trade and finance should be symmetrical, enabling all countries to pursue similar policies rather than suffering from a double standard. All countries could provide their own credit, for instance, rather than leaving this as the monopoly of a single nation at the expense of others.

The problem with this ideal was a growing recognition that symmetrical development along the lines pioneered first by Europe and then by America would involve rising raw-materials prices, and that countries would aim at achieving economic self-sufficiency by producing their own food and manufactures rather than remaining dependent on imports. Also, if Europe had an alternative to the dollar, Americans would have to finance their own government's budget deficit. U.S. interest rates would rise, while foreign treasuries could create their own credit rather depending on U.S. consumer demand, investment outflows and foreign military spending as the "engine of growth."

These perceptions prompted the Washington Consensus to be imposed, an economic order whose objectives, principles and policy precepts are in opposition to a NIEO and indeed, antithetical to those held almost universally a generation ago.

From currency stability to sinking exchange rates for debtor countries

In 1945 the United States opposed currency depreciation. The argument over the British Loan that year aimed at preventing Britain from establishing a competitive postwar exchange rate. The fear was that the Sterling Area and other countries might protect their economies against America's industrial and agricultural superiority by returning to the beggar-my-neighbor tactics of the 1930s. Devaluation of sterling had to be postponed until 1949, and currency stability was built into IMF prescriptions. The United States ran a heavy payments surplus but was not obliged to adjust, any more than other countries were allowed to devalue.

The U.S. balance of payments moved into deficit starting with the Korean War in 1950. By 1971 overseas military spending had forced America off gold and the dollar was devalued by 10 percent. Meanwhile, U.S. officials no longer feared the downward drift of sterling, given Britain's badly managed economy. They also saw that the Southern Hemisphere's social backwardness was locking it into the status of a raw-materials exporter and supplier of low-wage consumer goods. Latin America had dismantled its nascent industry, while its ex-colonial agriculture was based on absentee-owned plantations producing export crops rather than family farming producing grain and other food for the region's growing population. Its economies have become so export-oriented that devaluation alone would not suffice to change its trade patterns. It would merely reduce dollar prices for exports, along with the international price of domestic real estate, stocks and bonds—and for the public domain being sold off.

In recent years the IMF routinely has imposed devaluation on debtor countries in an attempt to reduce domestic purchasing power. This is supposed to leave more output available to export to pay foreign creditors. What is devalued in practice is mainly the price of labor, because prices for raw materials and capital goods are dollarized, as are foreign debts. The effect is to make exports cheaper and imports (especially of food) more costly, as each dollar of exports buys fewer and fewer imports. IMF planners claim that this will shift resources from domestic production to the export sector.

Debtor countries must provide more and more exports for each unit of foreign debt,[2] as devaluation impairs the Third World's terms of trade while increasing the debt burden in terms of domestic currency. The effect is to prevent debtors from working their way out of debt. Their unpaid balances are rolled over to grow exponentially, throwing them even further into dependency on the IMF and World Bank.

The NIEO sought to improve the terms of trade, but did not tackle the problems of land reform and backward economic institutions called for more progressive systems of taxation and income distribution. Proposals for a NIEO also never tackled the problem of debts that had mounted up beyond the ability of countries to pay. Such shortcomings reflect the degree to which the NIEO aimed at merely marginal amelioration within the context of the existing institutions rather than recognizing the need for more far-reaching structural transformation.

Regional economic groupings that did emerge, most notably the European Community, have been organized under monetarist principles. The European Central Bank is committed not to finance more than marginal budget deficits, regardless of employment conditions.

From full-employment objectives to financial and fiscal austerity

Roosevelt's New Deal was followed by postwar Keynesian fiscal policy endorsing budget deficits to promote full employment. This also was the objective of Keynes's proposed Clearing Union and of the International Trade Organization (ITO) proposed at Havana in 1948. Since the 1980s, however, the IMF and World Bank have demanded fiscal austerity and heavy taxation (of labor and industry, not finance and land), while dismantling protective tariffs and subsidies such as those the U.S. Government routinely has given to American farmers since 1933.

As noted above, austerity plans deliberately create unemployment that blocks wage levels from rising. The hope is that this will squeeze out more exports to pay foreign creditors. There is little thought of developing domestic markets and modernizing economies. Under monetarist direction neither Third World countries nor Europe were to achieve full employment. They are supposed to rely on American consumers rather than their own citizens to supply "demand." Full employment is to be ensured only for the United States.

In this respect the advice that the IMF and World Bank give to debtor countries is like that of a parasite telling the host to give the intrusive *rentier* all the revenue it demands for its own growth, neglecting that of the host. To make debtor countries "good investment markets," the IMF demands that taxes be raised—not on finance, real estate or other business, but on labor.

Devaluation holds down the price of labor regardless of union agreements in domestic currency, while privatization enables the traditionally unionized public-sector labor force to be replaced with non-union workers. High domestic taxation, coupled with low employment and purchasing power, shrinks the domestic market and reduces investment, making even less output available for export. And policies to hold down wage levels slow the growth of labor productivity, which requires rising educational, health and dietary standards. On a national scale the effect of mean-spirited austerity programs is to increase trade dependency and hence the balance-of-payments deficit, pushing countries even more deeply into debt and dependency.

These destructive effects may seem strange for ostensibly free-market philosophy to promote. The explanation is that the term "free-market" has become almost synonymous with dismantling government and replacing it with planning by global financial managers, whose business involves loading down economies with debt while "solving" the problem by dismantling and selling off public enterprises.

Few national leaders pressing for a NIEO showed an interest in improving labor's remuneration. Most plans were nationalistic rather than social-democratic, and no alternative economic theory yet has been put forth to counter the Chicago School monetarism that has spread throughout the world since the 1980s. It has taken the abject failure of the Washington Consensus reformers in Russia in recent years to spur thoughts of shifting the tax burden off labor and onto land and finance capital.

From budget deficits to fiscal surpluses (outside of the United States)
Worried that the cessation of military demand would lead to unemployment after World War II, governments were persuaded to inject purchasing power into economies by running budget deficits. But today the IMF directs economies to run budget surpluses so as to "absorb" local purchasing power and divert output to export markets. (So much for Say's Law, which posits that on an economy-wide basis, payments to employees are spent on buying the output they produce.)

One might think that the postwar epoch would have learned the lesson that governments should denominate debts in their own currency. But the Washington Consensus promotes dollar borrowing with central-bank guarantees. In post-Soviet Russia even domestic deficit spending was supposed to be backed with dollar reserves. This policy denies indebted economies of using the traditional means of eroding the national debt burden by gradually inflating away their purchasing power. The value of dollarized debt is out of their control, becoming heavier (in domestic-currency terms) as their inflation rates rise and their currencies fall in value.

It is deemed to be inflationary to create domestic credit but not to borrow abroad in hard currency, on the specious logic that foreign bankers will not lend for risky or bad purposes. The reality is that it is no more inflationary for governments to create their own credit than to leave this to private-sector bankers. In fact, public credit tends (if not corrupt) to be created for more social, long-term purposes aimed at raising living standards and promoting employment.

The financial sector claims that it is good for central banks to be "independent" and not answerable to elected governments and hence to voters. In practice, central bank independence turns out to be a euphemism for dependence on the Washington Consensus, whose control over fiscal and monetary affairs prescribes self-defeating policies that reward creditors at the expense of debtors, while permitting only the United States to run large and chronic budget deficits.

From neo-protectionism to neoliberal economics

The world seemed to be moving beyond laissez faire in 1945, and the NIEO seemed poised to usher in a neo-protectionist era (as described in Chapter 12, "The Ending of Laissez Faire"). By the 1970s hardly anyone expected to see the backlash of neoconservative "market fundamentalism" that was about to occur in the 1980s. Instead of promoting government power, today's fine print of the WTO aims at elevating finance capital over governments. In political terms, checking the government's regulatory power, public enterprise and taxation has turned the planning process over to financial managers.

The World Bank and IMF originally were empowered to lend only to governments, and hence were obliged to work with them. This caused complaints in the 1950s from economists advocating land reform. Nearly all the World Bank reports urged family-based food production, which required land reform in oligarchic former colonies. But the Bank claimed that it was powerless to impose reforms on client countries, and most of its agricultural loans were for large plantation projects to produce export crops.

Since 1980, however, the World Bank has not been at all shy at demanding privatization, deflation and other oligarchic policies. Today the Bank devotes its efforts to "nation building," a euphemism for the monetarist philosophy that blocks governments from raising living standards and breaking free of foreign finance capital. What began on the far-right periphery in Chile under General Pinochet in 1974 has now become mainstream policy.

It is a starkly creditor-oriented policy. Debtors throughout history have forfeited their property to foreclosing creditors, but today entire economies are told to begin selling off their land and mineral rights, along with government monopolies in railroads and airlines, power, water, gas, telephones and broadcasting in the public domain, capped by the privatization of Social Security. Given the financial austerity dictated by the IMF and World Bank, such sell-offs must be made primarily to foreigners, who cause a chronic balance-of-payments drain by "repatriating" their subsequent earnings.

Although the United States remained highly protectionist, its diplomats sought to block foreign governments from supplying credit to agriculture and industry on concessionary terms. Its own government had been doing this for a generation, but U.S. officials realized that financial charges are the largest cost of modern production, funded as it is by interest-bearing debt. The fact that socialist economies did not charge interest or rent was viewed as giving them a cost advantage. They alone could conduct planning along purely engineering lines using subsidized prices and virtually free credit and land use instead of having to give priority to financial pay-offs and other payments to *rentiers*.

American fears that such governments might "interfere with markets" led it to scuttle proposals to create an ITO and to exclude the Soviet Union and other centrally-planned economies from membership in the World Bank and IMF. Foreign countries that set out to emulate U.S. policies by subsidizing their production and trade were isolated (Cuba and China), destabilized or overthrown (Iran, Guatemala and Chile).

From symmetrical international law to a double standard favoring the United States

Trade negotiations have foundered on America's agricultural subsidies and quotas that block Third World economies from developing their own food production. U.S. refusal to relinquish the farm protectionism that has been "grandfathered" into trade agreements has left little to negotiate, as the remaining trade issues seem marginal by comparison. U.S. support of "free markets" rests on U.S. Government manipulation and support of its own domestic market.

There is a further fear that America's go-it-alone policy will lead it to ignore the international agreements it signs. Steel is a notorious example, most recently in 2002 when Pres. Bush sought to attract voters in Pennsylvania and other steel-producing states by imposing illegal import quotas (*viz*. Chapter 11, "America's Steel Quotas Herald a New Protectionism").

A similar double standard emerged in the sphere of foreign investment. Despite the rising U.S. balance-of-payments deficit, America blocked foreigners from buying control of its banks, airlines, military and technology companies. OPEC governments were told in the 1970s that they could use their dollars only to buy small marginal shares of major U.S. companies. In the 1980s Japan was permitted to invest only in overpriced real estate, movie studios or troubled companies, while the United States demanded that foreign economies sell their own commanding heights.

The most striking double standard since the 1970s has been America's ability to pursue a debtor and a creditor strategy simultaneously. The United States is a debtor vis-à-vis Europe and Asia, but remains a creditor vis-à-vis "developing nations," that is, economies fallen into the debt trap and food dependency rather than really developing. As described in *Global Fracture* (p. 257):

> America's strategy in the face of the New International Economic Order is to render it no more than a tentative scenario, and to reestablish the pre-1973 state of affairs wherever possible. The Treasury-bill standard is to be reinstated while gold, sterling or a Eurocurrency are rejected as viable alternatives. . . . American export prices are to be supported as foreign countries continue to depend on U.S. grain, arms and aircraft, in payment for which Third World countries are to compete among themselves once again to export their raw materials at falling terms of trade. . . . U.S. economic strategy is to continue drawing upon foreign resources in order to sustain growth in its living standards and government spending.

A major U.S. fear is that foreign countries might expand their own monetary and credit systems through Keynesian budget-deficit policies of the sort that the United States has been running all along. Domestic money and credit creation would free foreign countries from dollar dependency on foreign capital, while land reform and subsidies to promote self-dependency in food would reduce U.S. grain exports.

This is precisely what the Washington Consensus opposes. The double standard, after all, provides a free ride for the U.S. economy, as well as for creditors in client oligarchies.

From foreign trade and investment to currency speculation

Trade and financial dependency were deemed to be part of an economically efficient global specialization of labor and credit. But Mexico's insolvency in 1982 interrupted lending and investment until 1990, by which time Argentina and Brazil were obliged to pay 45 percent interest on dollar-denominated debts. This exorbitant rate reflected their failure to develop along lines leading to economic and financial self sufficiency.

Investors nonetheless started to lend again, having discovered a new source of foreign exchange. Debtor-country governments might pay their creditors by selling off public enterprises. These privatization programs were voluntary pre-bankruptcy forfeitures, as if governments were not sovereign debtors able to retain the public domain under their own control by obliging bankers and bondholders to absorb the losses resulting from their bad loans.

A quantum leap occurred. Whereas creditors in times past appropriated the property of individual debtors piece by piece, they now have taken aim at the entire public domain of national economies. Appropriation of public enterprises is passing into the hands of financial managers.

A byproduct of the resulting "free capital movement" (that is, capital flight and "repatriation") is that foreign trade no longer plays the major role in determining exchange rates. The frenetic currency speculation now being conducted minute by minute each trading day far exceeds the entire annual volume of trade and direct investment.

From government monetary control to creditor control

Ending of the Cold War has given way to a reversion to the classical conflict between creditors and debtors. Today's characteristic mode of exploitation is not to seek industrial profits by employing wage labor, but to get governments to promote (and un-tax) *rentier* economies yielding interest and rent. This is achieved by bringing financial leverage to bear over indebted countries, and in the creditor nations as well.

The post-1980 order thus has been primarily financial in character. Instead of enabling Third World debtors to monetize their own credit, the IMF's role has been to make them dependent on credit creation by foreign banks, in a way that reflects specifically U.S. national interests.[3]

Acquiescence in this state of affairs could not have developed without a distracting array of euphemisms and ideological blinders. Less developed countries (called "backward" in 1945 because of the property ownership patterns and financial dependency put in place under colonial rule) were indoctrinated to believe that the path to wealth lay in developing as export-oriented raw-materials monocultures. Meanwhile, the assumption that credit relationships should be controlled abroad—and in "hard currency"—deterred countries from becoming self-reliant by implementing what G. F. Knapp called the State Theory of Money.

From Cold War isolation of Russia to neoliberal buyout

In the 1970s the Cold War metamorphosed into détente as America and Russia formed trade ties, capped by U.S. grain sales. Russia's opening to the West led to *glasnost* and *perestroika* in 1986, and five years later the USSR was dissolved. In one of the greatest economic about-faces in history, Russia was persuaded to assign its mineral wealth, land and enterprises to insiders drawn mainly from the ranks of the old Soviet *nomenklatura* and *mafiya*. When the dust had cleared, Russia discovered that its industrial, agricultural and military production had been dismantled. America had ringed it with military bases from Central Asia to outer space, and was using the flight capital of its kleptocrats to buy out what remained of the nation's natural resources and other assets.

During the past decade the Washington Consensus has shown itself to be anything but a policy that promotes growth. Given a freer hand in Russia than anywhere else, neoliberal "reformers" managed to destroy Russia as a potential rival of the United States.

Neoliberals claimed that the new proprietors would respond to the logic of market incentives as described in economics textbooks and build up production by recycling their income into new investment. But the appropriators realized the political risks inherent in grabbing assets in which they were seen not to have had any role in creating. The safest way to preserve their gains was to move as much as they could out of the country as quickly as possible, away from the tax collector and criminal authorities. The oligarchs moved their takings abroad at the rate of $25 billion annually for a decade—and then followed their bank accounts by obtaining citizenship in Israel, Britain and other countries.

By 2001, ten years after Yeltsin's attack on Russia's Parliament, a quarter-trillion dollars had been siphoned off and spirited out of the country through embezzlement, false invoicing of exports and flipping ownership rights to foreign buyers. Over and above this capital flight was the brain drain of Russian scientists and skilled workers. Life spans shortened, disease spread (headed by AIDS) and suicide rates rose as Russian society fell into depression psychologically as well as economically.

The Soviet Union thus was conquered financially rather than militarily, broken into a set of Third World countries that relinquished policy control to the U.S. AID, World Bank and IMF. By 1994 the government and many private companies had stopped paying salaries to labor, and no domestic credit was made even to finance government deficits. The "reformers" had wiped out domestic rouble savings through hyperinflation, prompting people to keep their savings mainly in the form of the $100 bills, accumulating more U.S. currency than was circulating in America itself.

Farm machinery rusted, factories rotted and investment plunged without finance, causing a deepening import dependency. Neoliberals insisted that government payments be backed by U.S. dollars, as if employees would spend all their money on imports. (The neoliberal showcase of Argentina followed dollarization even more stringently, crashing in 2002 and leaving a decade's worth of unpaid debt in its wake.)

Yet rather than being perceived as an object lesson illustrating the failure of such policies as a program of economic growth, the dismantling of Russia by neoliberal financial policies is being lauded as a victory of market efficiency over the inherently inefficient role of government planning and investment. The private fortunes created by these reforms were made by carving up the public enterprises that the government had built up, not by enterprise in the classical sense of increasing productive capacity.

Meanwhile, the era of world peace envisioned in 1945 is giving way to a global network of U.S. military bases and even the militarization of outer space. Still, the main mode of conquest remains financial, by dismantling government regulatory and taxing power outside of the United States. Toward this end the World Trade Organization (WTO), IMF and World Bank oppose government economic intervention, thereby promoting just the opposite program from what originally was envisioned for postwar development.

From Cold War to class war

Collapse of the Soviet Union in 1991 ended the Cold War, leaving the United States as the world's undisputed military and economic power. No longer checked by a Communist threat, it sought to make its gains irreversible by depicting its victory as evidence that government planning, price subsidies, taxation, income redistribution and public credit all were wasteful *ipso facto*. Public regulation and an active social role for government appeared to be discredited even in Social Democratic countries, including proposals to create a more equitable economic order in the sphere of foreign trade, financing and government planning to modernize agriculture, industry and social welfare.

Could so great an inversion of the social and economic philosophy reasonably have been forecast in the decades when free-marketers were isolated on the right-wing fringe? Certainly the final paragraph of *Global Fracture* (p. 267) was off the mark in concluding that "whether led by socialist governments or monarchies, countries are regulating market forces to serve their own national or regional self-interest." Financial interests are now doing most of the world's economic planning, and Chicago School monetarism has become so dominant since the 1980s that by the 1990s even China's leadership had developed an eclectic tendency, prompting Deng Xiaching to remark that "black cat or white cat, it doesn't matter as long as it catches mice."

The question is, why hasn't a more symmetrical and equitable mode of international development emerged? If the strategizing of the 1970s has failed, what then is the most likely path to a more workable post-neoliberal order to replace the Washington Consensus? It is easy enough to understand America's desire to act in its own self-interest. But why have Europe, Asia and Third World countries acquiesced in this American-centered world instead of promoting their own distinct interests? They are not "playing the game" that economic textbooks and those of international power politics assign to sovereign nations.

This poses the question of what America will do with its unprecedented power. The logic of empires is to promote growth of the imperial center, not of the periphery and hence the empire as a whole. Rome's experience affords a lesson. As Tacitus described Roman policy, *solitudinem faciunt pacem appellant*: "They have made a wilderness and call it peace." The *rentier* oligarchy used its control to shift the tax burden onto the shoulders of agricultural and handicraft producers, leading to debt foreclosures, demographic shrinkage and a deepening dependency that settled into serfdom.

Ending of the Cold War bears many similarities to the conflict between creditors and debtors in times past. By the 1980s this conflict took on a political dimension as right-wing governments came to power in the United States, Britain and other countries. Mexico is an example of how Latin American regimes served financial interests. Its 1988 presidential election was stolen by the PRI, blocking the populist leader Cuauhémoc Cárdenas. In 1991 the authoritarian PRI allied itself with the right-wing National Action Party (PAN) to maintain the crony capitalism that led to financial collapse of the Mexican stock exchange in 1994, headed by the telephone company and other enterprises that insiders had privatized.

From empirical economics to free-market sloganeering

For decades, IMF financial managers have stripped debtor countries of the credit and revenue needed to grow. It is as if a parasite has taken over host economies and their guiding brain, bleeding away their nourishment to feed its own body. Its takings have been mistaken for growth in the host countries rather than destroying the host's own investment needs. Most biological parasites have learned to establish a symbiosis with their hosts and even to help them thrive, but empires never have succeeded in regulating themselves so rationally.

The financial sector's dominance over governments today is illustrated most nakedly in the Russian reforms that culminated in "grabitization" and subsequent sell-offs, and refusal by the European Community's central bankers to permit budget deficits to provide the credit needed to reflate its economies.

Orwellian double-think has given such reform the meaning of regressive taxation, insider privatizations, flight capital ("free capital transfers"), and a dismantling of government regulation. For its victims, "reform" along these neoliberal lines has become a bad word, diametrically opposed to the principles of the NIEO and progressive reforms prior to the 1980s—Social Democratic policies to build up the home market, and budget deficits to spur full employment at rising educational, health and living standards.

Yet quite apart from American arm-twisting, the lack of an alternative logic to today's trickle-down ideology of wealth creation has left a *tabula rasa* to be filled in to explain how governments best might act independently along such lines.

The Path to a Post-*Rentier* Economic Order

It is not hard to see what is needed to counter the polarizing effects of today's neoliberal reforms. A better world order would provide government credit to finance budget deficits to spur investment and employment; denominate international debts in domestic currency and make debt service subject to the capacity to pay, as the Dawes and Young Plans did for German reparations in the 1920s; and shift the tax burden away from labor and industry onto land, subsoil resources and monopolies.

To bring about such a world order, it is necessary to create new international institutions whose development philosophy would replace that of the IMF, World Bank and ITO; negotiate an alternative to the U.S. Treasury-bill standard; enact U.S.-style tariffs and subsidies to complement land reform; constrain U.S. military expansionism; and develop a post-neoliberal theory to restore the classical distinction between earned and unearned income.

Government credit to finance budget deficits aimed at spurring investment and employment

Economies do not require foreign exchange and savings to pay labor and other domestic factors of production. There is no reason for governments not to do what the United States has been doing all along—running budget deficits to support domestic market demand at a rate that keeps labor fully employed. Although monetarists claim that government credit is inherently inflationary, there is no reason why government credit should be any more inflationary than private credit. In fact, public credit under democratic regimes tends to be spent in ways that are conducive to the long-term raising of living standards, while banks prefer to finance property bubbles and the acquisition of real estate or other assets already in place.

Denomination of international debts in domestic currency

Most countries may benefit from importing technology and capital goods, but the past half-century's experience with debt dependency (euphemized as "resource flows") has shown that such borrowing should be made only in their domestic currency, as only its value remains under their control. If self-determination is desirable and indeed, part of the political definition of sovereign states, it follows that currency and debt control is a *sine qua non*. This requires that dollarization be replaced with debts denominated in domestic currency.

The objective is to create a form of economic balance that promotes development rather than being merely redistributive in character. Today's economic orthodoxy defines "equilibrium" as the rate at which debtors need to sell off their assets to pay creditors (*viz.* the demands of Argentina's bondholders since 2002). American diplomats define financial equilibrium as the amount of U.S. Treasury debt that foreign central banks must buy in order to finance the U.S. budget deficit as it cuts taxes, while trade equilibrium seems to be the volume of products that foreign countries need to supply America to enable its citizens to maintain their living standards even as their economy deindustrializes and the population is turned into *rentiers*.

The problem is that today's trade and payments system aims at rewarding *rentiers* rather than helping countries develop. The disastrous effect of neoliberal logic has been demonstrated most notably in Russia's deflation of the domestic market in the mid-1990s, and in the European Community's fiscal austerity. Future generations no doubt will find it remarkable that this doctrinaire monetarist consensus was self-imposed voluntarily without a General Pinochet being in place to enforce it at gunpoint.

Today (2004), Argentina is trying to establish conditions under which dollar debts must be converted into its own national currency. This need was learned the hard way, following the country's 2002 default after a decade of hyper-dollarization that required each issue of domestic currency to be backed by a parallel loan to the U.S. Treasury, as if Argentina were part of the U.S. fiscal system rather than a sovereign country. Although international bondholders and bank lenders have protested, the precedent for Argentina's negotiating stance was created by none other than Franklin Roosevelt himself when he unilaterally negated the "gold clause" in pre-1933 financial contracts. (The clause made all debts payable in gold valued at the price prior to dollar devaluation.)

A rent and resource tax on land, subsoil endowments and monopolies

Today's global financial grab seeks above all to obtain resource rents (including monopoly profits) by acquiring public monopolies, raw materials and real estate, not by investing in new capital formation to earn industrial profits. The extraction of property rents has been maximized by blocking governments from collecting them as taxes. As financiers know, what the tax collector gives up is available to be paid out as interest, dividends and management fees.

It is fairly easy for governments to counter this kind of resource grab. All they need do is to tax the land, subsoil mineral wealth and natural monopolies that have been privatized. The virtue of such a tax is that it reduces the fiscal burden levied on industry and labor. This shifts the tax system away from wages and industrial profits onto the "free ride" of rental revenue produced by nature (favorable land sites or natural resources) or monopoly power. It would enable governments to recover the revenue that *rentier* asset-grabbers hope to siphon off.

Rent and property taxation is legal under international law as long as it is applied evenly to domestic and foreign owners alike. It has a long pedigree, having been the focal point of classical political economy culminating in John Stuart Mill and subsequently was espoused by the 19th century's major economic reformers ranging from the German socialists Ferdinand Lasalle and Karl Marx to Henry George and Thorstein Veblen in the United States, Alfred Wallace, George Bernard Shaw and Winston Churchill in Britain, Sun-Yat Sen in China, Jose Marti in Cuba, and Leo Tolstoy and Alexander Kerensky in Russia.

A rent tax does not involve nationalization of property, which would require compensation under international law, recalling the arguments over "just compensation" that became such a thorn in relations with Cuba and other Communist nations after their revolutions. Every government is permitted to tax its property and income in any way it chooses.

Even Milton Friedman and other neoliberals have acknowledged that a rent tax is the fairest and most equitable form of taxation. Rather than pressing this perception, however, they realize that the political appeal of their monetarist doctrines is mainly to property owners. They tend to conflate profit with rent, as if land and other property and monopoly rights belonged in the same category as manmade capital that requires labor for its creation rather than merely the act of appropriation. This confusion between land and capital is politically motivated in failing to distinguish between profits earned from tangible capital investment and the "free lunch" of economic rent—the free lunch that Milton Friedman and other neoliberals publicly claim does not exist, despite their preference for a rent tax over all other forms of taxation.

Squeezing out a surplus that has no counterpart in direct production costs is not "profit" in the classical sense of the term. It is economic rent, or what John Stuart Mill's generation of reformers called the "unearned increment." Vladimir Putin's counter-liberal reformation in Russia in support of resource-rent taxation is based on the perception that globalism has become mainly an exercise in appropriating property and rent.

Western countries, by contrast, have seen a steady reduction in the proportion of taxes levied on property since the end of World War II. The tax burden has been shifted onto labor and fixed capital formation. This trend needs to be reversed under an economic order that aims at growth and development rather than rewarding *rentiers* for using borrowed credit to gain control of property and monopoly rights whose prices are being inflated.

New international institutions to replace the IMF, World Bank and ITO

The IMF and World Bank hardly can be expected to support proposals that would loosen their control over debtor economies. Although their original aim was to support stable exchange rates and finance economic modernization, their economic doctrines now support *rentier* resource grabs and debt dependency. These two institutions need to be replaced because they are not reformable.

There is no need for countries to remain members of these two institutions, or of the ITO with its opposition to government enterprise and regulatory activity. Member countries simply need ask that their gold subscriptions to be returned, thereby rejecting the Washington

Consensus and its opposition to rent taxation, deficit financing and public credit creation.

U.S.-style protective tariffs and subsidies

As late as the 1950s, United Nations economists saw land reform as essential to the policies needed to enable food-deficit countries to supply their own grain rather than remaining dependent on imports. This policy requires a break from the ITO's imposition of free-trade principles on countries outside of the United States and Europe. The alternative is for food-dependent regions to import whatever the United States produces in crop surpluses, and to supply the tropical plantation plants that America does not produce in sufficient quantities to satisfy its home market.

Grain-deficit countries need to feed themselves in order to break free of the food weapon wielded by highly protected U.S. and European agriculture. Self-sufficiency requires a shift away from foreign-owned plantation production for export markets. To modernize agriculture and industry in the face of the heavily subsidized investment that has characterized Europe and the United States during their industrial and agricultural revolution, countries need to do what they did: provide protective tariffs to subsidize the capital investment needed. In other words, they should do what America actually has done, not what its diplomats say to do.

An alternative to the U.S. Treasury-bill standard

Foreign countries that run balance-of-payments surpluses presently are obliged to keep their central bank reserves in the form of loans to the U.S. Treasury *ad infinitum*. These savings become part of the U.S. financial system rather than building up their own productive capacity. There is no hard-currency guarantee for the value of these loans as the dollar falls against the euro, yen and other currencies of economies running trade and payments surpluses. In domestic-currency terms, the value of dollars held in central bank reserves declines.

The problem is how to constrain the United States from running a payments deficit without limit, and how to compensate countries for their foreign-exchange losses resulting from a buildup of dollar reserves in their central banks. Prior to 1971 a constraint was imposed by countries holding their foreign-exchange reserves in gold and using this metal to settle international balances. In the absence of a shift to some such asset today, or into currencies issued by European and Asian economies, the problem can be solved only by spending dollar surpluses as they accumulate.

The most natural and symmetrical option would be to impose on the United States the same demand that it imposes on other countries: let dollar holders buy control of industry and high technology, forests and other natural resources. A related alternative would be to use surplus foreign-owned dollars to buy out U.S. corporate investments abroad.

Yet another alternative would be to do what America did in 1921 when the German mark and other European currencies were plunging in value. The United States applied tariff duties according to the American Selling Price (ASP) rather than to the nominal import price. This resulted in a floating tariff, rising to reflect currency depreciation and hence preventing financial fluctuations from disrupting existing production-cost patterns.

A logical extension of this practice would be to use tariff revenues and other foreign-exchange proceeds to provide a subsidy to exports made to countries whose currencies were depreciating in value. The objective here would be to normalize costs and achieve in practice the assumption of "pure cost values" that underlies traditional trade theory.

Isolation of offshore flight-capital and tax-avoidance centers, and regulation of transfer pricing

National tax laws and regulations have been countered in recent years by dummy corporations registered in tax-avoidance havens as vehicles to enable companies to use intra-corporate transfer pricing to evade taxes and other laws.[4]

The counter-strategy is simple. National financial systems and tax collectors can refuse to acknowledge such centers, much as the United States and its allies isolated China, Russia, Cuba, Libya and Iraq for many years. It is to be expected, however, that attempts to create a better economic order along these lines will be confronted by U.S. pressure to prevent its emergence. This requires regional agreements to achieve strength in numbers.

Constraints on U.S. military expansionism

As Chalmers Johnson recently has observed in *The Sorrows of Empire*: "According to the Pentagon's annual inventory of real estate—its so-called Base Structure Report—we have over 725 military bases in some 132 countries around the world. This vast network of American bases constitutes a new form of empire—an empire of military enclaves rather than of colonies as in older forms of imperialism. . . . To dominate the oceans and seas of the world, we maintain some thirteen carrier task-forces, which constitute floating bases." Most recently, the United States has started to militarize outer space with satellite-based weaponry.

All this spending increases the deficits in the U.S. balance-of-payments and domestic budget, which the central banks of Europe and Asia are subsidizing on a much vaster scale today than in the Vietnam War years prior to 1971, when the gold-exchange standard imposed a limit on overseas military spending. It has long been an axiom of world geopolitics that imperial ambitions can be sustained only by falling into a debtor status and hence sacrificing financial power, as Britain and the rest of Europe discovered after World War I. Since America went off gold, however, this check on foreign military spending no longer operates.

The key to limiting imperial ambitions in the modern world lies in re-establishing the link between the costs of empire and the dissipation of economic position. No nation can afford to pay these costs by itself, given the expense of modern military technology. Yet the costs of empire have broken every imperial design in modern history, as exemplified most dramatically by the British Empire's dissipation after World Wars I and II. Its maintenance costs drove sterling into a financial dependence on the U.S. dollar—a dependency that America deftly turned into a political and diplomatic dependency that remains in place even today, even as it maintains its global military power by shifting the costs onto Europe and Asia.

If the key to military strength lies in shifting the costs of empire onto the periphery (as Rome did, bleeding its colonies dry in the process), the key to dissolving empire must lie in resisting this shift. To paraphrase the slogan that inspired the American Revolution in 1776, "No taxation without representation." The United States taxes the world by running a balance-of-payments deficit, thanks to its ability to negotiate credit without limit from foreign central banks while enjoying a free ride as *rentier*-in-chief.

A post-neoliberal theory to restore the classical distinction between earned and unearned income

It seems absurd to call the present system's high taxes and public guarantees to foreign bondholders "free enterprise." Under these conditions "market fundamentalism" becomes a euphemism for financial dominance over governments. It is merely another form of centralized planning, not the absence of planning. It is planning to impose dependency, not self-reliance.

A more equitable and peaceful world order would reverse today's trend of turning planning power over to financial institutions. Economies need to produce output rather than be turned into vehicles to generate interest, dividends and capital gains. The role hitherto assigned to government has been taken over by creditors and foreign investors.

Neither foreign loans nor prior savings are needed to fund capital investment and employment. National credit can be produced by any country, and indeed is a prerogative of sovereignty. What need to be developed are internal markets rather than reliance on U.S. consumers and military spending to act as the world's "engine of growth."

The emerging oligarchy is euphemized by the term "managed democracy," which is antithetical to democracy in the traditional meaning of the term. It goes together with "post-industrial," as if modern finance is promoting progress rather than retrogression.

The solution must be as much political as economic. American imperial designs have produced a doctrine of financial austerity rather than one designed to modernize economies by moving them along the lines that the United States itself pursued to achieve its position of world leadership.

On the other hand, China has followed a path that may be emulated by India and perhaps Venezuela, Argentina and Brazil, while Russia under Putin's resource-rent tax may revive its industrial base along lines that go far beyond those contemplated in the 1970s when *Global Fracture* first was published. The alternative is for the U.S.-centered world to crash into a financially imposed austerity, Roman Empire style, leading to neo-feudalism.

Notes

1. Joshua Cooper Ramo, "China has discovered its own economic consensus," *Financial Times* (London), May 7, 2004, summarizing his report on *The Beijing Consensus*, published by the Foreign Policy Centre in London.
2. My *Trade, Development and Foreign Debt* (Pluto Press, 1972, Chapter 6 and especially Chapter 15) provides a historical analysis of how capital transfers depress the terms of trade.
3. I have discussed these North–South issues in a series of UNITAR reports published by Pergamon Press: "The United States and the NIEO," in Erwin Laszlo and Joel Kurtzman, eds., *The United States, Canada and the New International Economic Order* (1979); "The Structure of the World Economy: A Northern Perspective," in Laszlo and Kurtzman, eds., *The Structure of the World Economy and Prospects for a New International Economic Order* (1980); and "The Logic of Regionalism in History and Today," "The Objectives of Regionalism in the 1980s," and "A Regional Strategy to Finance the New International Economic Order," in Davidson Nicol, Luis Excheverria and Aurelio Peccei, eds., *Regionalism and the New International Economic Order* (1981).
4. I describe this phenomenon in detail in my introduction to a new 2004 edition of Prof. Tom Naylor's *Hot Money* (McGill-Queens University Press).

Introduction

The New International Economic Order involves far more than higher prices for oil and other Third World raw materials. It connotes a movement by Europe and Third World countries both to become independent of the U.S. economic orbit and more closely integrated economically and politically with one another. In the realm of international finance it promises an alternative to the dollar standard, hence a winding down of foreign credits to the U.S. Treasury and other federal agencies—which currently owes over $90 billion to the central banks of Europe, Japan and OPEC. In world commerce it aims to replace the Third World's depletable mineral resources with viable industrial and agricultural sectors designed to provide economic independence from the industrial nations. Both world trade and investment are passing out of the hands of multinational firms as governments are buying into them or regulating them in the national interest. New criteria based on long-term regional development objectives are taking the place of the narrow profit motive in allocating world resources.

More publicity has been given to the rhetorical principles of the New International Economic Order than to its substance and specific mechanisms. It is hardly surprising that when any nation cites principles of international equality or "restoration of world equilibrium" to justify its policies, it construes these principles in terms of its own specific economic advantage. When Third World countries speak of international equilibrium they mean stabilizing the terms of trade, so that their export prices may keep pace with rising prices for imported food and arms—at the cost of increasing trade deficits for the industrial nations. From the Third World's vantage point these trade deficits should be financed by a transfer of ownership of heavy industry and capital goods. By contrast, when the industrial nations speak of restoring

1

equilibrium they are referring to their balance of payments. They envision the Third World rolling back its price increases for oil, coffee and other raw materials, or at least relending its export earnings to central banks in the industrial nations on easy terms. Thus, equilibrium for the industrial nations means continued enrichment at the expense of Third World countries (and possibly each other as well, as in the case of American strategy vis-à-vis Europe and Japan). Equilibrium for the Third World means the opportunity to catch up with and perhaps overtake the richer nations.

The resulting shift in trade structure as Third World countries seek to realize this ideal has far-reaching implications for world commodity prices, hence for international finance, the flow of world investment and the locus of world economic growth generally. By increasing U.S. import prices for raw materials while eroding foreign dependency on U.S. grain and other products, the New International Economic Order threatens to turn the terms of trade against the United States as foreign countries move toward regional autonomy and internal diversification of their economies. In this objective Third World countries finally are emulating the state-directed forms of industrial and agricultural development enacted a century ago in continental Europe and the United States. They have broken free from the intellectual sway of laissez faire by recognizing that equality of per capita world incomes and productive powers must be brought about by their own deliberate efforts under the guiding hands of governments. The myth of riches resulting automatically from the so-called invisible hand of world market forces is dead.

What, after all, is the world marketplace and its seemingly neutral market forces? Recent congressional investigations in the United States have thrust into the limelight the previously invisible hand of bribery of foreign officials by multinational firms, as well as covert operations of the Central Intelligence Agency against regimes that have followed economic policies contrary to U.S. national interest—most recently the Allende government in Chile. (A story remains to be told in Greece.) The U.S. Government has consistently opposed foreign moves toward economic or political independence, the undertaking of basic institutional land reform throughout the Third World, the assertion of national authority over domestic affiliates of U.S. multinational corporations, and any other attempts to alter world trade and investment in favor of foreign countries. The United States is seeking unilaterally to regulate its international trade via import and export quotas and insistence that foreign countries guarantee a fixed share of their markets to U.S. suppliers. It has provided export subsidies in violation of existing world trade rules. It has regulated the overseas activities of U.S. firms while blocking foreign takeovers of American companies. It has used foreign aid as a diplomatic lever and as a means to tap foreign resources for specific U.S. objectives. Most important—but least recognized—it has borrowed at will from foreign economies by the simple expedient of running balance-of-payments deficits that it refuses to settle with anything better than Treasury bills of depreciating value.

In short, by 1973 American nationalism had produced so blatant a double standard that the postwar structure of world trade, investment and payments fractured. Third World countries rebelled against the system of world trade and investment that had failed to develop their economies while building up the industrial nations. "Resource allocation" by world market forces had become a euphemism for the workings of the international mineral cartel operating hand in hand with industrial governments in the face of deepening Third World dependency. World market forces, backed by U.S. foreign aid and related diplomacy, led foreign countries to produce the type of goods Americans chose to import and to buy the type of goods America chose to produce and export, even if they could produce these goods themselves as in the case of food.

To counter this manipulative superstructure, Third World countries joined forces with each other (and subsequently with Europe on specific issues) to create their own intergovernmental economic system. The first successful alliance, the Organization of Petroleum-Exporting Countries (OPEC), was emulated by exporters of bauxite, copper and other key commodities. The result has been a return to the classical adversary system of world diplomacy that existed for centuries prior to World War II, a system in which each country looked after its own interests. However, there is one vital difference: individual nations are no longer acting alone but forming geographically associated common markets characterized by an economic complementarity provid-

ing regional self-sufficiency in vital necessities, i.e., food, arms
and heavy industry. The Near East and Africa recognize that they
cannot attain their objectives without the support of major industrial nations, and their logical strategy is to pry Europe out of the
U.S. economic orbit. Japan is seeking to deepen its economic and
financial ties with Asian countries. Thus, what seemed to be a
cosmopolitan laissez faire world order in 1945 has become transformed into one of regional self-sufficiency and increasing government control.

PART I

An American World

CHAPTER 1

Pax Americana

The postwar economic order is fragmenting because it was designed to solve the problems of 1945 in a backward-looking not a forward-looking manner, and because it aimed to curtail European nationalism but not that of the United States. In 1945 the immediate political issue was how to supersede the diplomacy of nationalism that had led to world breakdown and war. The pressing economic issue was how to avoid postwar recession by supporting international purchasing power. These objectives inspired the most idealistic sentiments among their proponents. However, their proposed solutions were preoccupied with the trauma of the Great Depression and its associated tariff and currency wars, and with specifically U.S. economic objectives. By looking backward, by concentrating overwhelmingly on the problems of the industrial nations and those of the U.S. economy in particular, the postwar move toward a cosmopolitan world economy under American aegis lay the ground for new and unanticipated problems.

The devastation wrought by World War II transformed political philosophy just as it altered economic circumstances. Avoidance of war, and of statism generally, became a higher political principle than the nationalism which had formed the basis of world relations for over four centuries. Only twelve years had elapsed since breakdown of the 1933 London Economic Conference led to internecine tariff and currency wars. With these spectres in mind European countries virtually abandoned the traditional adversary system of world diplomacy based on negotiations among men representing their own nations' self-interests. Alliances historically had been formed and broken, compromises made and national wealth promoted or lost through a combination of negotiated tradeoffs, direct coercion or

threat thereof. All this was now changed, heralding an era unique
in international relations.

At the outset, the world's diplomats were determined that the
economic problems and upheavals that followed the First World
War would not recur. Defeated nations would not have to pay
reparations which could bankrupt them and leave them vulnera-
ble to renewed nationalist, socialist or communist movements.
The European Allies would not have to repay armaments debts
out of depleted international reserves and an almost non-existent
net export income. The world could start afresh, at least from the
economic vantage point.

Europe for its part felt a revulsion against the nationalism that
had culminated in depression and war. Its means of production
had to be rebuilt or redirected to peacetime applications, while
its financial resources had been drained. The continent no longer
could afford the enormous military and bureaucratic overhead
imposed by its colonial systems. Even if it desired the trappings
of imperialism (as did France for awhile in Southeast Asia and
Algeria), it could hardly pay for them. England found itself nearly
bankrupted by the costs of occupying its zone of defeated Germany, and could not reassert imperial authority without cutting
itself off from American aid. In fact, it was heavily in debt to its
own colonies for its wartime purchases of raw materials and military support, so that growth in its exports would be earmarked
largely to repay these debts. Furthermore, production of commodities for export would divert resources from the task of
reconstruction. These factors muted Europe's desire to enter
into export competition with America.

Most important of all, Europe's leaders believed that U.S.
financial leadership and resources were preconditions for postwar economic stability, hence for political and military stability.
They chose not to start a new rivalry for export markets, not to
engage in competitive currency devaluations, tariff protection or
export subsidies, nor to move toward either full-scale socialist
planning or economic integration with one another. Instead of
pressing their own national interests they merged themselves
into a U.S.-oriented world order.

Meanwhile, the first concern of U.S. officials was to secure full
employment and production at home. America's productive capacity in both agriculture and industry exceeded domestic needs.
Now that the war demand was over and the economy was return-

ing to civilian production, demand for its economic surplus would have to be met through exports. The National Planning Association estimated that the United States would have to export about $10 billion annually in order to ensure full employment. Its most obvious markets were the devastated countries that needed these products.

Cordell Hull and other U.S. officials feared that European nations might seek to regain their former international positions by entering into a new export competition, beginning with their own colonies and spreading out to absorb the markets and raw-materials supplies of other powers. National rivalries, with their alignment of competing satellite systems, would prevent economic recovery (especially in the United States) and thereby threaten peaceful world relations. In particular the Sterling Area and the Franc Zone threatened the concept of a unified trade and investment area based on the dollar and on preeminent U.S. export capacity. America's postwar planners therefore pressed for a regime of free trade and an open door to international investment. The world was to become integrated along lines highly favorable for the United States.

Both Europe and America looked forward to a cosmopolitan One Worldism that seemed to dovetail neatly into U.S. economic objectives while providing substantial inducements to Europe in the form of foreign aid, U.S. military support, and a reciprocal demand for exports. However, the textbook principles underlying the postwar economic order rested on the simplistic hope that the economic and political self-interests of nations might easily complement each other without much sacrifice of any single nation's economic potential or established interests. Prosperity for all would be promoted through a harmonious specialization of world labor and production, with the gains shared equitably among nations.

The specific terms on which this was to occur were highly self-serving to America. Foreign countries would purchase enough surplus American output to guarantee full employment for the United States, and they would pay for these U.S. exports in two ways: by supplying raw materials and labor-intensive products desired by Americans, and by selling their resources to U.S. investors. America's own idea of One Worldism thus merged easily with its own national self-interest.

European governments meanwhile shifted their attention away

from imperial rivalry toward rebuilding their domestic economies. The world moved to dissolve the principles of nationalism
itself, along with protectionism, socialism, imperialism and any
other form of statism that might interfere with an open international economy.

The major threat to free trade and a universal open door policy
seemed to emanate from the communist countries, which might
manipulate foreign trade in such a way as to interfere with the
West's allocation of resources along market-oriented lines. U.S.
officials argued that laissez faire economies would be at a disad-
vantage in dealing with state-planned economies, inasmuch as
foreign trade and investment patterns would be established by
pricing and trade decisions made in the managed economies.
Furthermore, if the Soviet Union and its satellites were to be
permitted such practices, should not England and France be
entitled to follow suit? Economic planning seemed to connote
the paraphernalia of nationalism, and must therefore be stymied
at the outset. The solution to this problem was to isolate the
communist countries and cut them off from commerce with the
West. The Free World must remain integrated in order to prevent commerce from evolving on the basis of restrictive intra-
bloc markets that might once again lead the world into economic
fragmentation. A cosmopolitan world economy would set the
stage for prosperous and peaceful world relations. (The only
threat of war seemed to lie with the Soviet Bloc, and this could
be minimized by the U.S. nuclear deterrent, complemented by
the set of interlocking regional alliances established under U.S.
leadership—NATO, CENTO and SEATO.)

America's diplomats therefore presented both the Soviet
Union and its other allies with a choice: either to join the United
States in a dollar-oriented trade and investment area while being
helped by U.S. aid during their transition to this new epoch, or
to maintain their statist policies and colonial systems on a go-it-
alone basis. The Soviet Union chose the latter course while the
Europeans, led by England, readily accepted America's economic, financial and military umbrella. The world thus split into
two great blocs, one led by the United States, the other by Soviet
Russia.

Within the Western bloc, England was quickly stripped of its
world position and empire. The pound sterling was maintained

at so high a parity that British industry could hardly compete with American exporters in world markets. England entered the post-war world in debt to its colonies and to the United States (thanks to the British Loan of 1945–46). Like other countries it was obliged to settle its balance-of-payments deficits in gold or in U.S. dollars freely convertible into gold. England, France and other European countries watched their modest international reserves drain to the United States.

In order to finance European and other foreign purchases from America, that is, to ensure adequate financial resources to sustain U.S. exports ("world trade") under moderately laissez faire policies and currency convertibility, the U.S. Government had taken the lead (in 1944, at Bretton Woods, New Hampshire) in establishing the International Monetary Fund (IMF) and the World Bank (formally called the International Bank for Reconstruction and Development). Loans were provided by the U.S. Government and U.S. credit markets via the World Bank to European governments, which used them mainly to pay for goods supplied by American exporters. The source of the original loan funds provided by the IMF and the World Bank came from foreign currency and gold subscriptions by the participating nations. America's subscription amounted to almost $3 billion and entitled it to nearly 30 per cent of the voting power. The member nations agreed that an 80 per cent majority vote would be required for most rulings, thus conceding unique veto power to the United States. This enabled U.S. officials to dictate terms and refuse loans to governments that pursued policies opposed by the United States.

In this way a moderately open world economy was maintained. In fact, during 1944–46 an internationalist spirit merged naturally with laissez faire principles that hitherto had been considered idealistic rather than pragmatic. In place of the system of nation-states, with its colonial rivalries that had existed since the beginning of the modern industrial era, the victors of war acquiesced to an ally and voluntarily dismantled their empires, opening vast new areas to U.S. trade and investment. The Western Alliance was consolidated voluntarily into the postwar dollar-gold area. Europe gave up its empires but was at peace with itself. This was a major accomplishment. Whatever today's juncture in world affairs will bring, the epoch of European nationalism has passed from the world stage forever.

Europe was fully aware that it was ceding to America the option of determining its own currency values and tariffs. The United States was the only nation with sufficient foreign exchange to finance a program of overseas investment, long-term export financing, and foreign aid. Still, in Europe's exhausted state the concepts of internationalism and "free" market competition held tremendous appeal, particularly during the era of Marshall Plan aid. It was left to American diplomats to shape this war-weary world and, for all their internationalist rhetoric and ideals, one can hardly be surprised that they expressed their national interest by appropriating the markets and resources of Europe's dependencies and ensuring that the postwar international organizations were subject to U.S. veto power and diplomatic constraints. Inevitably, the particular form of internationalism emerging from World War II was dominated by U.S. economic strength (surplus productive capacity, especially in agriculture), backed by U.S. ownership of 59 per cent of the world's monetary gold (composed largely of Europe's refugee gold that had been transferred to the United States in the 1930s), and ultimately cemented by U.S. military force and police operations.

Even so, the resulting system seemed to connote stability, not one-sidedness. In the realm of world finance, for instance, currencies were assigned fixed values and gold once again became the standard of foreign exchange, with a defined value of 35 U.S. dollars per ounce. This return to fixed currencies freely convertible into gold prevented foreign countries from pursuing competitive devaluations or beggar-my-neighbor policies. But it also curtailed foreign ability to pursue expansionary economic policies. Relatively early in their business cycles foreign countries began to lose their rather modest holdings of gold as increasing domestic purchasing power reflected itself in a rising net demand for imports.

In the realm of world trade, the General Agreement on Tariffs and Trade (GATT) called for equal tariff treatment of all trading parties. Tariffs no longer could be unilaterally imposed, and more than two decades of international tariff concessions were negotiated. Other trade barriers, such as quotas and assigned values for imports, were disallowed. Even in those special cases where general trade restrictions were permitted for domestic or balance-of-payments purposes, discrimination among supplier countries was forbidden. The IMF, World Bank and GATT became interlocked into a single postwar system governing world trade, aid and investment. Withdrawal from any of these institutions would *de facto* involve withdrawal from the others as well. Nations that failed to participate could find their access to Western markets, foreign aid and investment resources blocked.

Nonetheless, the United States did not join GATT as a full member. U.S. representatives could negotiate trade agreements, but Congress could repudiate them and often did. After all, congressmen were elected to serve the interests of their particular districts, and protection of domestic industry and agriculture took precedence over more generalized foreign trade benefits. Other member nations accepted this double standard and agreed to adhere to rules and restrictions that did not constrain Americans. This became the original flaw that moved the world further and further away from the images conjured up by the egalitarian, laissez faire rhetoric that characterized early postwar diplomacy.

Pax Americana had been achieved. Europe set about rebuilding its domestic economies according to the Keynesian doctrine of supporting domestic employment and incomes (hence demand) by pursuing expansionist social-economic policies and growth in consumption standards. This was precisely what John Hobson had urged a half-century earlier as an alternative to economic imperialism, with its primary focus on foreign markets rather than on domestic demand. Europe abandoned its imperial ambitions, virtually ceding its empires to the United States as spheres of influence and as wards.

U.S. domination of the world's foreign-aid programs, and its position as the world's major source of capital equipment, foodstuffs and arms, led to even greater U.S. affluence. By 1949 the nation had acquired 72 per cent of the world's gold. Embarrassed by its riches, and aware that accumulating gold in only one country would destroy its function as the world's monetary standard, the United States made substantial outright grants to foreign governments via the United Nations Relief and Rehabilitation Administration (UNRRA) and through Marshall Plan aid. In 1950 it achieved its $10 billion annual export target. The United States stood at the pinnacle of its power and appeared invincible in the military, political and economic spheres.

There was little pressure to create a meaningful system of checks and balances against the possibility that America might abuse its postwar power by pressing its own self-interest directly at the expense of foreign economies. Perhaps Europe, which carried the main burden of postwar negotiations with the United States, felt it had no real choice. There was an almost universal belief that the U.S. economy would tend inexorably to run balance-of-payments surpluses. Therefore, the postwar economic order's financial institutions were designed to supply foreign countries with as many dollars as the United States could be induced to provide. No mechanism was created to curtail U.S. dollar creation beyond a given point, nor was much thought given to the prospect of an overabundance of dollar liquidity leading to a future world inflation. In order to obtain dollars, Europe felt obliged to follow the lead of American diplomats. Meanwhile the less industrialized countries and ex-colonies were left to fend for themselves in a world whose trade and investment patterns, and power relations generally, directed their economic development primarily to serve the collective needs of the industrial nations.

But clouds loomed on the horizon. War erupted in Korea during 1950–51, and America's ongoing involvement there and elsewhere throughout the world pushed its seemingly impregnable balance of payments into what turned out to be nearly chronic deficit status. Furthermore, despite the benefits which the United States derived from a cosmopolitan world economy, it proved unwilling to play by the rules of laissez faire that it lay down for Europe, Japan, Canada and Third World countries. It asked foreign countries to maintain free trade policies and an open door to world investment while it maintained, and even increased, its own protectionism in agriculture and raw materials, followed by textiles, steel and electronics. Congress in particular was unwilling to remove import quotas or to lower tariffs protecting U.S. agriculture and industry (especially chemicals). America used its leverage in world lending agencies to guarantee fixed market shares for its output, regardless of price considerations or other "free market forces." Countries that did not submit to U.S. pressure were isolated and boycotted. What had appeared as a free trade system in 1945 became increasingly regulative, coercive and exploitative.

World leaders did not anticipate that resolving the problem of nationalism would create a new set of international relations whereby Europe, Japan, Canada and Third World countries would find themselves becoming economic satellites of the United States. The institutions of the postwar economic order were not designed to cope with the Cold War and its subsequent U.S. balance-of-payments deficit, with the terms of trade shifting against Third World countries and the latter's underdevelopment, or with today's era of inflationary shortages and other features that have redefined the world economy. The economic ideology of Pax Americana was highly appealing to many nations by virtue of the simplicity of its assumptions and the fact that it was in many ways profitable, as far as it went. But as Europe and other industrial nations grew stronger they naturally evolved away from the domineering presence of the United States. They then found that American diplomats had created a hold on foreign nations that could not be broken except by a great wrenching of the very economies that were most abused by the process (Germany, Japan, England and Canada). The United States had evolved a system whereby its balance-of-payments *deficit* formed the basis of the Free World's monetary system and simultaneously financed America's vast Cold War military overhead.

Postwar world planners did not foresee in the 1940s, or even the 1950s, that America might exploit Europe financially. After all, Europe was broke. It seemed logical to take U.S. officials at their word when they pointed out that America had a stake in supporting European living standards and purchasing power, insofar as these were preconditions for supporting European demand for U.S. exports, hence full employment in the United States. An American balance-of-payments deficit was looked upon with favor, as providing Europe with international reserves which were—or at least seemed to be—as good as gold. An abuse of America's unique ability to provide dollars to the world simply was not foreseen. But it was this wedge that was to undo the entire edifice of the American-based Western world which seemed to be so tightly cemented by the postwar economic order.

Actually, the line of mutual accommodation was much narrower than originally anticipated. American officials had hoped that as Europe grew it would form a growing market for U.S. exports, but would neither displace U.S. exports through domestic competition, nor buy so much that it would create domestic

U.S. shortages. Europe and other nations were supposed to supply America with goods desired by Americans which U.S. industries did not choose to produce—e.g., raw materials and labor-
intensive products—but were not supposed to compete with
existing capital or threaten existing employment patterns. Inevitably, these forms of competition developed.

   Until the late 1950s economists throughout the world believed
that America's balance of payments tended to run a chronic surplus, except to the extent that the U.S. Government funded foreign-aid programs and military support which served to provide
the world economy with much-needed dollars. America was so
strong that any debilitating war seemed out of the question.
Europe could scarcely foresee that it would earn back its gold
plus that which the United States had earned on its trade with less
industrialized countries. When this began to occur, when the U.S.
balance of payments was thrown into ever-larger annual deficits,
American officials began to alter and warp the system which they
had taken the lead in creating. What began ostensibly as an
egalitarian diplomacy evolved into an engine of exploitation
whose mechanisms were almost entirely unanticipated, even by
the Americans themselves.

CHAPTER 2

The Treasury-bill Standard
Versus the Gold Standard

Since 1960 the United States has drawn on world resources through a novel monetary process: by running balance-of-payments deficits that it refuses to settle in gold, it has obliged foreign governments to invest their surplus dollar holdings in Treasury bills, that is, to relend their dollar inflows to the U.S. Treasury. In order to understand this process it is necessary to review the evolution of money itself. For in a historical sense the international U.S. Treasury-bill standard is the culmination of money's evolution from an asset form to a debit form, and from a private-sector to a government debt form. But this evolution has been pressed to an illogical and one-sided extreme.

From asset money to liability money

Before coinage was invented, society used commodities such as cows and silver as mediums of exchange and means of conserving the value of its savings (much as is done in India and Africa to this day). Because cows and silver were the ultimate forms in which society kept its wealth, they also served as common measuring rods of the value of grain, jewels and other goods. However, such commodities were often cumbersome, particularly for trade among distant communities. Metallic coins were eventually adopted which compressed a relatively high amount of value into a small and convenient space, and were capable of being transported at will. This was asset money pure and simple.

Governments first got into the picture by establishing mints to assay the commodity content of gold, silver or copper coins, and to attest to their stated weight and fineness. A modest seigniorage was charged by the mint. Some clipping and shaving of coins occurred by those seeking to pilfer their valuable metal, and coins wore down as they circulated. But this discrepancy between actual and stated value was relatively unimportant compared to what happened when governments began to issue coinage of their own. For the time inevitably arose when states needed money over and above what they could conveniently raise from taxes and the spoils of war. When this point arrived they began to debase their currencies by intermixing more copper with gold and silver. The commodity value of such coins thus fell below their nominal face value. Governments increased their seigniorage profits by issuing fiat currency whose worth rested mainly in local political authority, not metallic content. Wars were particularly instrumental in inducing governments to raise funds in this manner, and most of the inflations and currency debasements of antiquity were associated with wars. Coinage was still asset money, but there was a fiat aspect to its issue. Something was got for nothing. The state appropriated society's wealth for its own use by the money-creation process.

As the Middle Ages gave way to modern times, European commerce required a convenient and portable medium of exchange which was also relatively immune to robbery by highwaymen and other bandits. Monasteries (such as the Knights Templar) and private goldsmiths took the lead in issuing paper notes against the bullion held in their safes. This function evolved gradually into the institution of depository banks, which for many centuries held bullion in their vaults and issued notes against it. At first the banks maintained 100 per cent reserves, so that their note issue was fully backed by their bullion. But it soon became apparent that many of their notes were kept in circulation, with only a portion being cashed in for bullion in any given period. Banks were therefore able to lend some of their deposit balances at a profit. Thus, liability money, associated with bank loans and bank debts to depositors, began to develop alongside asset money. Money was evolving from a metallic commodity into an institution.

Inevitably, some banks were tempted to overextend their lending and note issues and subsequently failed. The public was thus periodically reminded of the obvious fact that no bank operating on a fractional-reserve basis could redeem all its notes and deposits if they were submitted at the same time. By definition, any bank operating on a fractional reserve basis would be insolvent in such a situation. It became clear that faith and confidence were required for the smooth functioning of any fractional reserve monetary system, and that under normal business conditions the liquid liabilities of banks need not be fully balanced by liquid assets.

The next institution to emerge was the central bank. Soon after England's "Glorious Revolution" of 1688 overthrew the Catholic Stuart monarchy and installed William III of Hanover, the new regime solicited proposals for financing its projected war with France. Many suggestions were made, especially for land banks. William Paterson, a Scotsman, proposed founding the Bank of England which would exchange the government's promissory notes for currency or deposit credits. In essence, the Bank of England (a private bank until it was nationalized in 1844) would stamp "legal tender" on government debt and circulate it (with the bank collecting interest for its service as an intermediary in the process). This expedient was emulated in country after country in a development that was early described by the German monetary theorist George Friedrich Knapp in *The State Theory of Money* (1905).

Each nation's central bank became the bank for the commercial banking system. It held deposits for and loaned funds to individual banks in order to stabilize the nation's credit by protecting deposits against seasonal and other special fluctuations in withdrawals and money flows. The central banks ultimately replaced the many smaller, private-sector institutions in issuing currency. National currencies became backed in part by the nation's monetary gold stock and in part by the government's promissory notes, that is, the national debt. Asset money was evolving more and more into liability money, and was becoming political by virtue of the fact that it was created and spent by national governments.

To most people, money still appears to be simply an asset. They may easily forget that the coins in their pockets, the folding money in their wallets, and the checking account balances at their commercial banks are also debts. Currency and coinage are debts of the government's Treasury, government IOUs marked "legal tender." Checking accounts are deposit liabilities of the commercial banks which hold them, against which bank loans are made. And, for every $7 deposited in a U.S. checking account, the bank must deposit roughly $1 with its central bank—the regional Federal Reserve Bank. These reserves in turn are invested by the Federal Reserve System in U.S. Treasury bills, that is, three-month or six-month notes issued when the government needs to borrow money. All domestic money is thus a form of credit—one that ultimately turns on the pivot of Treasury debt.

It is important to stress that not all monetary debts are expected to be repaid, particularly that component which is used as society's monetary base. If the U.S. Government repaid its entire federal debt, the nation would have no currency. Thus, a given proportion of society's monetary debt is a *de jure* but not a *de facto* liability: nobody ever expects a government to repay its domestic debt, merely to roll it over and refinance it.*

Alchemists failed to transmute base metals into gold, but national banks have succeeded in transmuting national debt into national money or legal tender. As a nation's debt grows, so does its monetary base, particularly in times of war when government cash needs are greatest. This explains why the great inflationary cycles of modern times have all coincided with wars—the American Revolutionary War, the Napoleonic Wars, the Civil War, World Wars I and II and, in more recent times, the Vietnam War.

Domestic money contrasted with international money

Trade within a single country can operate with currency based primarily on faith in domestic institutions. After all, each nation has its own taxing power and domestic money-issue privilege to finance its chosen policies. But international trade requires something more substantial than fiat money based on government debt. In modern times that something has been gold. To be sure, individual buyers did not actually use gold to pay for their imports. Instead, they exchanged their local currency for

---

*In the 1890s the U.S. Government's tariff revenues enabled it to begin repaying its outstanding debt. This created a shortage of the bonds needed by banks to hold as backing for their note issues. The national currency contracted and monetary panic ensued. Thus, it can hardly be claimed that it is in society's interest for a government to repay *all* its debt. Still, monetary cranks periodically warn of an imminent economic collapse on the ground that society has let its government become insolvent by issuing outstanding liabilities (its currency and Treasury bills) in excess of its short-term capacity to pay—as if it would ever be called upon to do so!

that of the seller's country, or paid in their own currency and let the seller himself make the exchange. These foreign currencies (or checks) were converted into domestic currency (or checking accounts) through the seller's or buyer's central bank, which periodically redeemed them for gold at the central banks of their countries of origin.

If trade and payments among countries were fairly evenly balanced, no gold actually changed hands: the currency claims going in one direction offset those going in the opposite direction. But when trade and payments were not exactly in balance, countries that bought or paid more than they sold or received found themselves with a balance-of-payments deficit, while nations that sold more than they bought enjoyed a surplus which they settled in gold. For many years it was an easy matter to judge a country's balance of payments: one had only to look at its gold movements. These movements rarely were large because each nation possessed only a given amount of gold, which was used to settle the balances as they occurred. If a country lost gold its monetary base would be contracted, interest rates would rise, and foreign short-term funds would be attracted to balance international trade movements. If the gold outflows persisted, the higher interest rates would deter new domestic investment and incomes would fall, thereby reducing the demand for imports until balance was restored in the country's international payments.

A unique form of international money developed in this century with the emergence of the so-called key currencies—first the pound sterling, and subsequently the U.S. dollar. For many years these currencies were desired universally. They functioned as a *store of value* as individuals, firms and governments across the globe conserved their international savings in bank accounts and investments denominated in sterling or dollars. They also functioned as a *medium of exchange* as many exporters—particularly in soft-currency countries—demanded payment for their goods and services in the form of these hard currencies. Finally, they functioned as a *stable measure of value* as shifts in the worth of soft currencies were measured in reference to them. In view of the ability of dollars or sterling to fulfil these three functions, the world was willing to accumulate working balances denominated in these currencies and held on deposit in the United States or England. However, demand for the key currencies could persist only so long as they were stable and liquid financial instruments, that is, only so long as they were readily convertible into real assets such as gold. For they remained a form of national debt, after all.

Emergence of the U.S. Treasury-bill standard in world finance

In the early postwar period the United States ran a substantial surplus in its international trade and payments. As Europe and Third World countries bought more from America than they sold to it, they shipped their little remaining gold to the United States, where it became part of the Treasury's gold stock and was used as backing for Federal Reserve notes. (Each dollar's worth of these notes was backed by 25 cents worth of gold.) If anything, the United States was concerned with how to provide the world with more gold so that foreign credit systems and prosperity (and hence, demand for U.S. exports) would not be brought to a halt by America's continued balance-of-payments surpluses. In fact, a major consideration underlying America's Cold War spending after the Korean War was the realization that the money spent by American troops abroad on local food, housing, rest and recreation, and general consumer goods, plus foreign oil to fuel American ships and aircraft, would provide foreign economies with much-needed dollars. U.S. payments slipped into deficit, but the Treasury had more than enough gold to meet all its net spending abroad.

During the 1960s America's overseas military spending represented the entire balance-of-payments deficit as the private sector and non-military government transactions remained in balance. By 1968 America's gold stock had shrunk to $10 billion (down from $22 billion in 1951) and foreign countries held much more than this amount in the form of dollar claims. America's debt to foreign central banks thus exceeded its ability to pay in gold. U.S. officials indicated that it would be "unfriendly" for foreign central banks to ask for settlement of any of their dollars in gold, and urged them to hold their dollar balances in the form of U.S. Treasury bills instead. Because America still provided the foundation for its allies' military defense, because it held veto power in the international organizations that provided foreign aid and other loans, and because of the pure inertia of its weight in postwar diplomacy, foreign countries (except France) acquiesced to American demands. The United States promised to curtail its balance-of-payments deficits—but took no real steps to do so.

Earlier key-currency countries, such as England, would have imposed domestic austerity programs to stem their payments deficits. Domestic employment and investment were periodically reduced by the deflationary "stop-go" policy that became a hallmark of Britain's attempt to support the international value of the pound sterling by pursuing balance-of-payments equilibrium. British government assets (such as its holdings in Woolworth) were even sold to foreign investors (mainly in the United States) to raise foreign exchange. But the United States had discovered how to avoid this, and indeed how to derive positive benefits from its balance-of-payments deficit. The nation was, after all, obtaining foreign resources for nothing more than promissory notes that quite visibly could not be repaid, at least not in gold at the going price of $35 per ounce. To be sure, the United States made repeated promises to put its financial house in order and restore balance in its international payments. But it escalated the war in Southeast Asia and its foreign spending continued unabated.

In fact, the U.S. Treasury was enjoying a built-in market for its debt, making it much easier to run domestic budget deficits. Not only were Americans able to obtain foreign goods, services, companies and other assets in exchange for mere pieces of paper, but these pieces of paper were U.S. Treasury IOUs. All the United States needed to do was to run a payments deficit and foreign central banks were deluged with dollars which they could only invest in U.S. Government promissory notes. To be sure, they could refuse to accept these dollars. But this would collapse the dollar's value on world currency markets, thereby allowing U.S. exports to undersell their own countries' products.

Europe's predicament soon became the basis of explicit U.S. strategy. The Chase Manhattan Bank's publication *Business in Brief* featured an article in April 1967 by its foreign economist, John Deaver, showing how the economic burden of America's payments deficit could be thrown onto foreign shoulders. Noting that U.S. military spending abroad showed little sign of slowing down in the face of an escalating war in Southeast Asia, and that private-sector trade and investment were moving more deeply into deficit, Dr. Deaver observed that:

> As dollar liabilities continue to grow, the question arises as to what would happen if foreign central banks wished to cash in all their dollars. By now total liquid liabilities of U.S. banks to foreigners is over two times the amount of our gold stock and about ten times the amount of free gold beyond that required to back the nation's currency. Thus, a run on the U.S. gold stock could not possibly be satisfied.

"Although no one knows what might occur in a crisis, two options are very clear," the author continued. First, the United States might revalue gold upwards, so that it could pay off foreign central banks in a lower volume of higher-priced gold. But this would reward America's enemies, Soviet Russia and South Africa, the world's two major gold producers. It also would reward France, whose policy of cashing in its surplus dollars for gold on a monthly basis irked U.S. officials to the point of francophobia. The alternative strategy was for the U.S. Treasury simply to stop selling (and buying) gold. This would confront foreign central banks with a serious dilemma:

> With their dollars no longer freely convertible into gold, they would have to decide what to do with the dollars they own, and how to deal with the dollars that would be presented to them by their own commercial banks for conversion into local currencies.
>
> But this would be a most disagreeable choice. On the one hand, if they permitted the dollar to depreciate, prices of U.S. goods would drop relative to domestically produced goods. Furthermore, it would make U.S. exports more competitive in third markets. This solution would be vigorously opposed by most exporters and businessmen abroad.
>
> On the other hand, if foreign central banks continued to support the dollar at its present [foreign exchange]rate, this would place them more unequivocally than ever on a dollar standard, a politically embarrassing solution to countries that had participated in the run on the dollar in the first place.
>
> If it is made unmistakably clear that in the event of a crisis the U.S. would simply terminate the privilege now given to foreign central banks of buying [U.S.] gold freely, then the burden of decision regarding the defense of the dollar would be shifted even more than now from the U.S. to the shoulders of European and other central banks.[1]

It also would create an international financial crisis that would hurt Europe more than the United States. About one-quarter of foreign national income involved exports or imports, compared to only 4 per cent for the U.S. economy. Thus, U.S. officials were able to hold a Sword of Damocles over Europe's head. "In any case," Dr. Deaver concluded, "foreign central banks cannot easily escape from dollars they now hold. . . . Thus, for the dollar holder, there is no place to go," that is, no place except leaving these dollars invested in Treasury bills.

The Federal Reserve System, which had guaranteed a 25 per cent gold backing for its paper currency since 1945, removed all gold cover in 1968. The last vestige of U.S. asset money was gone. In the international sphere, foreign dollar reserves had become the unrepayable debt of the U.S. Government. America's payments deficits became so large that the London Gold Pool, designed by world central banks to stabilize the price of publicly traded gold at $35 an ounce, was closed down in the face of massive speculation against the dollar. Henceforth there were two prices for gold, a pegged price of $35 an ounce among world central banks themselves, and a free-floating price for private sector transactions. In August 1971 President Nixon stated officially that America would no longer exchange its dollars for gold. In the absence of any other medium of exchange, the United States succeeded in establishing its own government debt as the key international monetary standard.

U.S. exploitation of its creditors

Foreign acceptance of the U.S. Treasury bill as the world monetary standard had a dramatic impact on the American economy. The nation's payments deficit was creating a built-in market for its national debt, and the government saw no need for economic restraint. Expansionary monetary and fiscal policies were pursued irrespective of their balance-of-payments consequences. In the face of a growing payments deficit the U.S. Government accelerated federal spending and money creation, and watched foreigners bear the cost of financing this spending spree. As government spending accelerated (without a corresponding rise in taxes) the federal debt rose sharply. During the 23-year period 1946–69 the publicly held federal debt grew by $14 billion—of which foreigners financed over $9 billion. Then, in only 39 months (from the beginning of 1970 through March 1973), as the U.S. payments deficit pushed massive amounts of dollars into foreign hands, the Treasury's net public debt jumped by $44 billion. Foreign central banks actually financed $52 billion of new federal debt, enabling U.S. private investors to actually reduce their holdings of Treasury securities by $7.5 billion (Figure 2.1).

The enormous growth in America's domestic money and credit supply drove up prices and thus reduced the dollar's purchasing power. The sharp increase in foreign central bank purchases of Treasury bills forced down the interest rates on these securities even though yields were rising in other areas of the U.S. money market. Americans wisely put their money into more profitable investments.

The dollars created by the United States in the process of running its balance-of-payments deficit and federal budget deficit not only inflated the U.S. money supply and U.S. prices, they inflated the whole world economy as these dollars were con-

FIGURE 2.1
Growth in the U.S. Federal Debt, 1946–76
(billions of dollars)

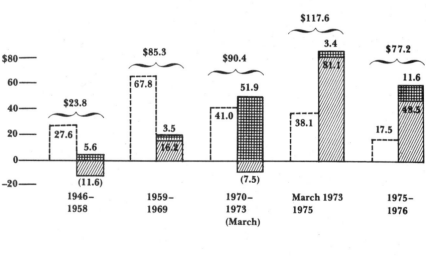

FIGURE 2.2

Ownership of U.S. Public Debt, 1945–76

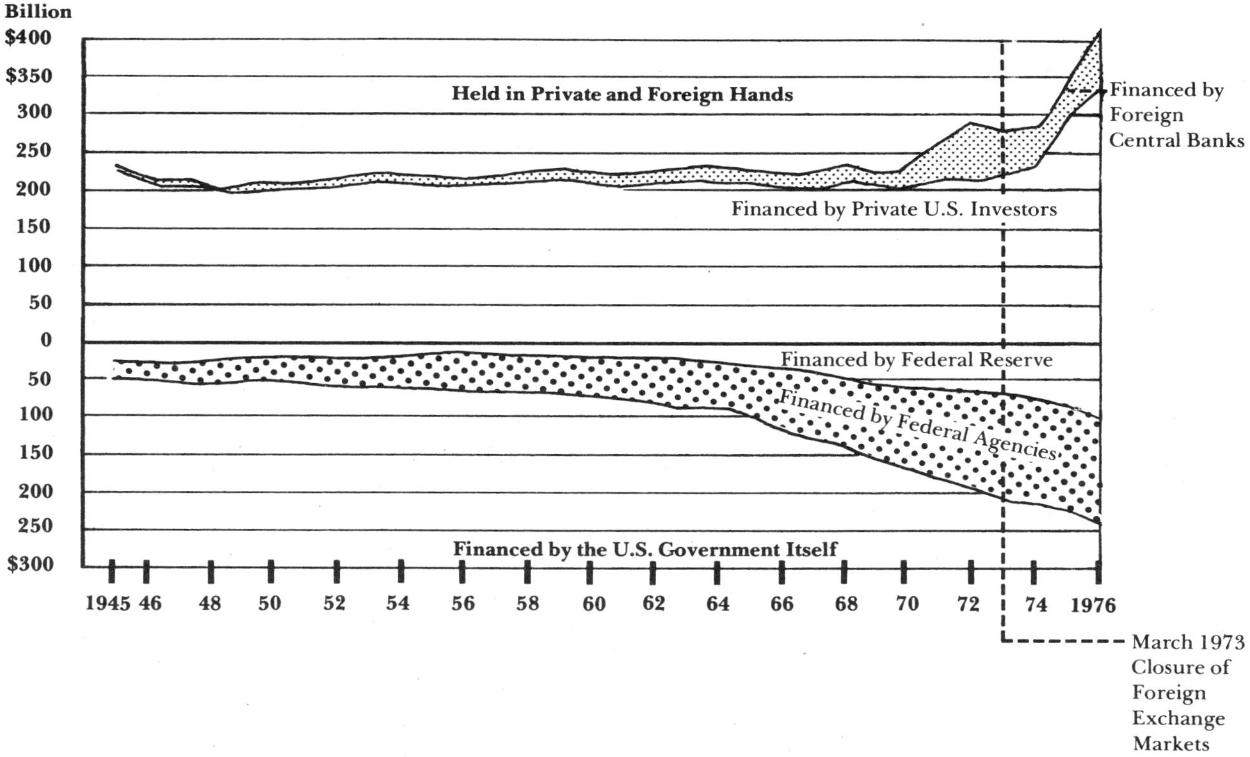

TABLE 2.1

America's Debt to Foreign Governments and Other Foreigners

(millions of dollars)

	1973	1974	1975	1976	1977
Foreign Official Assets in the U.S.	**$63,088**	**$69,317**	**$ 80,298**	**$ 87,197**	**$105,341**
U.S. Treasury securities	53,038	53,152	56,434	60,772	70,111
Bills and certificates	*31,910*	*31,909*	*35,054*	*34,181*	*37,675*
Bonds and notes, marketable	*5,209*	*5,674*	*5,032*	*6,613*	*11,788*
Bonds and notes, nonmarketable	*15,918*	*15,568*	*16,348*	*19,978*	*20,648*
Other U.S. Government securities	57	639	1,541	2,432	2,998
Other U.S. Government liabilities	1,606	2,759	3,483	5,215	10,227
U.S. liabilities reported by U.S. banks	8,340	12,466	18,284	16,126	17,138
Other foreign official assets	–	303	557	2,652	4,867
Other Foreign Assets in the U.S.	**22,284**	**26,772**	**43,486**	**46,800**	**60,522**
INTERNATIONAL FINANCIAL INSTITUTIONS	2,206	2,764	4,143	6,043	8,739
U.S. Treasury securities	539	344	647	2,890	5,730
Bills and certificates	*327*	*297*	*497*	*2,555*	*2,702*
Marketable bonds and notes	*212*	*47*	*150*	*335*	*3,028*
U.S. liabilities reported by U.S. banks	1,667	2,420	3,496	3,153	3,009

FOREIGN COMMERCIAL BANKS	14,687	17,768	30,360	29,880	38,022
U.S. Treasury bills and certificates	2	8	229	332	169
U.S. liabilities reported by U.S. banks	14,685	17,760	30,131	29,880	37,853
OTHER PRIVATE FOREIGN RESIDENTS	5,391	6,240	8,983	10,877	13,761
U.S. Treasury securities	621	596	769	1,090	1,174
U.S. liabilities reported by U.S. banks	4,770	5,644	8,214	9,787	12,587
Total	**$85,372**	**$96,089**	**$123,784**	**$133,998**	**$ 90,409**
U.S. Treasury Securities	*54,200*	*54,100*	*58,079*	*65,084*	*77,184*
Other U.S. Government Obligations	*1,663*	*3,398*	*5,024*	*7,647*	*13,225*

Source: U.S. Department of Commerce, Office of Business Economics, *Survey of Current Business*, December 1976 and earlier dates, Table 9.

verted into foreign currencies. Foreign central banks reluctantly invested their dollar inflows in U.S. Treasury bills whose interest rates were substantially below world levels and the pace of world inflation. These central banks had little choice: they were hardly about to invest their money in the U.S. private-sector capital market. (One can imagine the political embarassment that would have confronted Germany's central bank had it invested its surplus dollars in Con Edison or Penn Central stock, in New York City securities, or in the money market paper of real estate investment trusts and other businesses that soon became insolvent in the face of America's inflationary problems.)

The new situation became especially problematic in the case of Germany, the fruits of whose export-oriented prosperity were being siphoned off by the U.S. Treasury. German industry had hired millions of immigrants from Turkey, Greece, Italy, Yugoslavia and other Mediterranean countries. By 1971 some 3 per cent of the entire Greek population was living in Germany, producing cars and other export goods and thus earning profits for their companies as well as foreign exchange for Germany. Many private firms profited from this export trade, but when Volkswagens and other goods were shipped to the United States, the German economy lost. Companies could exchange their dollar receipts for deutsche marks with the German central bank and thus secure their profit on export sales, but Germany's central bank could only hold these dollar claims in the form of U.S. Treasury bills and bonds. It lost the equivalent of one-third the value of its dollar holdings during 1970–74 when the dollar fell by some 52 per cent against the deutsche mark, largely because the domestic U.S. inflation eroded 34 per cent of the dollar's domestic purchasing power. To add insult to economic injury, Germany found itself, along with Japan, Canada and Switzerland, financing America's domestic and foreign spending programs which included the war in Southeast Asia and military support of Israel, policies to which these governments had refused to contribute directly.

In the past, nations had sought to run payments surpluses in order to build up their gold reserves. But now all they were building up was a line of credit to the U.S. Government to finance its programs at home and abroad, programs which these central banks had no voice in formulating, and which were in some cases designed to secure foreign policy ends not desired by their governments. The U.S. Government showed no eagerness to stem either its payments deficit or its domestic budget deficit, for both were being financed in a painless way. "It is rather remarkable," observed France's president, Giscard d'Estaing in 1975, "that the war in Vietnam, a localized conflict of a very special nature involving a great power and a small power, could have such far-reaching effects on world economic equilibrium. . . . Any other country that was faced with a balance-of-payments deficit of this magnitude would have been obliged to take steps to restore balance whereas the United States was not obliged to do so; the method of financing its deficit exempted it from having to restore equilibrium and it was therefore a system which caused considerable inequality in the interplay of monetary power."[2] Financial disruption led to trade instability, as the process of financing America's deficit induced an inflation among the industrial nations collectively. By dislodging foreign-exchange rates it altered price relationships between industrial exporters and raw-materials exporters, and induced political shifts in the direction of world trade.

The world inflation stemming from America's domestic and foreign overspending distorted the industrial economies at the same time that it turned the terms of trade against Third World countries. But much more than the terms of trade was involved. Why should countries sell their exports if the foreign currency they received was effectively sterilized in the form of forced loans to the United States or other customers?

A new kind of disequilibrium mechanism was established. U.S. strategy apparently was to consolidate the evolution of asset money into liability money—gold into dollars in the form of Treasury bills—as a permanent development in the world economy, just as it had come to characterize the domestic monetary system. It seemed only logical to U.S. monetary authorities that what had evolved domestically should also evolve internationally. But this did not take account of the reality of national divisions among the world's governments. These divisions rendered irrational the ideal that any one nation's debt might serve as international money, to be issued at will by a single government to finance acquisition of other nations' resources.

Europe, Japan and Canada were transformed into an utterly novel form of satellite. Their apparent prosperity may have increased on a wave of exports to the United States and sale of their firms to U.S. investors, but the Treasury-bill standard obliged them to relend their resulting balance-of-payments surpluses to the U.S. Government. American consumers might choose to spend their incomes on foreign goods rather than to save, American business might choose to buy foreign companies or to undertake new direct investment at home rather than to buy government bonds, and the American government might finance a growing world military program, but this overseas consumption and spending would nonetheless be translated into savings and channeled back to the United States. Higher consumer expenditures on Volkswagens or on oil thus had the same effect as an increase in excise taxes on these products: they accrued to the U.S. Treasury in a kind of forced saving. Stepped-up U.S. purchases of European firms, and even U.S. military spending abroad provided more money to the government, whose spending did not have to be financed on a pay-as-you-go basis. (At least, Americans did not have to pay taxes to finance the spending for which foreign central banks, and hence foreign taxpayers, bore the cost.) It became increasingly questionable whether this debt would ever be repaid. The American strategy was to roll it over continually, preferably at interest rates lagging the rate of inflation.

To the extent that American business appropriated the major growth areas of European industry, the latter's prosperity would entail rising profits remitted back to the United States. It also would spur European demand for U.S. exports, thereby supporting new U.S. investment, employment and profits. And, it would help Europe to take over the burden of financing its own defense costs within NATO. America thus benefited from its net creditor status as world investor via its multinational firms, while on intergovernmental account it benefited from its net debtor status. Two types of international economic strategy therefore were developed for two different situations—a debtor strategy vis-à-vis other industrial nations to tap their central-bank resources, and a creditor strategy vis-à-vis Third World countries over which the United States held a financial leverage that it objected to when used by its own creditors (i.e., Europe, Japan, Canada, and subsequently OPEC).

As long as Europe remained dependent on the dollar and on

American economic and military aid, and as long as it remained divided into rival national entities with separate currency systems, monetary independence and an alternative to the dollar standard were not really feasible. The pound and the French franc could not serve as buttresses of a common European monetary system, at least given the currency parities assigned to them in discussions with U.S. officials during the closing days of World War II. A European alternative to the dollar would have to be pan-European. Its development would require a European balance of payments surplus, plus the creation of a common taxing authority (inasmuch as currency represents a form of national debt and hence a transfer of economic resources to the fiscal authorities). This in turn presupposed creation of a European parliament to represent the countries being taxed and to allocate expenditures of the funds raised. Europe was hardly prepared to approach this task in 1945, and three decades later it is only on the threshold.

CHAPTER 3

Third World Problems

While America was tapping the resources of its fellow industrial nations by drawing on foreign central-bank credit almost at will via its balance-of-payments deficits, its multinational firms exploited Third World countries in a more familiar investor-creditor process. And yet neither the classical analysis of international investment nor the socialist theory of imperialism anticipated the postwar system of Third World underdevelopment that resulted from market forces shaped by the international commodity cartel and reinforced by international aid-lending policies.

The phenomenon of Third World underdevelopment

Until the 1960s the policy of free trade and an open door to foreign investment was presumed to accelerate growth in less industrialized countries as well as to yield high profits to international investors. This belief, however, rested on a number of simplistic assumptions.

First of all, classical growth theory held that profits were highest in "young" countries and declined as industrial maturity was approached. As capital accumulated in increasing amounts in Britain, America and other industrial lead-nations, its earnings would tend to fall relative to the rents and wages earned by land and labor. This would lend domestic industry to invest abroad in search of higher profits. If all countries followed similar development patterns, in which economic growth was a direct function of the quantity of capital (relative to labor, land and natural resources), then foreign investment would help the less developed countries "catch up." It would raise their overall level of economic activity, generating higher incomes out of which to reimburse the original foreign investors. Foreign investment tended to be concentrated in the export sector, increasing output of Third World oil and minerals, tropical agricultural products and (in densely populated, low-wage countries) labor-intensive industrial manufactures in which younger countries enjoyed a comparative cost advantage. The export sector was expected to become a lead-sector, creating a source of domestic demand that would trigger a higher level of domestic economic activity. According to the Keynesian income-multiplier process, each new dollar of export demand was supposed to result in $3 to $5 worth of increased domestic spending and employment. It also was supposed to finance a general economic infrastructure to sustain and broaden the domestic development process.

Orthodox theory promised a mutually rewarding specialization of production between advanced and less developed countries. Each would produce what it was best at producing. "Nature" itself seemed to have destined some countries to be industrial while others remained raw-materials monocultures. Each country's "endowment" of labor, capital and land was supposed to be firmly established and employed at maximum efficiency. This meant that it could hardly be very responsive to government efforts to alter "factor proportions" by attracting capital or skilled labor, or to upgrade factor quality. Third World countries were advised to allocate their resources within boundaries set by existing world cost and productivity conditions, and in accordance with simple profit-maximizing principles. These criteria were not to be qualified by any long-term development strategy at odds with existing cost structures and trade patterns, by national security criteria such as increased economic independence and self-sufficiency, or by other policies designed to alter the world status quo. (And yet such overriding of market forces was applied consistently in the industrial nations.)

Lenin, Rosa Luxemburg and other socialists shared the classical view that industrial nations would compete to secure the world's less developed areas as investment outlets and export markets. They believed that foreign investment would industrialize these countries and thereby bring into being an urban working class along the lines experienced in the more advanced nations. Neither they nor classical economists anticipated that international investment would develop islands of foreign-controlled technology in the midst of deplorably backward economies and societies, or the degree to which foreign capital inflows would raise the economic level of those in power but not the general per capita income of the populace at large. Socialists believed that national revolution would vanquish right-wing, foreign-backed dictatorships, and that henceforth economic progress would be rapid. Only belatedly did they express the fear that foreign investment in and of itself might systematically warp the raw-materials exporting economies. Classical economists still have not accepted this almost universal fact. They point to specific mismanagement of Third World economies on a case by case basis, without searching into the general dilemmas that have led to this political-economic malformation.

The fact is that only a rudimentary working and middle class developed in most Third World countries. A rural exodus occurred without a subsequent urban prosperity. Growth in national output occurred mainly in the export sector, not in the production of goods destined for domestic consumption. Even people were exported, as the most talented, richest or best endowed were trained abroad, where many chose to stay. The landed aristocracies that dominated many Third World governments successfully opposed social-economic modernization. Non-progressive regimes were supported by the covert arms of industrial governments and by large international investors, as exemplified by America's overthrow of the Mossadegh government in Iran in 1953, the Arbenz government in Guatemala in 1954 and the Allende government in Chile in 1973.

Another unforeseen development was that concentration on export-oriented mineral and agricultural production retarded development of the Third World's domestic agricultural self-sufficiency. (Economists writing prior to World War I would have been amazed by the emergence of the most highly industrialized nations (i.e., those of North America and Europe) as the world's major food-surplus regions.) In country after country, the lack of progress in land reform and related agricultural modernization led to food deficits that consumed the modest balance-of-payments gains from foreign investment. (This process has been termed the Chile syndrome.)

To the extent that a development problem was recognized at all, it was viewed from the perspective of the industrial nations and their raw-materials requirements. The dollar and sterling balances held by Third World countries after the war were seen simply as sources of demand for European and American exports, and indeed were soon spent in the industrial nations without being invested in meaningful Third World capital formation or modernization. Third World countries were presumed to benefit indirectly from the North's economic reconstruction: demand for their primary products would grow in accordance with peacetime economic resurgence in North America and Europe, tacitly assuming an export-oriented pattern of development to be in the Third World's long-term interests. (After all, this was at a time when economic growth was viewed simply in terms of demand—e.g., consumption—not in terms of productive relations, capital formation and the modernization of institutional structures.) The World Bank did not even begin development lending until the Korean War in 1951. During its first five years it concentrated almost exclusively on reconstructing the economies of the industrial nations, while American bilateral aid was concentrated on Marshall Plan grants to Europe. When the World Bank did turn to Third World countries it was to finance an export-oriented infrastructure based on transportation, port development and related projects designed to make it less costly for foreign investors to extract their minerals. Little concern was paid to the fact that Third World imports were being financed increasingly by loans rather than by growth in net earning power through greater self-sufficiency or improved terms of trade.

To be sure, American economic spokesmen hoped that moderately egalitarian patterns of world trade and development would result. Perhaps the demand for raw materials would be supported as economic growth occurred in the industrial nations. (This was a sort of international "trickle down" theory.) Perhaps the international investment process would help Third World countries catch up. Perhaps latecomers might even enjoy an advantage in being able to proceed directly to the most modern technology. But little attention was paid to what was actually occurring— because reality proved offensive both to theory and to self-interest on the part of the industrial nations in perpetuating the process. Throughout the 1950s and 1960s the Third World fell further and further behind as measured by living standards and productivity differentials, domestic rates of capital formation and international dependency.

Foreign investment was viewed as involving few external costs. Its main effect seemed to lie in providing Third World governments with an extraordinary source of foreign exchange stemming from increased export earnings. Precisely because it helped create an "advanced" capital-intensive export sector it seemed to accelerate economic growth. But this growth was occurring in the midst of a backward domestic economy. Third World import dependency increased as rapidly as its exports were spurred by foreign investment. These raw materials were being worked up and consumed by labor in the industrial nations rather than forming the foundation for a broadly based Third World domestic industry (or what economists call forward linkages).

These facts were not perceived and emphasized mainly because the perspective underlying postwar world relations was the product of a simplistic and above all self-serving ideology. Economic growth was being channeled to service the industrial nations. The Third World's trade deficits were financed by capital inflows that connoted foreign appropriation of its resources and by foreign-aid borrowing to finance an export-oriented infrastructure. Export sectors became islands that were more a part of the industrial nations' economies than their own. Following the Korean War boom Third World resources were sold to foreign investors at declining relative prices (i.e., terms of trade) while the price for imports rose steadily. Policies based on this warped philosophy of development led to a declining spiral of poverty. When world demand for Third World products weakened during recession conditions in the industrial nations, or when the Third World's import prices rose (as they did following America's 1972 grain sale to the Soviet Union), the only option was to sell mineral resources even faster in a vain attempt to stabilize export income to obtain the foreign goods on which these countries had become dependent. This accelerated sale of resources glutted world markets all the more, holding down the international price of raw materials and thus creating an apparent "need" for even more foreign investment. Meanwhile, the Third World's growing foreign debt found no counterpart in domestic self-sufficiency or in balance-of-payments capacity to repay this debt. Thus, most former colonies relapsed into their prewar trade and borrowing patterns even though they were given their nominal political independence by European powers. They did not participate in the epoch of Keynesian social democracy and growth in living standards enjoyed by the industrial nations. Many entered periods of dictatorship and economic polarization as they became export monocultures.

With the benefit of hindsight it is clear that this monoculture syndrome and its associated agricultural backwardness was by no means inevitable. The Third World's enforced economic isolation during World War II had obliged it to provide its own foodstuffs and other essentials, laying a foundation for its future development. Many countries held substantial dollar and sterling balances as a result of their wartime raw-materials exports. But instead of using these funds to create a broad domestic capital base to elevate their economic status, their regimes seemed to prefer government luxury spending on monuments and arms, or infrastructure spending on roads and port development to facilitate their export growth. Their concept of capital formation was devoid of any purposeful definition in terms of their own development needs or options. For instance, the Argentine government paid over $1 billion to take over ownership of its rather dilapidated railroads that had been financed by British capital, instead of leaving them in British hands, regulating them in the "national interest" (i.e., at low profitability), and spending the billion to create a vast agricultural and industrial infrastructure.

In short, Third World countries let themselves be convinced that self-sufficiency in food production was not worth the price. Given food aid by the United States on relatively easy terms, and granted foreign exchange by the World Bank to finance an export-oriented development of their economies, they found the path of least economic resistance to lie in exchanging their minerals and plantation crops for grain and industrial manufactures imported from the United States and Europe. To have increased domestic food production would have required land reform and hence a confrontation with vested landowning interests. Furthermore, economic advisers from the industrial nations urged Third World governments to concentrate on seemingly high value-added (or high foreign-exchange earning) minerals and plantation crops without taking account of the social or structural economic consequences involved.

The postwar division of world labor and production was accepted as something natural, as if existing cost structures were not subject to deliberate transformation. A growing international dependency reinforced the domestic polarization between rich and poor. To be sure, many Third World countries extended their manufacturing sectors, but their industry often was dominated by local affiliates of multinational corporations that remitted their profits back home rather than reinvesting them in the host country. In this way the world saving function was concentrated in the industrial nations rather than extended to the less developed countries as forecast by both orthodox and socialist economic models.

Thus, what appeared in 1945–50 to be a process of world enrichment was perceived to have decayed into a process of international exploitation. The raw-materials exports that previously were viewed as increasing Third World GNP and export earnings (hence wealth) had an overwhelming offsetting aspect: they accelerated mineral depletion, warped host-country economies, contributed to food deficits, and caused a general deterioration in the Third World's terms of trade. Raw-materials exporters were selling their mineral endowments without putting in place an equivalent value of capital to enable them to sustain their economic growth once these minerals ran out. Their capital was being consumed rather than reproducing itself. This problem had not been considered by architects of the postwar economic order.

Workings of the world minerals cartel

The system of world commodity cartels, backed by the industrial governments and supported by their foreign-aid systems, shaped and dominated the "world marketplace" during the 1945–73 period. Most of the profits resulting from exploitation of relatively low-cost Third World mineral resources were appropriated by investors from the industrial nations. Host countries were left with as little as possible over and above local production costs and taxes. For instance, one-third of Chile's export price for copper was kept abroad by Anaconda, Kennecott and Cerro during the 1960s, and this ratio seems representative of many raw-materials exporting countries.

The Chilean economy thus received only about 67 cents out of each dollar's worth of copper exports. (The remaining 33 cents represented profits, depreciation, depletion, shipping and management charges retained in the United States, plus the cost of imported equipment used in producing Chilean copper.) The rich nations grew richer and more diversified while the Third World was depleted of its minerals and the pattern of its economic development was warped.

The industrial nations stood to benefit whatever the evolution of Third World terms of trade. If a world raw-materials oversupply held down Third World export prices, this would lower production costs in the industrial nations. If the terms of trade improved for Third World exports, the proceeds would accrue to the international minerals cartel which would use its profits to expand mineral output throughout the Third World. The world minerals industry has been described by Terence McCarthy as representing, physically, "the extraction of ores, and coal, and petroleum, etc., from the earth, but functionally something very different and very peculiar. On a world scale it is—or has been until now—a means by which capitalist cartels and trusts shift, gallon by gallon or ton by ton, bits of one country to other countries. And as they sell off one country bit by bit they use the proceeds to buy up leases on other countries mile by mile which they then sell off bit by bit until nothing is left behind but holes in the ground, some narrow and deep, some broad and shallow —until all the Third World becomes West Virginia."[1] The end of this so-called market process is to leave the raw-materials exporters with no remaining natural resources, a neglected agriculture, and thus with little productive capacity to support their domestic populations.

Oil represents the most obvious example of this type of exploitation. Prior to 1973 the oil-exporting countries were beholden to the international cartel sometimes known as the Seven Sisters: British Petroleum, Royal Dutch-Shell, and five U.S. companies— Exxon (formerly Standard Oil of New Jersey), Standard Oil of California (Socal), Texaco, Mobil and Gulf. These Seven Sisters had three brothers—the governments of the United States, Britain and Holland—and at least two cousins, the governments of France and Italy (which held shares in Companie des Pétroles and Ente Nazionale Idrocarburi, respectively). These five governments together supported the cartel's operations so long as they provided enough oil to sustain the Western world's 4 per cent average annual growth in petroleum demand at prices that declined steadily during a generation in which nearly all other prices were rising.

If the oil cartel had not controlled every aspect of the petroleum industry, or as economists say, if it had not been vertically integrated, prices at each stage of its operations would have reflected costs plus "normal" profits. However, by keeping crude oil prices so high that refining and marketing operations had to pay nearly as much for their crude oil as they received for their finished product (and far more than the oil companies paid to the oil-exporting countries), the industry's overall profits were artificially concentrated at the tax-exempt, crude-oil production stage. American companies managed to pay virtually no taxes. They enjoyed a depletion allowance on crude oil production, were able to write off all exploration and development costs against current income (rather than capitalizing them over a number of years), and could count their royalty payments to oil-exporting countries as credits against net U.S. income taxes (rather than simply as gross costs). Similar tax advantages were granted by England and Holland to their firms.

Despite the fact that the Third World had an absolute cost advantage in producing raw minerals, it could not translate this into a competitive advantage for industries based on these materials. For instance, its fertilizer and brass industries were obliged to pay the same price for their oil and copper inputs as did firms in the industrial nations. Both sets of firms bought their raw materials from the world minerals cartel at common world prices that did not reflect national cost disparities. Market forces established a single price for oil and for copper no matter where these commodities came from, even if it cost much less to take oil out of the ground in Arabia or copper out of Chile than to produce these minerals in the United States.

This warping of "true" economic relations was potentially unstable. For one thing, it left few profits to be taxed by governments of the countries in which the refineries and marketing networks were located—generally the politically and militarily secure industrial nations. It also tempted governments in the oil-exporting countries to tax reported earnings—which actually represented the earnings on oil-cartel investment spread over both crude-oil production and downstream operations taken together. This temptation grew larger as the relatively low export prices increased American and European dependence on Third World oil.

However, oil-exporting countries were stymied by the way in which the world oil cartel was organized. Although it allocated its profits in Third World countries, these countries were prevented from entering world markets and taking these profits themselves. For one thing, by operating its refineries and other downstream operations at a nominal loss, the international oil cartel deterred new entrants into the industry. Who would invest in expensive refineries and marketing systems that were dependent on high-priced crude oil and thus were unable to earn normal profits? On the other hand, what oil producer (or oil-producing country) could enter the oil industry without securing a market outlet for its crude oil? Both the production and downstream ends of the world oil industry thus were effectively controlled by the cartel.

Location of oil refineries in the industrial oil-consuming nations (and their island dependencies such as the Netherlands Antilles and Curaçao, off the coast of Venezuela) protected the industry against expropriation by oil-producing governments. The cartel was able to boycott any oil-producing country that might request a higher price for its oil: control over crude oil reserves would be of little avail to Third World mavericks without their own refineries and marketing outlets, for they would find no market for their output. The oil industry could turn elsewhere readily.

This did not stop some countries from trying to improve their lot. In 1953 Iran's socialist Prime Minister Mohammed Mossadegh moved to nationalize the British-owned concessions. But he found himself confronted by the oil industry's ultimate weapon, intervention by the U.S. Government and suspension of all foreign aid to Iran. As President Eisenhower wrote to Mossadegh:

> The failure of Iran and of the United Kingdom to reach an agreement with regard to compensation has handicapped the Government of the United States in its efforts to help Iran. There is a strong feeling in the United States, even among American citizens most sympathetic to Iran and friendly to the Iranian people, that it would not be fair to the

American taxpayers for the United States Government to extend any considerable amount of economic aid to Iran so long as Iran could have access to funds derived from the sale of its oil and oil products if a reasonable agreement were reached with regard to compensation whereby the large-scale marketing of Iranian oil would be resumed. Similarly, many American citizens would be deeply opposed to the purchase by the United States Government of Iranian oil in the absence of an oil settlement.

There is also considerable sentiment in the United States to the effect that a settlement based on the payment of compensation merely for losses of the physical assets of a firm which has been nationalized would not be what might be called a reasonable settlement.

Mr. Eisenhower concluded that "the Government of the United States is not presently in a position to extend more aid to Iran or to purchase Iranian oil."[2] Soon thereafter Mossadegh was overthrown and murdered. The new Shah, installed with Anglo-American support, negotiated the desired "reasonable agreement" with the British.

With this kind of leverage the oil cartel had no difficulty buying oil at the low-cost margin of production, i.e., that which it cost the oil-exporting countries to produce it, plus a comparatively modest royalty charge. This oil was then resold by the cartel to its own refineries at the same high price paid for oil from relatively high-cost producers in Texas, Oklahoma and offshore sites. The difference between these two margins of production was pocketed by the oil cartel.

A two-tier price system was thus created for world crude oil, and the system paid handsome rewards. On the one hand, high prices were supported to cover production costs and profits in the United States, and indeed to enable Europe to develop its North Sea oil. But there was no intention to permit foreign oil-producing countries to enjoy the benefit of their favorable cost differential. Artificial supply and demand forces were maintained to make sure that this accrued to the private cartel. For instance, import quotas were imposed to limit the volume of Third World oil that the multinationals could sell in the United States. Independent dealers could not import any oil, so that Third World countries could not find customers for their petroleum outside the cartel. A regulated flow of foreign oil thus was imported by major U.S. oil companies under government license at low world trade prices, and sold at enormous, virtually tax-free profits. To be sure, countries like Korea would have liked to buy their oil directly from Third World countries and thus saved the cartel's margin of profit. But they were told by their suppliers (in the case of Korea, Gulf Oil) that if they bought one gallon from any other supplier they would lose their "preferred customer" status, that is, would face the danger of being cut off in an emergency. When this threat of a cartel-sponsored oil embargo began to lose its force, direct bribery of government officials was resorted to in stories that are just now coming to light.

This state of affairs led a former editor of the U.S. Bureau of Mines' *Minerals Yearbook* to observe that the United States and other Western nations had bought foreign raw materials "under terms similar to those under which we got Manhattan Island from the Indians. We still claim, without a shred of justification, 'right of access' to everyone else's natural resources at prices of our own choosing." The United States had purchased oil at $2 or $3 per barrel, and in general "never allowed a price to be paid for minerals that reflected long-term scarcities of nonrenewable resources, kept up with the rising cost of traded manufactures or provided decent wages to those who did the mining."[3] Exhaustible resources of raw materials were being exchanged for the renewable resources of the industrial, food-surplus, capital-accumulating nations.

So rapid was the repayment of U.S. overseas oil investment in balance-of-payments terms that the oil cartel was exempted from the country's foreign investment controls imposed by the Johnson administration in 1964. In 1966 the Chase Manhattan Bank published a study of the *Balance of Payments of the Petroleum Industry* which examined the industry's worldwide operations in the years 1960 and 1964 and concluded that "the average dollar that leaves the country in the form of new petroleum investment is returned within three years. This is largely because of the many investment-related receipts that, in addition to remitted income, benefit the U.S. payments balance. Because of the shortness of this payback period a policy of tightening today's investment restraints would seriously impair the international operations of the U.S. petroleum industry. In balance-of-payments terms, it would yield little in the long run."[4]

To prevent the world oil cartel from playing the oil-exporting

countries against each other these governments joined together
to coordinate their export strategy. The purpose underlying the
formation of the Organization of Petroleum Exporting Countries
(OPEC), asserted the President of Venezuela, "was to protect the
basic wealth extracted from our subsoil at prices that have never
compensated for the costs of our imports and of the technology
needed for our development. . . . It is our countries that have
always borne the unacceptable burdens of international trade.
Our companies and demands have never been heeded, and our
legitimate aspirations have been frustrated."[5] The Shah of Iran
pointed out that "in 1947 the posted price of a barrel of oil in
the Persian Gulf was 2.17 dollars; in 1959 [it] was $1.79 . . . a
decrease of 38%" during a time when prices of "world commodities increased by between 300 and 400%."[6]

OPEC was not taken very seriously by the industrial nations
and, in fact, was generally ineffective in its early years. Brain-
washed by the multinationals and by economic advisers supplied
by the World Bank and other aid-lending institutions, and well
aware that foreign aid was granted only to right-thinking governments, OPEC officials accepted as a fact of life the dual price
system for world crude oil, foreign ownership of their national
resources, and a general laissez faire philosophy of world trade
and development. Perhaps the oil exporters did not recognize
the degree to which industrial nations were as dependent on
them (and on other raw-materials exporters) as the Third World
was dependent on industrial and food-exporting nations. Furthermore, they remained dependent on the U.S. military umbrella. Most important of all, their own native economists were
trained largely in American and British colleges which taught an
economic ideology that was highly self-serving to the industrial
nations.

The industrial nations and their cartels seemed to be consolidating their strength vis-à-vis Third World countries, for the
latter did not yet feel themselves in a position to act against the
postwar trade system. They finally did so only as a last resort,
when their alternative was imminent depletion and impoverish-
ment. Oil companies in the United States and Europe planned to
vastly increase Third World petroleum output in keeping with
their own mushrooming energy consumption. Cheap fuel was
powering a prosperity in which Third World populations were

hardly sharing. Gaps were widening in international incomes and productive powers, requiring ever greater transfers of foreign aid, loans and investments—hence debt—to balance international payments. While the world's economies became increasingly interlocked, largely through the vehicle of private investment by multinational firms, this involved a growing dependency on the part of many Third World countries that came to rely on the United States and other industrial powers for imports of vital foodstuffs, arms, and often for their domestic political support. Structural deficits emerged in their balance of payments as the choice between importing food and growing it at home became less a matter of comparative costs and choice than of outright necessity, e.g. limited productive capacity. The Third World's agricultural productivity stagnated, while in the industrial nations it even surpassed growth in industrial productivity. Earlier economic orthodoxy had held that the industrial nations would grow increasingly dependent on Third World food and raw-materials surpluses, which presumably would be priced at their high-cost margin of production. In fact just the opposite was occurring: it took an ever-growing quantity of Third World exports to pay for each unit of imported food, as well as for arms and other manufactures.

This system whereby economic affluence in the industrial nations was associated with Third World underdevelopment collapsed from its very strength: Third World countries were left with practically no choice but to assert themselves in the face of foreign control over their economies and diplomacy. The reasons for the United States and other industrial nations pressing their advantage to this extreme are to be found in the changing nature of the Cold War, which evolved from Western confrontation with the Soviet Bloc to a Soviet-American détente that threatened both Europe and the Third World.

CHAPTER 4

Cold War Strains Resolve Themselves in Détente

By year-end 1972 it seemed that Europe could not resist massive dollar inflows without risking a monetary crisis that would disrupt its foreign trade and domestic economic life. Third World countries for their part could not fight the international mineral cartel without facing market sanctions and a foreign-aid cutoff that also would result in social-economic crisis. Thus, both the industrial and Third World governments seemed hooked on new forms of international dependency that did not exist before World War II.

The United States alone seemed to maintain diplomatic initiative. U.S. foreign policy reflected its domestic economic drives, whereas countries historically were obliged to adjust their home economies to fit international financial constraints. Foreign countries still had to live within their means. Only the United States need not restrain its domestic economy in the face of balance-of-payments deficits. It alone could continue running into debt to foreign central banks without having to impose domestic austerity programs. In the face of America's economic initiative, foreign countries had to adjust their trade and financial policies to dovetail into domestic U.S. programs. Third World raw-materials sales (preferably at stable prices) were determined mainly by U.S. consumption needs, with the caveat that these exports must not compete with existing U.S. productive capacity. U.S. sales to Europe and Japan of grains and other exports (preferably at rising prices) were to expand so as to absorb full U.S. output. But if the American economy should experience domestic shortages, foreign countries would be cut off. In effect, foreign economies were to serve as residual suppliers and residual markets.

America thus dominated world affairs despite its apparent lack of economic self-control. Its multinational firms earned over $10 billion abroad in 1972, and were projected to earn as much as $20 billion annually by 1980—enough to restore surplus in the nation's balance of payments despite its continued overseas military involvement. American firms controlled world trade in raw materials, manufactured goods and arms, while U.S. bank branches dominated the Eurodollar and Asiadollar markets. International credit was created at will to finance the overseas expansion of American firms and to lend at a nice profit to central banks in payments-deficit countries. Foreign commercial banks rarely participated in consortium loans to debtor countries without being joined by major U.S. commercial banks and by U.S. Government participation. The U.S. Treasury for its part still held $10 billion in gold, more than any other single country. It retained veto power in the International Monetary Fund and World Bank, so that intergovernmental aid was not extended on terms opposed by the United States. Foreign countries still hesitated to pursue policies actively opposed by American diplomats; given the immediate costs versus benefits there seemed little alternative but to remain in America's economic orbit.

Internal contradictions of the Cold War

How did this system break down? How was America's seemingly impregnable economic power dissipated? The answer can be found largely in the Cold War's military costs, which rose steadily from 1951—when the Korean War first pushed the U.S. balance of payments into deficit—through the Vietnam years. Overseas military spending represented the whole of America's balance-of-payments deficit during the 1960s, deranging the Western economic system that the Cold War originally had sought to cement. Thus, whereas division of the world into two competing blocs in 1945–46 was designed to isolate statist economic systems from an American-oriented alliance based ostensibly on laissez faire principles, it ended by creating a growing economic rivalry among the Western capitalist nations. America's balance-of-payments deficits resulting from its war in Southeast Asia became an economic wedge dislodging the Bretton Woods system of international finance and its gold-based system of fixed exchange rates. The war's financial strains led to closure of the London Gold Pool in 1968, dollar devaluation and gold inconvertibility in 1971, and world financial and trade crises in 1973. Without a smoothly functioning financial system, the superstructure of relatively free trade and investment could not be maintained. The United States reverted to economic protectionism instead of supporting progress toward generalized tariff reductions. It closed its doors to world investors and tied its foreign aid to strictly self-serving objectives. Congress or the executive branch of government vetoed laissez faire principles whenever they did not serve U.S. interests. This created a double standard of economic diplomacy that virtually drove foreign countries to seek independence from America's expanded system of nationalism.

The inevitable economic consequence of the Cold War was therefore to create a growing antagonism between America and Europe, especially as Europe approached economic parity with the United States. For the basic Cold War division of the world into a capitalist West and a communist East implied a unipolarity within each of the two rival systems. Both lead-nations controlled the terms of trade for their exports vis-à-vis those of their supplier countries, and both controlled their respective international payments systems, as well as their military structures. American economic planners expected Europe and Japan to remain in a state of dependence stemming from an ongoing financial and economic reliance on scarce dollar credits and U.S. agricultural surpluses, just as the Comecon countries and China were supposed to depend on Soviet Russia.

However, this state of affairs contained the seeds of its own dissolution, especially within the West. Not only was the United States obliged to bear the major cost of defending the West, but U.S. officials aggravated their burden by viewing all left-wing movements abroad as potential extensions of Soviet power. This transformed domestic politics throughout the world into a conflict between right-wing regimes which often developed into military dictatorships supported by the United States, and left-wing regimes which were pushed increasingly into the Soviet camp by Western economic sanctions (as in the cases of Cuba and Vietnam). America's struggle against Soviet Russia and its associated bloc of nations thus took on the characteristics of a general struggle against land reform movements and emerging social systems in Latin America, Iran, Southeast Asia, Africa, and more recently in Greece, Portugal, Spain and Italy.

Only the United States and Russia seemed able to afford the costs of large-scale troop deployments abroad, not to mention atomic arms and the space race. Over time, however, they could afford these costs only by warping their own civilian economies. America's Cold War spending may have pulled the country out of economic recession in 1950 and again in 1958, but it distorted the shape of the ensuing prosperity, to the detriment of domestic capital formation.

Civilian economies outside of the United States avoided this military overhead and began to overtake America's civilian economy, just as in Eastern Europe living standards came to surpass those in Soviet Russia. These tendencies weakened the hold of both superpowers on their satellites and allies. But America still sought to maintain domination over its non-communist allies, and to prevent emergence of leftward-leaning governments throughout the world. Soviet Russia waged a parallel diplomacy to maintain its own satellite system and to prevent economic leakages to the West in trade, payments and emigration. Russia marched into Hungary and Czechoslovakia, while America involved itself in Vietnam. What began as a Cold War pitting the Western capitalist nations, led by the United States, against the state-planned economies, led by Soviet Russia, thus evolved into a struggle to perpetuate the West's and East's respective dependency systems. To support the military trappings of these two systems each superpower sought to tap the resources of its satellites. But the economic strength underlying both Soviet and American domination of their respective spheres of influence was being sapped. Military power was less and less grounded in economic strength.

European integration leads to growing rivalry with the United States

The year 1957 marked a turning point in world affairs with Russia's launching of Sputnik, formation of the European Economic Community (EEC) effective on the first day of 1958, and America's worst recession since World War II. Seeking both to close the missile gap with Russia and to spur economic recovery, the American government stepped up its military spending (particularly in rocket and missile technology) which set the stage for its subsequent debacle in Southeast Asia.

U.S. diplomats at first viewed the Common Market as little more than a customs union for the six nations—France, Germany, Italy, Holland, Belgium and Luxembourg (joined in 1970 by Britain, Ireland and Denmark). European economic integration promised greater prosperity and thus a growing market for U.S. exports, but no political move to independence from the United States or even a competition with American exporters. American firms had shown little interest in investing in Europe so long as it remained fragmented into segregated national markets, but a surge of U.S. investment occurred after the Treaty of Rome. The continent's prosperity subsequently helped it take over the costs of its own defense, thereby freeing it from American military subsidies and economic aid. It also inspired a move toward economic, political and military independence, particularly in the face of America's balance-of-payments deficits and the inflationary pressures these deficits conveyed to Europe.

An early source of U.S. antagonism with Europe was the Common Agricultural Policy (CAP), formulated in 1960. In order to transfer European labor from the countryside to the cities, the CAP emulated the American policy of price supports, crop subsidies and other paraphernalia of agricultural protectionism to induce farmers to consolidate their farmlands into larger units using less labor and more farm machinery. Europe refused to yield to America's demand that a fixed share of its grain markets be guaranteed to U.S. farmers irrespective of Europe's growing capacity to feed itself. France vetoed Britain's first two applications for membership in the EEC when the British government rejected the CAP while acquiescing to America's insistence on a guaranteed fixed share of Britain's grain market.

In the military sphere, U.S. antagonism grew when General de Gaulle withdrew France from NATO in the mid-1960s on the ground that it was run for American purposes which at some point might diverge from those of France and other European nations. Even Germany, despite its thriving economy, was unwilling to pay the cost of American occupation, although it did agree to make advance payments on arms purchases and to recycle

America's deutsche-mark troop-support costs by lending an off-setting sum to the U.S. Treasury. NATO thus remained a balance-of-payments burden for the United States, and the burden increased when the dollar was devalued in 1971 and 1973.

Cold War strains

While Europe's economy was strengthening, the Cold War's domestic and balance-of-payments costs were laying the groundwork for America's domestic inflation as well as dislodging the dollar's stable position in world finance. In 1964–65 President Johnson and his economists were unwilling to acknowledge that U.S. domestic spending programs must be curtailed if the war in Southeast Asia were to be financed on a noninflationary basis. The President struck a bargain with congressional liberals to sponsor their domestic spending programs if they would support his war. The American economy sought to consume both guns and butter, with the Federal Reserve System simply creating the credit to finance the resulting budget deficit. These surplus dollars spilled over to become a demand for foreign goods and services, ending up in foreign central banks which recycled them to the United States by purchasing Treasury securities. In this manner an amount equal to the entire foreign-exchange cost of America's war in Southeast Asia was financed by the central banks of Europe, Japan and Canada. America's inflationary money-surplus became a payments deficit which, in turn, was recycled to inflate domestic U.S. capital markets in a process that persisted during 1968–73. Government economists depicted the nation as becoming richer and richer.

America's unwillingness to pay for the unpopular war, coupled with foreign unwillingness to further underwrite the war-inspired U.S. payments deficit, began to fracture the West's political and military alliances. When West Germany protested against U.S. demands that its central bank recycle its dollar inflows into special nonmarketable U.S. Treasury securities, and when it threatened to refuse exchanging deutsche marks for future dollar inflows, American officials threatened to reduce their troop commitment to Germany's military bases. Acquiescence in financing the U.S. payments deficit, and in deteriorating terms of trade for countries outside the United States (in the face of sharply rising U.S. food and arms prices) seemed to be the price required for other countries to remain under the U.S. military umbrella. To U.S. eyes the price being asked of Germany and the rest of Europe was part of a *quid pro quo* compensating it for absorbing the lion's share of the West's defense costs. But to many European eyes these expenditures were better foregone, especially those in Third World areas. When Europe, Japan and Canada found themselves obliged to finance America's foreign spending they demanded a voice in the execution of Western defense policy. This was denied them. Europe therefore moved to design an international diplomatic and economic system that would better reflect its evolving interests.

The inflationary pressures stemming from America's attempt to transfer the war's costs to its allies led Europe, Japan, Canada, and finally the Third World countries to seek to extricate themselves from their position of subservience to the United States. This meant breaking away from the U.S.-sponsored system of world payments, trade and foreign aid. The economic process that had struck U.S. eyes as an ongoing success story was coming to be viewed abroad as a parasitic system. Instead of the world economy being geared for peace it was becoming enmeshed in financing America's worldwide military spending. U.S. economic interests thus evolved along a collision course with economic interests in both the industrial nations and the Third World. Each party, each hemisphere had come to interpret the other as wanting something for nothing.

The first antagonism had developed among the industrial nations themselves, between payments-surplus Europe, Japan and Canada on the one hand, and payments-deficit America on the other. The second antagonism was slower to develop—that between regions whose terms of trade were improving (i.e., the industrial nations generally) and the Third World raw-materials exporters whose terms of trade were suffering most from the worldwide inflation. The final conflict of interest arose in the military sphere. The U.S. Government asked members of NATO, SEATO and CENTO to bear an increasing share of their defense costs, but they were unwilling to do so in the face of America's domination of these regional defense organizations and, in particular, the unique U.S. veto power over their use of nuclear weapons.

America's *rapprochement* with Soviet Russia

America's trade and investment relationships with Europe had indebted it to the point where a U.S. trade-and-payments surplus would be a hollow benefit to the U.S. economy: real goods and services would merely be exchanged for its own paper-dollar assets. Unless it could continue to run a payments deficit with Europe, Japan and Canada, it could trade profitably only with the Communist nations. These nations had never extended dollar credits to America for the simple reason that they had been at odds with it for years. Thus, they had no Treasury bills to sell in the process of financing their trade deficits with the United States. Most important of all, their economies were complementary to that of the United States. The price of U.S. agricultural exports would be supported by demand from Communist countries, while the price of U.S. imports might be pressed down by communist sales of raw materials and gold (whether these were sold directly to U.S. buyers or to third countries). Europe and Japan would be left holding their U.S. Treasury bills.

America's trade and payments problems with other industrial nations therefore opened the door to its *rapprochement* with the Soviet Union. Cold War tensions between the United States and Soviet Russia had reached an unsupportable limit. Meanwhile, the economic and political tensions felt by the United States toward Europe and the Third World were also approaching a breaking point. America began to turn toward Russia to secure peaceful commercial advantages that it could no longer obtain from its Western allies.

Détente with the Communist countries might have the additional benefit of recementing the Western Alliance by conjuring up fears that America would not respond to an external Russian threat. At the very least it promised to impose upon Europe the type of military burden that had weighed down the U.S. and Russian economies since World War II. Only a little arms rattling by Russia or the United States toward the Near East or some other region would induce foreign governments to purchase more weaponry, thereby adding to the demand for American arms. At any rate, the joint Soviet-American pronouncements that war between themselves was becoming less and less probable made it increasingly apparent that other countries would have to look out for themselves militarily.

A common interest linked the United States and Soviet Russia in preventing emergence of any Third Force in world affairs, be it China or the emerging triangular axis comprised of Europe, the Near East and Africa. After all, the Third International and CIA both had fought communism in Europe and other areas outside the Soviet sphere. Together, the Russian and American governments hoped to stymie social revolution in the Third World, Asia and Europe—Russia by its control over the Communist parties in these areas, America through its domination of the Social Democratic parties. The Soviet Union for its part had always feared the advent of socialism outside of Russia as threatening the focal point for an ideology that had come to be used for strictly Russian national ends. This is why Kissinger remarked that "A Communist Western Europe would be a headache for us. It would be a headache for the Soviets as well. They probably prefer not to see Communist powers taking over in Western Europe." America's struggle against statist or socialist regimes in the Western Alliance could thus continue without extension of this struggle to conflict head-on with Soviet Russia, and without the earlier fears that Russia was behind every left-wing movement throughout the West.

Rising U.S. economic antagonism toward its Western allies was thus associated with a winding down of its antagonism toward Soviet Russia. In fact, Soviet-American détente confronted Europe, Asia and Africa with a dual colossus: Kissinger's Partnership of Strength between the two great superpowers threatened to smother development of any new countervailing power. In principle it was intended to consolidate the 1945 division of the world into two separate camps, each revolving around its respective nuclear superpower. However, both superpowers were caught off base by the 1973 Middle East War.

PART II

Global Fracture

CHAPTER 5

The Events of 1973

The postwar economic order culminated in four 1973 traumas: the March currency crisis followed by floating exchange rates; Dr. Kissinger's April proposal for a New Atlantic Charter and Europe's repudiation of its principles; America's summer export embargoes on forty agricultural commodities and scrap metal; and the October Middle East War, followed by Europe's grounding of U.S. troops and supplies, the Arab oil boycott of the United States and Netherlands, and capping it all, OPEC's quadrupling of world oil prices. Coming together in a relatively short span of time, these events reinforced one another. Like stresses in the earth's continental plates which finally result in an earthquake, the buildup of pressures on the world's economic foundations resulted in a vast slippage in the diplomacy of international trade and finance.

The so-called Smithsonian Agreements, reached by the world's major central bankers meeting in Washington in December 1971 to establish new par values for their currencies, had lasted only half a year. In June 1972 the pound sterling was floated (that is, left to sink from $2.61 to $2.44). Furthermore, America's payments deficits continued to grow despite the dollar's 11 per cent devaluation under the Smithsonian Agreements. In July the world's currency markets were swamped by massive speculative pressures and movements out of U.S. dollars into German marks, Swiss francs and other strong currencies. Finally, on February 12, 1973, the United States was obliged to devalue the dollar by a further 10 per cent. Japan and Italy joined Canada, Switzerland and England in letting their currencies float, that is, letting their value be established by market forces rather than by central-bank intervention. Since the Smithsonian Agreements, the dollar had fallen by a trade-weighted average of 23 per cent against the OECD currencies (excluding the Canadian dollar, which closely maintained its parity with the U.S. currency). But even this devaluation was insufficient to prevent massive funds from flowing out of the United States, as well as from Britain. Matters were not helped by the fact that on the very day the U.S. dollar was devalued, Secretary of the Treasury George Shultz announced his intention to abolish by yearend 1974 the Interest Equalization Tax and the foreign direct investment controls that had been imposed in 1963 and 1964 to curtail U.S. investment outflows. (These controls were removed ahead of schedule, in January 1974.) This indicated that America's "galloping benign neglect" of its balance of payments would continue indefinitely, and that the government would make little or no effort to curtail further dollar outflows. A renewed run on the dollar ensued, and $6 billion was converted into German marks during a single week at the beginning of March. European central banks finally acted to protect themselves by closing their currency markets while they met in Paris during the week of March 9–16.

Following a 3 per cent revaluation of the German mark, the EEC countries announced a joint float of their currencies, called the Snake by the financial press. Henceforth their currencies were to be regulated within a 2.25 per cent margin of one another (subject to periodic shifts, the first of which was a further 5.5 per cent revaluation of the German mark in June). Europe thus adopted a system of stable but adjustable exchange rates and urged other nations to follow suit. Even more important, their central banks announced that when European currency markets reopened they would no longer purchase unwanted dollars. This terminated the system of quasi-automatic European central bank credit to the U.S. Treasury. Gold was re-introduced as backing or collateral for intergovernmental loans, paving the way for the metal's return as a means of settling international payments imbalances. The dollar fell in value as currencies became free to float or sink against one another. This ended America's ability to draw upon foreign resources simply by creating dollar credits. Its refusal to settle its balance-of-payments deficits with anything except Treasury IOUs left it with only a paper-backed, fiat currency whose international value was determined by the state of its balance of payments, that is, by supply and demand conditions. The new floating currency system also imposed costs on foreign countries: it reduced the value of dollars already accumulated by their central banks, and also provided U.S. exporters with a competitive edge in world markets.

This was only the first shock. On April 23, Secretary of State Henry Kissinger delivered a speech designed to put Europe back in its place as a U.S. satellite. In this "Year of Europe" speech he called for a New Atlantic Charter to counteract Europe's moves toward economic, political and military independence, just as the first Atlantic Charter of 1941 had laid the foundation for stripping England of its preeminence in the world. "For us," Kissinger asserted, "European unity is what it has always been—not an end in itself but a means to the strengthening of the West," that is, of the U.S. diplomatic sphere. "The prospect of a closed trading system embracing the European community and a growing number of other nations in Europe, the Mediterranean and Africa appears to be at the expense of the United States and other nations which are excluded. In agriculture, where the United States has a comparative advantage, we are particularly concerned that Community protective policies may restrict access for our products." Kissinger called for new economic agreements to be reached by direct bilateral negotiation between national presidents not "burdened" by technicians, foreign parliaments and the Common Market's technical machinery for negotiating monetary and trade issues on a community-wide basis. The new negotiations "must engage the top political leaders. . . . If they are left solely to the experts, the inevitable competitiveness of economic interests will dominate the debate. The influence of pressure groups and special interests will become pervasive." The United States might express its national interest via congressional restrictions on presidential negotiating authority, but Europe was to relinquish its countervailing safeguards. Its members must negotiate not as a confederacy with a common purpose but as individual nations that could be divided and conquered.

Few Europeans were impressed. *Le Figaro* asserted that, "In Paris, there has always been considerable mistrust of an alliance that could appear a bit like that between the wolf and the sheep, because of the specific weight of the main partner." In Germany, Willy Brandt rejected the proposed New Atlantic Charter and insisted that economic, monetary and military discussions not be linked in a single package but retain their "formal separation."[1]

In the summer of 1973 the nine members of the European

Community commissioned a report outlining the indicated path for Europe to become a Third Force in world affairs in the face of U.S.-Soviet détente. This report, completed under the direction of the Belgian diplomat Leo Tindemans in 1975, endorsed a closer European monetary union and a common European voice in world diplomacy—including a single European ambassador to the United States—so as to prevent America from pursuing a divide-and-conquer strategy. It also urged closer economic and diplomatic collaboration among Europe, the Middle East and Africa to restore the Mediterranean to its historically central role in world affairs. These objectives were implicit in Europe's behavior through the balance of 1973.

America's growing antagonism toward Europe (and toward other areas asserting their own self-interest) contributed to "go it alone" policies on both sides of the Atlantic. It also helped cement U.S.-Soviet détente, capped by a June 22 agreement between the two superpowers to the effect that nuclear war between themselves was unthinkable. Europe's NATO members resented that this agreement was concluded without their being consulted, and surmised that their armed forces were viewed in the United States simply as pawns of America's world military system.

In June the United States imposed export embargoes on forty agricultural commodities in an attempt to hold down the U.S. inflation. Export contracts were abrogated so as to satisfy domestic demand by shifting onto foreign economies the price impact of America's grain deal with Soviet Russia. This "Nixon shock" not only cut off Japan from soybean supplies, it let the world know that foreign access to American food output would be limited to what the nation could produce over and above domestic consumption while maintaining relatively stable domestic prices.

Both Third World and European spokesmen announced their antagonism toward the new U.S.-Soviet détente and their hope of promoting themselves as a new third force in world affairs. In September, at the Fourth Conference of Heads of State of the Non-Aligned Countries, Algeria's President Houari Boumedienne noted that "in recent years spectacular meetings had taken place among the Great Powers, announcing profound changes in international relations [i.e., Soviet-American détente]. It is abundantly clear that these initiatives correspond essentially to the aims of developed countries anxious to find a common ground for the settlement of the serious disagreements that divided them hitherto and to create a context for reconciling their respective interests. We cannot fail to note that the gradual shift out of the Cold War context has not been accompanied by a corresponding improvement in the condition of the countries of the Third World. On the contrary, tension and war have been transferred to Asia, Africa and Latin America, which have become the zones where all the contradictions of our contemporary world are concentrated and exacerbated."[2] (He reiterated these views in April 1974 at the Sixth Special Session of the U.N. General Assembly.)

The Third World's economic position was meanwhile being sapped by the world inflation. Although the prosperity enjoyed by the industrial nations spilled over to benefit the Third World through increased demand for its exports, the terms of trade nonetheless were turning against Third World raw-materials exporting countries, especially those suffering food deficits. They were also penalized by the fact that their relatively meager holdings of foreign exchange were denominated in sterling and dollars. "The ten per cent U.S. dollar devaluation of 1973 cost the Arab-Iranian oil exporters some $350 million in foreign exchange. In addition, the 1973 worldwide rise in wholesale prices cost them another $525 million in effective purchasing power of their savings, for a total loss of $875 million in the intrinsic value of their holdings of foreign currencies and equivalents. . . . To have avoided a loss in accumulated savings and current purchasing power from operations, the African and Arabian producer countries in 1974 would have had to enlarge their output . . . by about 1.3 billion barrels, even if they were to retain the total proceeds of the increase for their national treasuries. In the absence of an increase in oil prices, they would have had to accelerate depletion of their irreplaceable resources in exchange, effectively for nothing."[3] Acting in concert to improve their terms of trade, they quadrupled their oil prices from the January 1973 level of $1.80–$2.48 per barrel, to over $10 per barrel in December (with some Libyan oil being sold for as much as $15 per barrel in January 1974).

Even before the Oil War, strains had set Europe at odds with the United States. On September 23 the European Community published its own draft of an acceptable joint New Atlantic Charter which emphasized its intention to "establish its position in world affairs as a distinct entity" rather than merely as a passive vehicle for greater American influence in the world. Nowhere was European self-assertion more apparent than in the document's stance on world monetary reform. It called for "closer international consultation within the framework of the IMF [and therefore subject to European veto power], fixed but adjustable parities, general convertibility of currencies [into gold], the effective working of the balance-of-payments adjustment process, the effective international regulation of the world supply of liquidity [to curtail America's ability to run balance-of-payments deficits at whatever rate it chose to do so], the reduction of the role of the reserve currencies [the dollar and the pound sterling], and equal rights and duties for all participants." Two days later, at the IMF meetings in Kenya, the Common Market succeeded in having the Committee of Twenty's report on monetary reform call for a similar program.[4]

In October the world rupture spread to the Third World. On Yom Kippur, Egypt and Syria attacked Israel, and imposed export embargoes on oil sales to the United States, Holland and Denmark until such time as these countries would withdraw their support from Israel. When America sought to supply Israel, Britain warned that U.S. aircraft taking off would not be permitted to reland, and Germany forbade the loading of U.S. munitions onto U.S. ships at Bremerhaven. Europe thus grounded American NATO supplies and troops. Italy's Foreign Minister Aldo Moro demanded that Israel withdraw from all occupied territories. The United States had become more of a military and economic threat to Europe than an ally and productive trading partner.

Saudi Arabia and Kuwait added to the pressure on America by threatening to embargo any nation passing on its oil to the United States. "Our policy is clear," they announced: "no supplies of our oil are to go to any United States military buyers," including fueling depots in Singapore, Japan, the Philippines and elsewhere.[5] This threatened to immobilize America's Seventh Fleet, its planes in Thailand, its ground units throughout Southeast Asia, and the armed forces of its allied military governments in South Vietnam, Cambodia and Thailand which depended upon the United States for their supplies. Nations henceforth could support the United States and Israel only at the cost of economic boycott by the Arab oil-exporting countries (OAPEC).

In December, when OPEC quadrupled the price of its oil, it found the market circumstances successfully prepared by this Arab oil boycott. The Near Eastern countries were transformed into the world's major creditors almost overnight, giving them a corresponding power in international financial reform. Furthermore, Europe was vitally dependent upon Middle Eastern oil, and the very thought of U.S. military hostilities against the Arab oil producers threatened Europe at its energy lifeline. A common set of interests thus suggested that the two regions join forces.

The OPEC action broke up the Nixon-Kissinger strategy of using détente to draw Europe and Japan back into the American orbit (while taking the Third World for granted). Whereas Kissinger had warned Europe not to make special arrangements with Mediterranean and Third World countries, Europe's *rapprochement* with these countries was greatly accelerated as its dependence on oil led it to seek a rapid agreement with the oil-exporting countries. Its refusal to support the United States in its worldwide military alert during the Yom Kippur war was followed by its refusal to join the United States in forming an oil-importers' cartel to confront OPEC. In fact, the United States was shown to be following a rather hypocritical course. It sought détente with Soviet Russia but forbade Europe to make its own *rapprochement* with the Near East, Africa and other historically associated regions. It imposed export embargoes on agricultural commodities and raw materials (such as steel scrap) in short supply, but insisted that foreign countries not follow suit in other raw-materials areas, such as energy. It demanded central bank credits without limit, while using to the hilt its creditor status vis-à-vis Third World debtor countries. Across the board it pursued its own national interest but resented Europe, Third World countries and other regions pursuing theirs. Perhaps these contradictions might have been papered over if all countries had enjoyed economic prosperity together. But by yearend 1973 all the Western industrial economies were falling into their most serious depression since World War II.

A major factor separating America's economic interests from those in most other industrial nations was its higher degree of economic flexibility. Thanks to its immense oil and coal reserves, the nation could achieve a higher degree of energy independence if it were willing to pay the price. The European Community had no such choice: it would be able to draw on its North Sea reserves in a few years, but this might be high-cost oil and its quantity was limited. It had little option but to settle its energy-trade deficit by exporting industrial manufactures and selling substantial portions of some of its major industrial firms to OPEC countries. International financial stability also was of greater urgency for trade-dependent Europe than for America.

The United States did not offer Europe equal partnership in its proposed world. As one observer summarized the situation, "The Middle East alert and subsequent Geneva consultations ('How can Europe be absent from this negotiation when she is so profoundly affected,' lamented French Foreign Minister Michel Jobert before the French Senate) were private affairs in which no one took any particular notice of Europe." Jobert described Western Europe as having been "treated like a nonperson, humiliated all along the line" by the U.S.-Soviet détente, which he termed "a veritable condominium. . . . Faced with the superpower understandings, [Jobert] said, Europe should 'untiringly pursue' European union." Willy Brandt demanded that the Common Market be treated as an "equal partner" with the United States and insisted that "partnership cannot mean subordination."[6]

On December 12, Kissinger spoke in London on the topic of energy and European problems and sought to assure Europeans that President Nixon would not "sacrifice Western Europe's security on the altar of condominium." He acknowledged that "Europe's economic strength, political cohesion, and new confidence . . . have radically altered a relationship that was originally shaped in an era of European weakness and American predominance." But he insisted that Japan, Europe and North America could not pursue divergent paths save "at the cost of their prosperity and their partnership. . . . Europe's unity must not be at the expense of Atlantic community, or both sides of the Atlantic will suffer. It is not that we are impatient with the cumbersome machinery of the emerging Europe. It is rather the tendency to highlight division rather than unity with us which concerns us. . . . we cannot be indifferent to the tendency to justify European identity as facilitating separateness from the United States."[7]

What actually had occurred was that Europe and the Third World had been compacted into an alliance with common purposes in the face of U.S.-Soviet détente and the nationalist tenor of American economic diplomacy. They began to contemplate their joint evolution into a true Third Force in world affairs. This new alliance of the previously fragmented Europe and the Third World (beginning with the Middle Eastern oil producers plus Africa) was the foundation for what both sets of nations called the New International Economic Order.

The Oil War thus posed greater problems for American diplomacy than for that of the Soviet Union, which had fewer links to be broken. By increasing oil prices the 1973 events strengthened Russia's economic domination of Eastern Europe, which obtained most of its oil from the Soviet Union and now had to pay much more for its energy as Russia followed the OPEC price lead. Russia's apparent benefit made some American strategists fearful of pursuing a policy of détente that would provide relatively stronger benefits for the Soviet Union.

Pressures that had been mounting since the origin of the Cold War had erupted in one area after another. Europe, the Middle East and the Third World began to emulate America's self-assertion on the world stage. The European Snake, and possibly even a nascent gold-backed Arab oil currency tied to that of the European Community, threatened at some future date to dislodge the dollar from its world position by serving as a vehicle for international savings as well as a unit of account. The prospect of a European-Arab currency, enabling international savings and monetary reserves to take non-dollar forms, would aggravate America's capital shortage as its own domestic savings function dried up. The United States therefore opposed a European currency which would be stronger and more threatening to the dollar than either the pound sterling or the French franc had appeared to be after World War II.

A second prospect was that Europe, OPEC and other Third World countries might enter into preferential trade agreements with one another on the basis of associate membership status in the European Community. Such agreements could help countries transform world economic relations to their own benefit— for instance, by promoting a greater focus on agricultural self-sufficiency—irrespective of the wishes of the United States or Soviet Russia, leaving Kissinger's "Partnership of Strength" with little option short of war to oppose the New International Economic Order.

In the 1960s the major Cold War problem had seemed to lie with the Third World countries which appeared most prone to communist revolutions, not with America's fellow industrial nations. However, closure of the world's foreign-exchange markets in March 1973, followed by the Oil War in October, created a financial and commercial domino effect more serious than the military domino effect imagined by American policy-makers to characterize regions at the fringes of the Western Alliance. This alliance was crumbling at its economic center, not its outer military reaches.

CHAPTER 6

U.S. Trade Strategy Culminates in Export Embargoes

The evolution of America's agricultural policy since World War II reflects the same dialectical movement that characterized the Cold War: the nation's attempt to consolidate free trade on specifically American terms led to a growing protectionism and statism at home and abroad.

America's vast farm surpluses resulted from the income- and price-support programs enacted under the Agricultural Adjustment Act of 1933. In an attempt to maintain farm incomes near "parity" with non-farm incomes, an index was developed to relate crop prices to farmers' living and operating costs. This "parity pricing" index would have succeeded in its intended purposes if farms continued to produce a given volume of crops with a fixed quantity of labor and capital. But the index made no reference to productivity change: it tacitly assumed that a given volume of crops, or dollar of farm income, was created with a constant amount of labor, capital inputs and land. As farm productivity increased, particularly on the most highly mechanized farms, agricultural producers grew increasing crop surpluses (at diminishing costs) which the government found itself obliged to purchase at a predetermined price "indexed" to that of overall farm inputs (seeds, fertilizer, machinery, etc.) and living costs. Crops were simply destroyed by the government. For instance, many potatoes were dyed blue and dropped in the ocean. An increasing proportion of the surpluses were transferred abroad in exchange for foreign-currency payments which were used to defray U.S. Government expenditures in the food-recipient countries. But beyond a point the foreign aid program developed an embarrassingly and uselessly large accumulation of foreign currencies. It also cost the American government large sums for crop acquisition, storage and transport.

In the early 1970s the Nixon Administration announced its intention to restore agriculture to free-market status. Secretary of Agriculture Earl Butz announced that ending the agricultural price- and income-support programs and selling the existing crop stockpile would (1) eliminate a major federal budget expense (crop purchases by the Commodity Credit Corporation designed to support agricultural prices), (2) gain much-needed sales revenue for the federal government, (3) restore a free market in farm produce, (4) cement America's détente with the Soviet Union by selling it American grain and other farm products, and (5) support the U.S. balance of payments by selling food mainly to cash customers, e.g., Communist bloc countries. This reasoning seemed logical as far as it went, and many Democratic liberals joined Republicans in supporting the plan.

On July 8, 1972, a joint Soviet-U.S. announcement stated that Russia would purchase $750 million worth of U.S. grains over a three-year period. The U.S. Government promised Russia a substantial plum by assuring it that Soviet food purchases would not be publicized, so that the latter might buy U.S. grains at the lowest possible market price. (At this time grain prices stood at about $1.68 per bushel.)

Russia, suffering from a disastrous domestic harvest, purchased $1 billion worth of U.S. farm commodities and stepped up its Canadian buying as well. Wheat represented about half the total, equivalent to one-fourth of the entire U.S. crop—nearly all of it purchased during a two-month summer period.[1] The balance comprised soybeans, corn, sorghum, rye, barley and oats, whose prices rose sharply once the magnitude of Russia's food purchases became known. Many Americans came to refer to the deal as the Great Grain Robbery.

The full impact of Russia's purchase on domestic food prices was not grasped at the time. Herbert Stein, chairman of the Council of Economic Advisers, announced, "My guess is that we're talking in the neighborhood of a one-tenth or two-tenths of a percentage point in the consumer price index, or not much more than that." It soon became apparent that the rise in food prices was much more than marginal. Consumer meat boycotts spread across the country. Arthur Burns suggested that Americans accept one meatless day per week to improve their health, emulating the policies of Latin American payments-deficit countries such as Argentina, or the meatless days ordered during World War II.[2]

The Department of Agriculture portrayed the grain deal as part of the U.S. strategy to use agriculture to improve its trade balance: Secretary Butz earlier had announced his hope to increase U.S. farm exports to $10 billion by 1980, and it now appeared that this level might almost be reached in 1972 (the actual figure was $9.5 billion).[3] In February 1973 administration officials announced their hope that the current dollar devaluation would spur farm exports even further. Mr. Butz called the devaluation "a big plus for farmers."

But the Russian grain deal had ambiguous effects on American foreign trade and payments. U.S. officials assumed that the Soviet Union would sell gold to purchase American grain, except for a portion financed by Eximbank credits. And indeed, Russia did sell some gold, putting modest downward pressure on world gold prices and thereby supporting the dollar-gold parity. However, as a major gold-producing nation its interest did not lie in stemming the rise in world gold prices. It borrowed Eurodollars —precisely those surplus dollars with which the United States had flooded Europe and Japan for so many years. In February the Soviet Union obtained substantial loans at only 6 per cent, including a seven-year credit of $600 million borrowed in Italy. In May it attempted to borrow $1 billion from European banks at just three-eighths of a percentage point over the London rate for short-term (three to six-month) dollar deposits. Instead of paying for U.S. wheat with gold, the Russians paid largely in these Eurodollars.[4]

The result, in balance-of-payments terms, was that U.S. grain exports to the Soviet Union were equivalent to domestic sales for American dollars, not for gold or foreign currencies as was the case with traditional exports. Under these conditions real goods, services and assets were exported for the equivalent of domestic dollars, not foreign-currency drafts and gold.

Export orders surged to over 1.1 billion bushels out of a total U.S. crop of 1.7 billion bushels. By summer the government's food stockpiles were exhausted. A free market in soybeans and grains was established for the first time since 1948. The price of grain passed $3 per bushel in July and moved toward an all-time

high of over $4 per bushel in August, two-and-one-half times its
level a year earlier. Prices for other crops rose even more. The
food component of the consumer price index rose by over 50 per
cent, reducing the purchasing-power of American incomes accordingly.

Adding to the sharp increase in food prices was the fact that
American farmers, who had sold their prospective harvests to the
large grain trading companies early in 1972 before they learned
of the vast magnitude of Russia's grain purchases, withheld sale
of their 1973 crops until the last minute in order to judge for
themselves what the market would bring at harvest time. So acute
was the crisis that the price of corn in July rose above that of grain
for the first time in the 125-year history of the Chicago Board of
Trade.[5]

U.S. trade strategists continued to pursue their own particular
concept of American national advantage. Eliot Janeway coined a
new word in pointing out that, in view of the worldwide grain
shortage resulting from Soviet Russia and China participating in
Western grain markets, "no country can manage, no government
can survive, no economy can stabilize itself without continuous
access to American agricultural products—especially American
feed crops. Why then should our new agripower not be exploited?" Mr. Janeway proposed a 20 per cent "add-on" to U.S.
food exports, a monopoly tactic that he thought might yield the
U.S. Government $4 billion based on a $20 billion crisis level in
annual farm exports. "At the same time, 'soft' suggestions that
foreign bidders for American farm exports take non-negotiable,
non-interest-bearing, long-term U.S. Government securities in
exchange for their present holdings of short-term, interest-bearing liabilities would make a beginning of funding the 'overhang'
of hot dollars. The American initiatives are simple. The world
protein revolution has put America's potential to control the
world balance of economic and monetary power within our
grasp."[6]

But serious problems were developing. On June 27, 1973,
under pressure from a 15 per cent increase in U.S. wholesale
prices and a 50 per cent jump in food prices, the government
retreated from its free-market stance and imposed export embargoes on soybeans, cottonseed and their products. This broke
American export commitments, hurting Japan in particular. Fur-

ther export controls were imposed in July on forty-one more farm commodities, including livestock feed, edible oils and animal fats, peanuts, lard and tallow, as well as on scrap metal exports. Mr. Butz announced that crop export orders accepted after June 3, for shipment on or after October 1, "will not be licensed until further notice."

Richard Kaufman, a New York bank economist, quipped that "in the past the dollar has been inconvertible in terms of gold, now it's also inconvertible in terms of soybeans." The head of one of the nation's largest foreign exchange firms reflected that "it had been the United States contention in the past that Europeans should use their accumulated dollars to buy more American goods. Now . . . the United States has prohibited the export of certain agricultural commodities," hardly facilitating U.S. demands for guaranteed access to EEC grain markets. The government announced that whether controls would be necessary after September and October would "depend on the size of price increases in the United States."[7] The level of world prices was deemed irrelevant to U.S. economic plans; only domestic price and supply considerations were taken into account.

America's export embargoes abrogated its commitments to Europe and Japan. It appeared that these regions could no longer depend on America if they wished to secure stability in their supply of foodstuffs. Third World countries were left high and dry, suffering grain shortages that threatened to cause local revolutions.

In short, world trade patterns were dislocated. When a Dutch soybean-crushing concern was forced into bankruptcy the director of the American Soybean Institute announced, "We have been wounded. We have cut across contracts, and they [the Europeans] think that if we did it once we'll do it again." In Japan, which consumed nearly three million tons of soybeans annually —of which about 92 per cent was imported from the United States—the "Nixon shock" was worse. The director general of the Ministry of Internal Trade and Industry announced that "the Nixon Administration's actions this summer in restricting grain and soybean exports would be used by Japan and the Europeans as ammunition against United States proposals for more open markets for farm products . . . small Japanese family farmers, whose plots average about two acres and who are a mainstay of

74 GLOBAL FRACTURE

the ruling Liberal Democratic Party, would be protected against competition by large American agribusinesses."[8] The entire house of cards that U.S. diplomats called the Free World threatened to come tumbling down. Governments were coming to power whose first priority was to achieve self-sufficiency from U.S. foodstuffs as well as from the U.S. dollar.

Even U.S. agribusiness suffered in the aftermath of the export embargoes. When wheat prices began to recede from their peak of $4.21 per bushel reached in early 1975, foreigners began to cancel their fixed-price orders, much as overseas orders had been canceled by the United States two years earlier. In May, when wheat prices fell to $2.73 per bushel, the Turkish government nullified existing wheat contracts by forbidding imports at prices above current market levels. This cancelled the contracts that Turks had signed with Cargill for grain to be delivered in July at prices set earlier in the year.[9] The so-called sanctity of contracts was breaking down on a worldwide basis. Only those negotiated directly among governments remained intact.

Meanwhile, renewed stockpile proposals were being voiced. In September 1974 the Brookings Institution proposed that GATT members create a grain stockpile of 100 million tons, five times the size of America's 1972 grain sale to Russia, to be built up in crop-surplus years. Target prices would be set to determine stockpile grain accumulation or sales. Two months later Secretary of State Kissinger proposed an international accumulation of grain reserves. In August 1975 he submitted to the International Wheat Council in London (a group of forty major exporting and importing countries) a "unified U.S. plan" approved by both the Department of Agriculture and the State Department.

Kissinger emphasized that the U.S. Government was "unwilling to carry the entire, or even most of the burden of holding grains for the rest of the world," although much of the grain reserves would be purchased from U.S. farmers. Other nations would have to play a major role in purchasing surplus grain stocks. Fears of American farmers that the projected stockpile might hang over the world market to depress prices (as had the earlier U.S. Government stockpile) were allayed by the argument that "reserves could help maintain prices, if . . . the reserve would take in excess supplies from overproduction." These reserves might include some 30 or 40 million tons of wheat, rice and feed grains in the event that these should accumulate over and above normal world working stocks (usually about one-tenth of current demand). However, U.S. officials found themselves at odds with other grain-exporting countries in arguing that stockpile sales be geared solely to production shortfalls, making no reference to sudden foreign demand pushing up world prices. Australia, Canada and Argentina preferred a price trigger mechanism whereby reserve stocks would be marketed if prices rose by a certain amount.

While this proposal was being argued, the U.S. Government opened negotiations with Soviet Russia and Poland to reach a set of long-term grain agreements. A new wave of sales to the Soviet Union had been announced in July when Russia, in the midst of a drought as serious as that of 1972, contracted to buy 10 million tons of U.S. grain, about half the amount of its 1973 grain purchase. Domestic U.S. food prices began to rise sharply once again. This spurred the International Longshoremen's Association (ILA), strongly backed by George Meany of the AFL-CIO, to boycott loading of the grain until some public agreement could be reached. (In hearings before the Senate Agriculture Committee, Senator Bellmon asked Secretary Butz whether "it is up to the labor unions whether we make more sales? Is that what you said?" Mr. Butz replied, "It's what you said, but I won't argue with it." "I think we're in a heck of a shape if George Meany is running our policy," answered the angry Senator.)[10]

George Meany, Secretary of Labor John Dunlop and five labor union leaders met with President Gerald Ford on August 27 to argue that the planned grain exports would injure U.S. consumers by pushing up food prices.[11] A trade-off was agreed upon which called for America to export grain to Russia and other Comecon countries on a regular, long-term basis, preferably in exchange for Soviet oil. Although an export volume of 8 million tons of U.S. grain annually would reduce domestic food supplies, the purchases would not "suddenly" push up prices, for American farmers could plant their crops in anticipation of a certain Russian demand. In mid-October Secretary Butz announced the outlines of an American-Polish grain deal whereby Poland would purchase about 2.5 million metric tons of grain annually for the next three to five years at going market prices as of the date of delivery.

Mr. Meany emphasized that the agreement's most important breakthrough was that "the negotiations are not going to be Cargill, Cook, Continental to the Soviet Union. They are going to be government to government. . . . And the instructions are to negotiate a grain sale deal that will protect the American consumer as well as the American farmer. . . . We can no longer trust this trade to private enterprise, whose only motive is profit."[12] A grand circle thus was brought to a close. In 1972 the U.S. Government sold its food stockpile to Russia ostensibly to help restore a free market for grain. But by autumn 1975, the price consequences of this act had forced world grain trade and pricing to become a function of intergovernmental negotiations.

The American government's attempt to fix its grain export prices at high levels culminated in one of the earliest proposals of the incoming Carter administration. The new Secretary of Agriculture Robert Bergland announced on February 25, 1977, immediately following Canadian Prime Minister Pierre Trudeau's visit to Washington, that a joint U.S.-Canada wheat board had been proposed to regulate grain exports and prices. Between them, the United States and Canada account for three-fourths of world wheat sales (40 per cent and 35 per cent respectively). Canada's government already buys wheat directly from farmers and handles its exportation, but grain exports historically have been left in private hands in the United States, even in the case of foreign-aid shipments. This is now changing as the United States joins Canada in nationalizing its grain exports. The two nations are explicitly creating the first industrial nation counter-cartel to OPEC. "I'd be willing to drop these talks with anybody when the oil cartel is dissolved," Mr. Bergland told reporters. "But until such time as that occurs, I don't intend to back down."[13] The head of Canada's Wheat Board, Otto Lang, suggested drawing other countries (presumably Australia and Argentina) into the export pact to prevent the price of wheat falling in the event that Soviet and Chinese demand abated.

Nor did matters stop with grain. A key element of the 1975 U.S.-Soviet agreement was the issue of international shipping. Assistant Secretary of Commerce Robert Blackwell went to Moscow to support the ILA's demand "to insure that the rates are high enough for U.S. bottoms to claim a one-third share of the transport." Because state-owned carriers were not covered by

GATT agreements (save for Rumania and Yugoslavia), "the Soviet tactic of cutting some liner rates to and from U.S. ports to levels 30 to 40 per cent below the rates American carriers consider compensatory cannot be put on GATT's agenda at this point." The American government's grain sale to the Russian government seemed a suitable arena in which to bring up this problem. In order to enable U.S.-flag ships to participate in the grain shipment, U.S. trade representatives demanded a transport price of $16 per ton (replacing the expired rate on Soviet-bound freight of $9.50 per ton).[14]

Taken together, these negotiations demonstrated how far the political reality of world trade had moved from the ideology of laissez faire. As a *Journal of Commerce* editorial put it, "any government-to-government deal with Moscow involving long-term grain purchases could set a particularly disturbing precedent if it specified what proportion of the grain should move in American ships and at what rates. True, such stipulations were made in previous grain deals going as far back as the Kennedy Administration. But these were one-shot deals worked out on a temporary basis because the Russians needed a large amount of grain they hadn't thought they would need, and because they needed it in a hurry." The temptation was for this new government-to-government pattern of negotiations to spread to other areas. "Why limit them to grain sales to the Soviets? What about other exports of American agricultural products such as rice and cotton? And why limit them to agricultural products? Why not bituminous coal and lumber, just to mention a few."[15] Why not indeed?

Thus the United States took world trade out of the hands of businessmen and economists and turned it over to lawyers and politicians. America's arbitrary action in not honoring contracts set the pattern for other nations. Its abrupt refusal to sell food to countries dependent on U.S. agriculture prompted efforts toward independence from the United States, adding to the growing antagonism between America and its trading partners— Europe, Japan and the Third World. Finally its raw attempt to maximize its food-export prices paved the way for OPEC's actions in the fall of 1973.

CHAPTER 7

The Oil War Transforms
World Diplomacy

By attacking Israel in October 1973, Egypt and Syria created
a parallel set of tensions between Soviet Russia and the United
States, arms suppliers of the Arabs and Israelis respectively. Détente was tested and survived the confrontation—indeed proved
to be an Entente Cordiale. For when America and the Soviet
Union joined in a "Partnership of Strength" cemented by America's grain sale to Russia in return for the latter's pressure on
North Vietnam to end the war, an alliance was formed between
the only two nations (excluding China) capable of becoming
self-sufficient in most basic essentials. Both nations could face a
breakdown of foreign trade without fear of destroying their own
economic foundations. Such a breakdown would be inconven-
ient, but as far as essentials were concerned each superpower
could make do.

This self-sufficiency threatened Europe, Japan and the Third
World, which could not share America's or Russia's independence of action. What would be only an adventure for Soviet
Russia or America would pose life-or-death risks for Europe and
Japan. They had become dependent on foreign suppliers for such
basic needs as energy, raw materials, arms, manufactured goods
and replacement parts. America and Russia could pursue world
strategies with relatively little fear of international repercussions,
while other countries had to qualify their policies in view of their
dependency.

Attempts to overcome this dependency led to geopolitical realignment in the wake of U.S.-Soviet détente: Europe and the
Third World began to break out of America's economic orbit to
emerge as an independent and mutually self-sufficient third force
in world affairs. Europe's breakaway from the Treasury-bill stan-

dard to create its own currency system based on the Snake was the first major move in this direction. The Oil War extended this process of self-assertion into the realm of international trade and investment relations.

Substantial inducements prompted Europe to join with the Middle East. Just as European integration had brought together nine nations that had often been at odds with one another, this integration process might now be extended to contiguous areas beginning with the Middle East and Africa. The question to be decided was whether these areas would "depend" on the United States for their economic complementarity (remaining dependent on an already self-sufficient unit that did not need them as much as they needed it), or on each other so as to establish a new self-sufficiency and reciprocity. In view of their mutual dependence in such an endeavor, and their inability to achieve it by themselves in the near future, here would be a more trustworthy alliance. It was as if OPEC were whispering in Europe's ear, "We, not America, can be your best friends. We will be good customers for your industry, especially in the areas of capital goods. We will hire your companies to build entire factories and turnkey projects for us. And we can supply you with the financial resources that your industries need to expand their operations. This new economic complementarity between us will therefore be profitable and mutual. We, unlike the Americans, will certainly not oppose your attempt to become agriculturally self-sufficient. And perhaps we can establish a currency link with your Snake in our mutual search for a stable world payments system."

America's attempts to prevent this development only aggravated its relations with Europe. In Dr. Kissinger's December 12 London briefing on energy problems he showed himself concerned not simply with European "separateness" from America in world affairs, but with the prospect of European economic integration with other Eastern Hemisphere nations. Both Europe's and the Middle East's dependency on the United States would be reduced by its newfound complementarity and self-sufficiency. Dr. Kissinger sought to restore Europe's adherence to the U.S. economic orbit rather than to move into an alliance with the Middle East and other Third World countries. "Can our common energy crisis be solved by anything but collective action?" he asked in a year-end review of U.S.-European diplomacy, demanding "prior consultation" with the United States on any European negotiations to be held with OPEC or other Third World countries.[1] The Oil War thus brought into the open America's opposition to Third World countries moving to improve their terms of trade. (It also showed how lukewarm was Russia's support for the Third World position.) The concept of "partnership" was shattered between America and Europe on the one hand (fracturing NATO in the process), and America and the Third World on the other. Only the Alliance between America and Russia remained in place.

Two days later the Common Market gave its response to the Kissinger Doctrine in Copenhagen, where its Council of Ministers proposed a new kind of relationship with the Third World that excluded America:

International developments and the growing concentration of power and responsibility in the hands of a very small number of great powers mean that Europe must unite and speak increasingly with a single voice if it wants to make itself heard and play its proper role in the world.

In bilateral contacts with other countries, the member states of the community will increasingly act on the basis of agreed common positions.

The community will implement its undertakings towards the Mediterranean and African countries in order to reinforce its long-standing links with these countries. The nine intend to preserve their historic links with the countries of the Middle East and to cooperate over the establishment and maintenance of peace, stability and progress in the region.

The nine will participate in international negotiations in an outward-looking spirit, while preserving the fundamental elements of their unity and their basic aims.

The French suggested "that the Arabs be represented at the Copenhagen meeting to insure that diplomatic lines be kept open," and four Arab ministers were invited. President Pompidou and Foreign Minister Jobert argued that "Europe must develop a special relationship with the Arab world to keep oil flowing and to give Arab nations the technology and financial assets they need. . . . The French want a triangular relationship in which Arab oil producers would subsidize development plans for poorer and more populous Arab nations such as Egypt and Syria by buying equipment from Europe, which in turn would finance Europe's oil purchases."[2]

Europe as a whole thus sought accommodation with the oil-exporting countries, well aware that Middle East oil receipts would provide purchasing power for Common Market capital goods, arms and industrial products, as well as investment capital to help European firms expand their operations. America viewed this accommodation as a betrayal of the Atlantic alliance, and urged a strategy of confrontation with the oil exporters. Kissinger suggested that "The only long-term solution [to the energy crisis] is a massive effort to provide producers [in the industrial nations with] an incentive to increase their supply, to encourage consumers to use existing supplies more rationally and to develop alternative energy sources." In fact, a world oversupply of oil must be maintained, if need be through high-cost North American and North Sea oil development in order to drive world export prices back down so as to defeat the oil-exporting countries and other raw-materials exporters who were watching OPEC moves as a model for their own future strategy. This would be difficult without a functioning collusion between the oil cartel (that is to say, the major international oil companies) and consumer-country governments. It would be nearly impossible if Europe supported a policy of what Giscard d'Estaing called "concertation" instead of confrontation with the Third World.

The United States therefore drafted plans to create an intergovernmental oil-consumer cartel to replace the Seven Sisters. The new thirteen-nation cartel, christened the International Energy Agency (IEA), was scheduled to convene for its first meeting in Washington on February 9–13, 1974, just four months after the Oil War. According to the U.S. plan, governments in the oil-importing countries would join together to manipulate world trade in energy so as to push down oil prices, by force if need be.

Europe already had found itself left out in the cold by U.S.-Soviet détente. Its economy was even more threatened by the prospect of an American invasion of the Middle East. OPEC governments warned Europe and Japan that they would destroy their oil wells, pipelines and port facilities in the event of an invasion, thus blocking all oil shipments to the West for at least a year. This threat was certain to prevent oil-dependent Europe and Japan from acquiescing in any U.S. invasion plan. Europe found its self-interest to lie in supporting the Arab position and in preventing any outside intervention in the region that might interrupt its oil supplies. Thus, on January 7, when Secretary of Defense James Schlesinger threatened that the United States might use military force against the Arabs if they continued their oil embargo, Europe stepped up its efforts toward conciliation. American threats against OPEC thus helped ensure Europe's opposition to the U.S. energy position at the February meetings.

Prior to these meetings French Foreign Minister Michel Jobert flew to the Middle East to offer French participation "in petrochemical and oil refinery projects in Kuwait in return for guaranteed yearly deliveries of crude and refined oil." In Saudi Arabia he reached agreement with King Faisal to obtain 5.6 billion barrels of Saudi crude oil over the next twenty years (enough to satisfy one-quarter of France's projected oil needs) in return for French aid in building refineries and a petrochemical complex. Discussions were initiated to provide industrial equipment, roads, hotels, mineral water, Concorde planes and weapons in exchange for a further 800 million tons of oil. Jobert voiced his hope that French technology could help Saudi Arabia and Syria break out of their respective U.S. and Russian orbits. He further proposed a joint French–Arab aid program to African nations so as to draw that continent into an emerging European-Middle Eastern alliance. Saudi and Kuwaiti officials told Mr. Jobert that they were "counting on France to check efforts to establish a bloc of oil-consuming countries to counter the oil producers," and France agreed to urge that the upcoming Oil Conference be held under the auspices of the United Nations, which was dominated by Third World nations rather than by the United States.[3] The emerging European-Middle East-Third World alliance would thus be able to refer economic issues to a forum in which it could drive through resolutions of its own choice. France proceeded to lead the opposition against "involvement in anything like the 'cooperative action program' proposed by the United States." The French viewed the IEA as "an attempt to establish a European-Japanese-American power triangle, with the United States at the commanding peak, so that the United States can confront the Arabs and others as spokesman for the whole non-Communist industrial world." In place of this pyramid France pressed for "a meeting of Arab and European countries and a vast United Nations conference on energy and raw materials." Britain's delegate added his voice to the effect that the IEA conference must not "perpetuate itself."[4] In effect, the European Community was saying to the Arab world that it, not America, was their friend.

Most of all, American intransigence played the major role in swinging the Common Market to the French position. The European Community had just voted eight-to-one against France when "they suddenly received Washington's aide-mémoire proposing a broad expansion of the conference and a follow-up group. This was taken as an unacceptable challenge by the Common Market countries, torn between their desire to reach a common position on energy and monetary issues and their sense of need to cooperate with the United States."[5] As a result, on February 5, a week before the IEA conference in Washington, the EC's Council of Ministers announced in Brussels that the forthcoming meeting must "avoid all confrontation between certain consumer countries on the one side and the producer countries on the other." Europe made explicit its intention to "reserve its total freedom to decide the form it will give to its Community energy policy and to its relations with producer countries." It warned that "the Washington conference cannot, above all in its present composition, be transformed into a permanent organization," but should simply issue a position paper analyzing "the implication of the energy situation for the general world economy." Europe might establish cooperation to allocate energy in case of supply difficulties (which the United States was pressing for so that neither it nor Holland could be selectively embargoed in the future) and to economize in the use of oil and other forms of energy. But the Common Market insisted that "by April 1, 1974, a dialogue should be established" with the oil-exporting countries—not what the French called a dialogue of the deaf but an equitable negotiation to implement a New International Economic Order. The Council of Ministers thus rejected an American proposal to "work toward a 'cooperative action program' to meet the energy crisis. At the same time the French Foreign Minister . . . served notice that he would press ahead for a conference between the Common Market and Middle Eastern countries to work out a regional pattern of energy and technology exchanges."[6] It was precisely this *rapprochement* that disturbed American officials.

European representatives traveled actively throughout the Mideast. Mr. Jobert negotiated a bilateral oil deal with Iraq to

expand France's 1972 barter agreement to provide huge irriga-
tion projects, petroleum and petrochemical industry development, and salt factories in exchange for 130 million tons of Iraqi
oil. On February 9, the first day of the Washington energy meetings, France announced its largest barter deal yet, a $5 billion
agreement with Iran.

Kissinger achieved success in obtaining agreement from all
IEA members to share their oil with fellow IEA members in the
event of any new embargo. (The following month the Arabs lifted
their embargo against the United States.) But his design for a
New Atlantic Partnership died on the vine on March 3, when the
European Community acting as a unit made a broad offer of
cooperation to twenty Arab countries. The State Department
accused the Common Market of failing to consult the United
States first. Germany pointed out that "Foreign Minister Walter
Scheel had discussed the initiative extensively with Secretary of
State Kissinger Sunday night" and on earlier occasions. *Le Monde*
declared that even this discussion had been a betrayal of European autonomy: "What is hard to understand is Mr. Kissinger's
trying to force the Europeans to an explicit choice between an
American Europe and a more or less European Europe, from
which the United States has nothing to fear. . . . In plain words,
what that means is that Europe must not speak or act without
Washington's consent." West Germany sought an agreement
from its Common Market partners at least to consult with U.S.
officials before undertaking diplomatic overtures to Mideastern
countries. But Kissinger was angered when "Mr. Scheel failed to
get the mention of the [Arab-European] conference removed
from the European communiqué, although the draft was changed
to meet other American objections. High-level German sources
said the changes consisted of omitting any reference to oil policy
and Middle East peace efforts as possible topics for an Arab-
European 'dialogue,' and omitting a pledge to try to hold a conference before the end of this year." The resulting offer to the
Arab countries, Kissinger insisted, "could put Europe in direct
conflict with American efforts to conclude a Middle East peace,
and also with its attempt to forge a unified Western policy toward
the oil-producing countries."[7]

France remained adamant that the United States not be given
any option "of deciding which issues it ought to be consulted

on." The United States canceled a meeting with Europeans to review the draft of the joint declaration of principles defining the relationship between the United States and the Common Market when France refused to allow the declaration to contain the term "partnership," a term that the State Department hoped would establish a common identity among America and its allies. The ceremonial signing of the stillborn New Atlantic Charter was put off indefinitely, as was a parallel NATO document that President Nixon had hoped to sign on his planned April visit to Europe. "I can say one thing," warned Mr. Nixon. "I have had great difficulty in getting the Congress to continue to support American forces in Europe at a level that we need to keep them there. In the event that the Congress gets the idea that we are going to be faced with economic confrontation and hostility from the nine, you will find it almost impossible to get Congressional support for continued American presence at present levels on the security front." The proposed NATO document had called the alliance "indivisible," but just as in the economic document France refused to permit the word "partnership" to be included.[8] And France was supported by its Common Market partners. The new schism in world diplomacy had been drawn.

Germany tried to soften the blow by recycling some $2.2 billion of American military occupation costs, including purchase of $843 million of low-interest U.S. Treasury securities and over $1 billion in U.S. arms. It unsuccessfully asked its Common Market partners to "invite American officials to meet with it on obviously far-reaching matters before these are given to the ministers for final decision." When the Labour Party returned to office in Britain in March, Prime Minister James Callaghan insisted on the "fullest cooperation" between the Europeans and Washington in its first foreign-policy talk, adding that "we repudiate the view that Europe will emerge only after a process of struggle against America." Indeed, he warned of withdrawing from the Common Market, implying that "close ties with the United States . . . might well be placed ahead of links with Europe," and announcing that his country wished "to remain a member of an effective Atlantic alliance, and there is therefore concern about the degree of disagreement between the Community and the United States." Britain thereupon demanded renegotiation of its entry status, including renegotiation of the Common Agricultural Policy.

But the rest of the Common Market countries remained firm in their insistence on an independent identity from the United States. France reportedly feared that "in a free-ranging consultation system the United States could employ wide powers of persuasion, and much of the French suspicion on this score appears directed at Britain's new Labour Government, which has taken a strongly pro-American attitude since taking office early in March."[9] Quite simply, Europe's relations with the Middle East and with other raw-materials exporting regions of the world—indeed, with the Third World as a whole—had become just as critical as its relations with the United States. It was buying from and selling more to the Arabs than it was with the United States. Its Middle Eastern trade was more critical and more remunerative. It needed the Third World. Did it really need America?

This line of reasoning led the Common Market to act with a single voice in the United Nations, the International Monetary Fund and other world agencies to become a counterpoise to "the increased activity of the United States in international economic affairs."[10] The weight of a united Europe was now thrown behind the policy decisions of the U.N. Conference on Trade and Development (UNCTAD), the World Bank and most international economic organizations.

On May 13, in Kansas City, Kissinger deplored the attempt by "the so-called Third World" to disrupt the postwar order that had "served the world well." Two weeks later, on May 28, he attempted to dismiss "the theoretical debate over whether we are seeking a new world order or improving the existing one." In Milwaukee he warned that the United States would not deal with countries whose demands "simply do not reflect [preexisting] economic reality." As one writer observed, "What might still, a year ago, have been handled as a purely practical negotiation about oil payments and debt transfers has turned into a question of principle and ideology. . . . As a result of Kissinger's delaying tactics, the stakes have been raised. . . . When Kissinger ignored the OPEC overtures, threatened military action, and did all he could to line up the oil consumers into a hostile bloc, the obvious —almost an inevitable—reply from the world producers was to look for compensatory support in the Third World."[11] And in the industrial nations as well.

In a December 1974 *Business Week* interview Kissinger avoided ruling out U.S. use of force in the event that the OPEC actions "strangled" the American economy. Europe was stunned—and frightened. The outgoing chairman of NATO's military committee (a German air force officer), said that the NATO reaction to Kissinger's words had been "an exasperated 'For God's sake!' " The general secretary of Germany's Free Democratic Party deplored what he called Kissinger's " 'gunboat diplomacy' practiced by the Americans in China in the early part of this century." Even the pro-American Helmut Schmidt observed that the thought "that we could be drawn into conflicts against our will is something new in German political history. Until a generation ago, most of the time we were part of the cause when conflicts arose." *Le Monde* announced that France had much to fear from the return of the "tough Kissinger" who had already threatened French national security by oil-confrontation brinkmanship during the October War.[12]

On the other hand, it was only natural that such talk would spur Middle Eastern arms spending. In fact, the United States sought to finance part of its rising oil-import bill by selling additional arms to the region—about $8 billion in 1974. Iran and Saudi Arabia purchased the most advanced U.S. aircraft, making their air forces even more modern than that of the United States—but at the same time rendering them dependent on U.S. firms for replacement parts and related military hardware and software. Some 3,500 U.S. military advisers were reported to be working in Saudi Arabia, to which the United States was the prime arms supplier. Iran announced its intention to become a major arms manufacturer, and spoke with U.S. and German firms about purchasing tank plants and other manufacturing capability. Saudi Arabia helped other Arab countries, particularly Egypt, purchase U.S. jet fighters and other arms.[13]

In January 1975 a *Commentary* magazine article by Robert Tucker urged invasion of the Persian Gulf. Egyptian President Sadat replied that the Arabs "would blow up their oil wells before allowing them to fall under the control of invading forces from the United States or elsewhere." The Shah of Iran asked whether the United States was planning to invade Venezuela in view of its unlikelihood of getting European support for a Middle Eastern adventure. President Sadat added that Iran and the Arabs should settle their problems in the interests of a broader goal. "We are in the same boat, whether we like it or not, and we face the same fate, whether we like it or not."[14] Expansionist Iran and socialist Iraq rapidly settled a long-standing territorial dispute when Iraq ceded one side of the straits thereby assuring Iran access to the Oil Gulf. In return Iran closed its borders with Iraq and ceased to support the Kurdish rebels that had been conducting guerrilla warfare for decades in the mountain regions of Iraq from bases within Iran's borders. This paved the way for a settlement with the Kurds (followed by negotiations with the Turkish government). Thus, in the process of defending themselves against external danger from the United States, the Middle Eastern nations achieved at least a tentative peace in this region for virtually the first time in five thousand years.

A prime U.S. objective was to drive the world export price of oil back down. The increase in energy prices worked naturally to spur European and Japanese moves toward energy conservation, to render domestic energy production (especially of coal) more attractive, and to promote research into new energy sources such as nuclear and solar power. Europe already was developing its North Sea oil when President Nixon called for total U.S. energy independence by 1980. In principle, increasing energy self-sufficiency among the industrial nations would enable them to reduce their demand for OPEC oil, thereby putting downward pressure on its export price. This would indicate to other raw-materials exporters that if they attempted to raise their prices, the industrial nations might well reduce their raw-materials needs by developing synthetics and other substitutes. But the growth trend of energy consumption seemed too steep to sustain a rollback in energy prices, despite the increased spending on exploration and development of domestic energy. During 1974–75 the United States became increasingly dependent upon OPEC oil, and indeed on Arab oil. Nuclear power investments by electric utilities tailed off sharply as a result of the capital shortage, which threatened to be aggravated by the Ford-Rockefeller $100 billion Project Independence designed to develop synthetic fuels (coal liquefaction and gasification), shale oil and thermopower over the 1975–85 decade. Furthermore, despite the inducement of higher energy prices, the number of new U.S. wells brought into production declined sharply after 1973. U.S. strategy could not cope with the realities of the world's supply of and demand for oil.

Kissinger tried to persuade Europe to create and operate an intergovernmental oil-consumer cartel that would secure low-priced oil imports by such tactics as submitting common bids to OPEC. But this effort failed because the oil exporters were under no compulsion to accept such bids, a fact that threatened to leave Europe and Japan with almost no oil whatsoever if they stuck to this strategy. Saudi Arabia's oil minister, Sheik Yamani, warned that "any efforts to purchase oil collectively could result in further increases in prices."[15] Most important of all, Europe found that its higher oil payments could have a silver lining if they could be recycled on terms favorable to its industrial and banking systems. This perception paved the way for subsequent European competition with the United States to attract petrodollars.

Kissinger hinted that if OPEC would reduce the price of its oil to about $8 per barrel he might agree to index the world price of oil to industrial export prices. On February 8, 1975 (nearly a year after the Washington energy conference) he "proposed a world price guarantee for oil exporting nations in return for their 'assurances of supply,' " by which he probably meant oversupply sufficient to drive down the price of oil. "They can accept a significant price reduction now . . . for stability over a longer period, or they can run the risk of a dramatic break in prices" when alternative energy sources come on stream, presumably in 1985 given the long lead-times required to develop new energy resources. But instead of scaling down their prices, the OPEC governments increased them by about 9 per cent in October 1975, despite the fact that a world oversupply of oil seemed to be developing.

The Third World had discovered its power and intended to use it. Europe was being pulled toward it by virtue of the continent's need for raw materials and investment capital, as well as cover from U.S.-Soviet détente and American arms-brandishing. As France's president, Giscard d'Estaing, expressed matters in November 1975, "In our view, détente does not mean that we must accept a concept of détente that has been decided somewhere else, any more than in the question of France's security would we accept a concept of defense decided elsewhere. . . . If we didn't have a policy, then everything would actually be very clear since we'd be part of a system. It would probably be the American system. . . . There are some countries in the world whose foreign policy consists in not having one, in accepting the policy of another, and they don't have to contend with any questions in this respect."[16] The time had come for industrial nations outside the United States to reassert their own autonomy. Third World countries stood to benefit collectively by this European-American division. Instead of Kissinger succeeding in dividing America's allies he had driven them together!

Even Europe's internal politics became a matter of conflict with the United States. In particular, Mr. Kissinger and other U.S. officials opposed any *rapprochement* between European social democratic parties and their local Communist parties. As the *Manchester Guardian* paraphrased statements and briefings by U.S. officials, "The United States will adamantly maintain its refusal to give the political nod to the Communists of Western Europe. It has not the slightest intention of lending itself to any move that might legitimise them on the international scene or recognise their claims for a share in coalition Governments." Italy was the first case in point, as massive CIA funding for its noncommunist parties and those of other European countries was just becoming public knowledge. The possibility of Spain's legitimizing its Communist Party also disturbed U.S. officials.

At first glance, America's rejection of the Western European Communist parties seemed curious in view of its détente with Soviet Russia. Even Dr. Kissinger observed that "We are accused of being soft on communism and hard on Communist parties. . . . There is an inconsistency perceived in the United States between our opposing Communist governments in Western Europe and our talking to them in Eastern Europe." But he defended these policies as being quite logical: the danger of an independent Europe, whose possible communism might represent a breakaway from Soviet domination, lay precisely in the fact that it could not be controlled by mutual bargaining between Washington and Moscow. Furthermore, it seemed probable that communist European governments would reduce their defense expenditures. And of course there was the problem of "trusting" partially communist governments participating in NATO defense plans. Dr. Kissinger insisted that communist European governments would side with the Soviet Union in a military crisis. It followed that a European communist movement would (therefore) unbalance the world military system in Russia's favor, tempting it to veer beyond détente and leave the United States with only "a ruthless balance-of-power policy" to stem this process.[17]

Europe strove not to be deterred by either superpower. On January 22, 1976, Willy Brandt explained in an interview with *Der Spiegel,* "It would be wrong if by our conduct we contributed to halting the developments that have led to a break-up of the former monolithic block of communism." A few weeks later France's Communist Party unanimously approved a declaration of independence from Moscow at its Twenty-second Party Congress. European socialists dropped their support for Israel and moved toward advocating participation by the Palestinian Liberation Organization in the United Nations Middle East debate. The stage was set for a coordination of European political parties across national borders, electing representatives to the European Parliament, scheduled for 1978. Social Democratic parties would join in a broad EEC alliance, along with conservative Christian parties and Communist parties, all espousing an independent Europe that would decide its own fate irrespective of the wishes of Moscow or Washington.[18]

The final repudiation of Kissinger's European Doctrine came in a report by Belgium's prime minister, Leo Tindemans, which was commissioned in 1974 at the Paris summit and completed in January 1976. The report explained, "European union implies that we present a united front to the outside world. We must coordinate our action in all the main fields of our external relations whether it is a question of foreign policy, security, economic relations, or development aid." European federal union could best be supported in the realm of foreign policy: the existing mixture of nine national foreign policies should give way to a common European diplomacy, with EC. members dropping their veto power so that "the minority must rally to the view of the majority at the conclusion of a debate." Europe's foreign policy toward the United States should be coordinated by appointment of a single European ambassador to Washington, acting on behalf of the nine member countries and their majority position. European union, the report specified, "cannot occur without a transfer of competences to common bodies. . . . What price would we pay for inaction? The crumbling away of the Community, voices isolated and often going unheard in the theatre of the world, less and less control over our destiny, an unconvincing

Europe without a future. . . . European union obviously implies, within the fields covered by the union that the European states should always appear to be united, otherwise the term would be meaningless. . . . To carry conviction, progress must be irreversible."[19]

At some point Europe's weaker currencies (the pound sterling and the Italian lira) must join the Snake, and none of the existing Snake members must pull out of the agreement except in "manifest crisis." Coordination of international financial policies (establishment of currency values, etc.) must evolve toward coordination of internal monetary and fiscal policies. At some point this would require a single Finance Minister instead of nine, a single central bank and a single taxing authority. Because the power of taxation involves the power to spend, it presupposed an elected Congress or European Parliament, and elections were scheduled for spring 1978. Europe's individual national sovereignties thus would be ceded in favor of a common European identity, beginning in foreign policy and extending throughout the domestic policy mechanisms. Passport union within the European Community, a European Court of Justice, common medical and health policies, and a European arms agency to achieve economies of scale in arms manufacture were also implicit in the Tindemans report.

Thus did Europe declare its independence. The Third World had tested its strength and won its first battle. While the United States fought to regain control of the Free World by dividing and conquering the Third World and Europe, the latter sought to establish a new system of international finance, trade, aid and technology transfer that did not include America. Even on the military front the United States found itself musclebound, unable to wage further conventional wars in the face of its bankrupt international position.

Turkey fell out of the American sphere when Congress, supporting Greece in its invasion of Cyprus, cut off arms aid to Turkey until such time as it might withdraw from the island and terminate its cultivation and export of the opium poppy. Greece already seemed to have been lost through U.S. support of the military dictatorship of Colonel Papandopolous. Portugal was lost. Spain was in danger of being lost following the death of Franco and the emergence of the Communist Party as the nation's most active opposition party. Italy was threatening to admit communists into its government, supported in January 1976 by France and other European socialist parties that hitherto had opposed any united front with the Communists.

The United States, architect of Pax Americana, found itself isolated except for its relationship with the one nation, Soviet Russia, that it had designed the Cold War to isolate. It was left with little but détente to reassert its authority over its waning satellites, plus whatever momentum or inertia remained from its postwar position as military and economic leader of the noncommunist world.

CHAPTER 8

America's New
Financial Strategy

In rebelling against U.S. economic domination, Europe and Japan faced a more problematic situation than did OPEC and the Third World. Raw-materials producers could stop subsidizing America and other industrial nations by increasing their export prices while tightening their control and taxation of multinational firms. But the industrial nations were caught on the horns of a dilemma. As long as they sold their products for dollars that they held in the form of Treasury bills, they lost by exchanging real resources for pieces of paper whose purchasing power fell faster than their interest accrued. On the other hand, if they stopped the process by refusing to recycle their surplus dollars in this way, American currency would immediately fall in value, threatening European and Japanese exports and employment by enabling U.S. producers to undersell them. Dollar devaluation also would reduce the foreign-exchange value of foreign dollar reserves already accumulated. Thus, the longer Europe and Japan accepted the Treasury-bill standard, the more their interest lay in supporting the dollar. Despite this dilemma, in March 1973 European central banks finally refused to accept further dollar inflows. Japan went so far as to subsidize dollar expenditures by its businessmen in an attempt to divest its central bank of unwanted dollars.

European and Japanese firms continued to sell their goods to American consumers, but the supply and demand for dollars was now determined mainly by private-sector trade and financial transactions: exporters exchanged their dollar receipts for domestic currency on the open market where the oversupply of dollars reduced their value relative to foreign currencies. The price of U.S. goods and services dropped somewhat for foreign buyers, while the price of foreign goods rose for U.S. consumers. Foreigners began to buy more U.S. products, both to take advantage of the favorable price and to dispose of their existing dollars before they depreciated further. They also began to invest more heavily in the United States. Volkswagen and Volvo, for instance, found it less expensive to produce cars destined for U.S. consumption in America rather than in Germany or Sweden. The U.S. balance of payments moved into modest surplus.

Under a creditor-oriented system of international finance this payments surplus would have seemed highly desirable and would have had a positive effect on American capital markets. But under the Treasury-bill standard it created novel problems for the U.S. economy. These problems were as unanticipated as the benefits that arose from the nation's earlier balance-of-payments deficit. Europe and Japan were settling their new payments deficits with the United States (and subsequently with OPEC) by selling their Treasury bills on U.S. money markets. This sale of Treasury bills for cash competed with U.S. private-sector borrowing and with the Treasury's own sale of securities to finance the mushrooming federal budget deficit. American capital markets thus experienced an unprecedented credit squeeze as the demand for funds exceeded the supply of new savings in highly inflationary circumstances. The resulting financial stringency pushed up interest rates to all-time highs.

Meanwhile, Europe and Japan were obliged to deal with floating currencies whose instability complicated their long-term trade and investment. For when their central banks stopped accepting surplus dollars they lost control not only of the dollar's exchange rate but also that of all other currencies, hence for all practical purposes their own exchange rates. Many international investors moved out of the dollar into the Swiss franc or German mark, driving up the latters' value in terms of other European currencies. This uneven currency appreciation threatened the European Snake. It also began to price German and Swiss exports out of world markets, thereby threatening domestic unemployment in their export industries. (This problem might be solved if Switzerland's watchmakers all became bankers, or if Germany sent its "guest workers" home to Greece, Yugoslavia or Turkey, but economic life is not that readily flexible.) The European Community rejected Switzerland's request to associate its currency officially with the Snake, out of fear that its appreciation might boost the value of all Common Market currencies. Furthermore, the complex pricing mechanisms underlying the Common Agricultural Policy threatened Europe's general program of price supports.

In the absence of stable currency values, Giscard d'Estaing pointed out, "the unforeseeable reigns. The investor hesitates to make a commitment; the importer limits himself to short-term orders; the exporter inflates his prices as a hedge against uncertain developments. Only with the return of a predictable world will our businesses, both public and private, and our workers be able to decide on new initiatives and pick up the thread of progress. Greater stability must be sought in currency relationships, thereby returning them to their role as standards to measure the value of trade and as factors on which to calculate the return on investments."[1]

Trade patterns began to shift not because of changes in productivity or even domestic price movements but because of currency instability. Rather than allow America to outsell its former competitors through this process, central banks accepted enough dollars to maintain a reasonable minimum value for the currency. Europeans called this support a "managed float" while Americans called it a "dirty float," apparently wishing to see foreign currencies appreciate even further, and incidentally make European monetary integration more difficult as pressures pushed individual currencies away from the Snake range of 2.25 per cent.

The world's weak currencies therefore did not decline fully in keeping with their degree of payments imbalance. Central banks continued to support the dollar and other foreign currencies rather than let their own currency parities appreciate to the point where this would threaten established trading and investment relationships. Within a year central bank holdings of dollars, sterling and other national currencies had grown by about one-third—from $115 billion to about $150 billion, most of it in dollars. In December 1974 Alfred Hayes of the New York Federal Reserve Bank observed that, "since March 1973 (when floating began) official intervention in the exchange markets to moderate exchange rate fluctuations had totaled some $52 billion by the Group of Ten countries alone."[2] The hard-currency nations showed themselves unwilling to see a major decline in the value of Dollar Area currencies—those of the United States, Canada, Latin America and Japan—or their own associated weak currencies such as the Italian lira and the pound sterling. Support operations therefore continued, and Europe asserted itself with increasing force in demanding world monetary reform so as to stem altogether the need for official currency intervention. At the 1973 IMF meetings it called for "an effective and symmetrical adjustment process . . . based on stable but adjustable par values," with floating currency rates providing a useful technique only in "particular situations." Europe also pressed for "cooperation in dealing with disequilibrating capital flows," putting pressure on the Nixon Administration not to revoke its 1964 controls over foreign investment and bank lending. And it urged that gold convertibility be restored as a means of settling payments imbalances so as to put economic pressure on payments-deficit countries to correct their deficits.[3]

The Oil War adds to international monetary stresses

The Middle East War and its subsequent quadrupling of oil-export prices—from $2.50 per barrel to over $10 per barrel—threw the world into immediate financial upheaval. Dependence on imported oil by the industrial nations gave them little choice but to pay the price. But where was the money to come from? The World Bank, OECD and other organizations published scenarios projecting OPEC's foreign-exchange reserves to reach as much as $650 billion by 1980 and $1.32 trillion by 1985, a level equal to about fifty times existing U.S. official monetary reserves. This presumably would enable OPEC governments to "blackmail" the industrial nations and oil-deficit Third World countries by shifting their holdings of monetary assets away from nations not deemed politically subservient. However, these scenarios simplistically assumed that the higher oil prices would have little impact on discouraging oil consumption or spurring energy conservation measures. They also seriously underestimated the ability of OPEC countries to "absorb" capital goods and modern technology from the industrial nations. By 1975 most observers had scaled down their projections to forecast total international reserves for the twelve oil-exporting countries as peaking at around $250 billion by 1980 and then declining.

The immediate effect of higher oil prices was to throw Europe, Japan and the United States into payments-deficit status. European central bankers urged that a special Oil Facility be established within the International Monetary Fund to finance this deficit. In January 1974 the IMF's managing director, H. Johannes Witteveen, proposed a fund totaling as much as $12 billion for loans to oil-importing nations. About half the financing would come from OPEC members, giving oil exporters both an assurance of foreign buying power and a safe means of investing their export proceeds.

U.S. officials opposed this fund for several reasons. They did not accept the new oil prices as representing a lasting plateau, and spoke of rolling them back to as little as $3 per barrel. They perceived that creation of an Oil Facility within the IMF would provide purchasing power to support higher oil prices; without such funding they hoped that the oil-importing nations would have to forgo buying oil (thereby reducing effective world market demand and putting downward pressure on oil prices), or pay OPEC with IOUs of questionable value. Furthermore, it would provide OPEC with an alternative to U.S. Treasury bills as a means of conserving its export earnings: these earnings would be invested through the IMF rather than through the U.S. Treasury, in securities guaranteed by all IMF members rather than by the good will of the U.S. Government alone. Despite U.S. objections the so-called Witteveen Fund was activated in June 1974, but it was limited to only $3.6 billion. (Within six months it lent $2 billion to 33 countries.)

Secretary Kissinger countered with a plan for oil consumers to reduce their imports by three million barrels per day (valued at about $11 billion per year), and to cooperate in other actions designed to weaken the price of world oil. He offered U.S. support for a massive $25 billion fund to finance a confrontation between industrial nations and OPEC, but not to pay for higher oil imports without steps being taken to promote energy conservation and development of domestic energy substitutes for OPEC oil. As matters were put by former Standard Oil officer Jack Bennett in his new capacity as Under Secretary of the Treasury for Monetary Affairs, "The U.S. opposes IMF borrowing from the oil states to finance the Fund . . . and it opposes any plan that rather automatically links a country's ability to borrow to the size of its oil-trade deficit—a key feature of the IMF facility. . . . The U.S. would prefer to see the IMF oil-loan facility phased out of business as it lends out its remaining funds." Britain's Chancellor of the Exchequer Denis Healey insisted upon the urgency of an extension of the Oil Facility or establishment of some other fund under the leadership of European governments outside of the IMF. Failure to establish such a fund would induce the oil exporters to decide "that oil in the ground will be worth more than surplus dollars."[4] On this ground Europe pressed to enlarge the Witteveen Fund in January 1975.

Alfred Hayes accused the fund of taking the "riskiness" out of how oil-exporting countries might preserve the value of their international reserves: "The term 'recycling' has become very popular in recent months," he observed. "To me it is a misnomer. . . . It tends to conceal the basic question of who should assume the credit risk in lending to countries beset with economic difficulties. . . . More fundamentally, the oil-exporting countries will have to take on themselves an increasing share of the risk of the financing of the oil deficits through bilateral credits and grants."[5] In other words, OPEC was to be given intergovernmental notes of questionable value that were not backed by IMF resources.

For a number of years U.S. officials had proposed a special IMF facility to make low-interest loans to food-deficit Third World countries enabling them to pay for their increasingly expensive food imports, largely from the United States. This proposal was presented to the world as an example of humanitarian aid. But these same officials opposed IMF sponsorship of loans to pay OPEC members. This was termed "caving in to Arab blackmail" rather than helping oil-importers warm their homes during the winter. (In this respect U.S. policy reflected the sentiments of a popular bumper sticker in the southwestern United States following the Arab oil embargo of October 1973: "Let the Yankee bastards freeze in the dark.")

The *New York Times* was hardly disturbed at the thought of oil-debtors declaring bankruptcy and repudiating their international debts. Likening payments to OPEC to Europe's reparation debts following World War I, the newspaper observed that, "in effect, the oil-producing countries are asking the stronger industrial countries to take the risks involved in lending OPEC's surplus earnings to the less-creditworthy nations. The United States has been asking the oil producers to share these risks by investing in or lending directly to the countries that buy their oil, particularly the developing countries," that is, those with the lowest credit ratings and highest prospects of default. Senator Henry Jackson warned that if the United States supported an oil fund, "Uncle Sam" would end up "with all the funny money." Former Under Secretary of State George Ball was more urbane in proposing a plan designed to "involve the oil-producing states in assuming part of the burden" of extending loans to bad credit-risks among the oil-consuming nations.[6] OPEC was to be given little choice but to invest its oil revenues in economically non-creditworthy Third World countries and politically antagonistic industrial nations. (As Cuba's Deputy Premier Carlos Rafael Rodriguez recognized at the Rome food conference in November 1974, investments in the United States would make the oil countries "hostages of imperialism.") Can one wonder that their response was to take settlement of their oil surpluses in real goods and productive capital assets rather than in central bank promissory notes?

The United States apparently wanted to be the sole nation permitted to draw upon world central bank credit. If international financial aid were to be provided for Third World countries (or other nations) it should—from the U.S. vantage point—be part of a triangular process by which this credit would repay foreign-aid debts to the U.S. Government or purchase American farm exports, but not end up with the Arabs and other oil exporters. U.S. officials were not interested in contributing to IMF resources that would be lent to industrial rivals or Third World countries to be conveyed to the oil exporters (bidding up the price of world oil to American consumers in the process).

U.S. strategy to maintain the Treasury-bill standard

"The energy crisis and the persistence of inflation," observed France's ambassador to the United States, Jacques Kosciusko-Morizet, "are linked to international monetary and financial disorder, and behind that lies the instability of the dollar. It is futile to expect any permanent recovery until the American leaders, who on August 15, 1971 released their currency from all direct outside constraint [by suspending dollar-convertibility into gold], agree to return to the internal and external disciplines required by their international liabilities."[7] But Europe's demand for fiscal responsibility was unacceptable to the United States. The Treasury's debt to foreign governments had reached $90 billion by the end of 1976, so that if it were to run a trade and payments surplus its earnings would be spent in working off this debt, not in acquiring new ownership of foreign productive assets. Furthermore, inasmuch as this dollar debt had been used to finance the domestic federal budget, its repayment would involve a fresh budgetary expense. Redeeming foreign-owned Treasury obligations would throw the burden of financing past deficits onto current U.S. money markets. This would lead to three equally difficult options: (1) the government could reduce its net federal spending by an amount equal to repayment of its foreign-owned debt; (2) the debt could be financed by the private sector, thus depriving it of capital funds as domestic investors cut back their spending to pay for the Treasury bills being sold by foreign governments; or (3) America could accelerate its inflationary policies so as to substantially reduce the real burden (i.e., purchasing power) of its debt. (Of these three options the government chose the latter, even at the cost of deranging its domestic economy.)

U.S. officials sought to create yet a fourth option: to "fund the dollar overhang" by transforming this debt into part of world monetary reserves that would no more be repaid than the U.S. Treasury would be expected to redeem its domestic currency. Gold would be removed from the world monetary system and replaced by fiat dollars, while Americans got a free ride in creating these dollar credits in the process of paying for real foreign resources.

The U.S. plan was readied by June 1974. It called for creation of a new "substitution account" in the IMF aimed at liquidating (or more specifically, evaporating) the huge "overhang" of dollars and, to a lesser extent, British pounds held in other nations' monetary reserves. "Holders of 'excess' dollars would turn them in to the new account and receive Special Drawing Rights in return," that is, artificial IMF money.[8] The main feature of the plan was that this debt would no longer be owed by the United

States specifically. It would become an asset within the world monetary system for central banks owning dollars (and sterling), but would lose its debt aspect as it became consolidated permanently into world monetary reserves. The Treasury's IOUs thus would be converted into "IOU-nothings."

The greater the debt held by a central bank the more attractive such a scheme would be, especially to creditor governments holding debts of questionable value. In point of fact U.S. monetary officials faced the reality that many of the world's official debts to foreign governments were uncollectible. India already had negotiated to wipe out most of its foreign-aid debt to the United States, and the U.S. Government seemed unlikely to collect on much of its other foreign-aid lending. But it might convert these foreign-aid credits into an international monetary asset by funding national intergovernmental debts without national liability. The most questionable debt of all was the Inter-Ally debt dating from World War I. This too was thrown into the hopper by the U.S. plan. As the National Advisory Council reported in its 1974 annual report:

As of December 31, 1973, the outstanding World War I debt owed to the United States, including unmatured principal and interest, amounted to $25.2 billion, of which $20.8 billion was delinquent. The largest due and unpaid accounts are with the United Kingdom ($9.1 billion), France ($6.4 billion), Germany ($1.6 billion), and Italy ($1.5 billion).

The countries with large World War I obligations to the U.S. have never denied the juridical validity of these debts. They have, however, linked payment to the U.S. to the simultaneous payment of World War I reparations by Germany to them in amounts which roughly offset their war debts to the United States. Resolution of the problem of governmental claims against Germany arising out of World War I was deferred "until a final general settlement of this matter" by the London Agreement on German external debts, to which the United States is a party, concluded in 1953. This agreement was ratified by the United States Senate and has the status of a treaty.

While the United States Government has never recognized any legal connection between World War I obligations owed us and reparations claims on Germany, there is a linkage in reality, which makes this issue sensitive politically as well as economically. A National Advisory Council Working Group is studying the matter and is expected to make concrete proposals in the near future.[9]

So reads the final page of the National Advisory Council annual report published early in 1975. Any such plan would involve adherence by all the World War I allies, including presumably Soviet Russia. The Third World's interest would be attracted by the prospect of being able to wipe its own foreign-aid debts off the books. In fact every nation would be starting debt-free on intergovernmental account: only their assets would be carried over from the past.

This seemed to be the "cleanest" political strategy for America to wipe out its foreign debt. The crudest strategy, by contrast, would be to simply announce one day that it was repudiating it. This would create a monetary and trade crisis that would injure the entire (capitalist) world economy, and probably would hurt foreign countries more than the United States because of the greater role played by foreign trade in overseas economic activity. Still, this strategy was best used only as an ultimate threat to bandy about as a means of securing some more "voluntary" resolution of the Dollar Overhang problem.

Meanwhile, U.S. officials pursued their objective of phasing out gold from the world monetary system as the *numéraire par excellence* and the major alternative to U.S. Treasury bills for central banks to hold their monetary reserves and to settle their payments imbalances. A four-part strategy was suggested. First, the world's central banks would agree not to sell gold to one another (although they could sell it to the public). Second, the link between the value of gold and that of SDRs would be cut so that gold would have no fixed monetary value in central bank reserves. Third, the U.S. Treasury would lead the way by auctioning off part of its own gold stock. Finally, the IMF would help the U.S. Treasury drive down the world price of gold by selling off its own gold, thereby making it less attractive as a world monetary asset —less attractive as a stable measure of value, as a store of value, and thus as a means to settle payments imbalances.

When the Gold Pool was disbanded in 1968 the U.S. Government obtained agreement from foreign central banks not to sell their gold to one another. This effectively froze gold within the world monetary system. To be sure, there were ways to circumvent this agreement. For instance, Italy supported the shaky value of its lira by using its gold as collateral to borrow funds from Germany's central bank, mortgaging this gold at a reported value of about $130 per ounce. In June 1974 the Group of Ten endorsed this practice in an agreement that U.S. officials tried to portray as phasing gold out of the world monetary system rather than letting it reenter through the side door.[10]

But the world's central banks were still bound to evaluate their gold holdings only at the nominal rate of $44.22 per ounce (after September 1973), more than $100 below world market levels which had soared to the $170–$180 range by late 1974. Finally, on December 20, 1974, the French government announced its intention to revalue its monetary gold closer to going market levels. On January 9, 1975 it revalued its official gold holdings to $170.40 per ounce (the average London gold price as of January 7). This set the stage for France and other nations to begin to transfer gold among themselves at existing world prices, contrary to U.S. desires.

Meanwhile, on December 3, 1974 the U.S. Treasury announced it would sell some two million ounces of gold (less than 1 per cent of its total holdings of 276 million ounces) as soon as the new law permitting U.S. private citizens to own gold went into effect on January 1, 1975. For the first time in over thirty years American citizens would be legally permitted to hold gold, and Treasury officials wanted to make sure that this potential demand did not push the price of gold even higher than it already was. (European gold prices fell by $9 per ounce to the $175-per-ounce level following announcement of the Treasury sale, and continued down into the $160s.) Senator William Proxmire announced that he would introduce a bill in Congress requiring the Treasury to sell 25 million ounces of gold in 1975 in an effort to exert further downward pressure on world gold prices.

Response to the Treasury auction was somewhat light, and only 59 of the total 209 bids received were high enough to qualify for the Treasury's cutoff level of $153 per ounce. Less than one million ounces were sold, at an average price of $168.67 (most of it going to European bidders). At the Treasury's next sale, held on July 1, 1975, only half a million ounces was auctioned. This time world demand seemed to be growing, and it sold virtually all its offering for some $82 million, although the average price fell slightly to $165.05 per ounce. (The nickel add-on was designed to cut out the Dresdner Bank of West Germany, which bid on a total of 265,000 ounces at prices ranging from $153 to

$165 an ounce.) Once again, most of this gold was sold to European bidders.* The fact that a total of 758 bids was received this time, for eight times the amount of gold to be sold (i.e., for four million ounces), was reportedly "viewed by gold advocates as a sharp setback for government officials who want to eliminate the metal from the world monetary system."[11]

At a special June IMF meeting held in Washington, U.S. officials extracted further agreement by Fund members to remove gold from the SDR base. Instead of maintaining the SDR's value as equal to that of one ounce of gold (as it was originally established in 1970) it was redefined on the basis of a "basket" of sixteen national currencies, with no reference being made to the price of gold or that of any other commodity. What had been known as paper gold became "paper paper."

At the IMF annual meeting held in Washington at the beginning of September 1975 a compromise was reached on central bank gold policy: they could sell gold to whomever they wanted, even to one another, as long as the aggregate volume of their gold holdings plus that of the IMF did not increase. IMF members further agreed to abolish any official price for gold, an act that U.S. monetary authorities hoped would "end the central role of gold that existed in the former world monetary system."[12] In keeping with the spirit of this decision, the IMF agreed to proceed with the plan suggested by Managing Director Witteveen in Washington the previous June: it would sell one-third of its gold. In an accommodation mainly to Europe—which had argued that the IMF's gold should be returned to its member nations now that it presumably was being phased out of "official" world finance—one-sixth of its total gold was given back to the central banks that originally had pledged it. The other sixth would be sold on the open market, with profits (over and above the original $35 per ounce subscription price) being used to establish a special soft-loan "trust fund" to aid the world's poorer countries in need of balance-of-payments stabilization loans. (This became known as the Witteveen Fund No. 2.)

This agreement triggered a new wave of selling on world gold

---

*The largest bidder was the Swiss Bank Corporation at 140,000 ounces. Other foreign bidders included M. Rothschild & Sons, London [90,000 ounces], Compte de Banque et d'Investissements [29,750 ounces], and the Swiss Credit Bank [23,000 ounces].

markets. On September 1, 1975 the price of gold fell by over $5 per ounce to $155, and dropped another $6 per ounce the following day, reaching its lowest level in more than a year. By yearend it had stabilized around $130 per ounce.

IMF gold holdings were worth about $27 billion at going market prices in autumn 1975, in contrast to a nominal $8 billion at the artificial "official" price of $44.22 per ounce. Sale of one-sixth of this gold would provide a $3.3 billion profit to finance the trust fund that would replace the former Oil Facility, scheduled to expire at the end of the year. Central banks seemed likely to be major buyers of this gold. This would hardly demonetize the metal. Reality and rhetoric seemed to be opposed to one another.

There was a caveat attached to the IMF agreements: they were not to be submitted to national parliaments of the IMF members until the argument over fixed versus floating exchange rates was settled. The Interim Committee of the IMF scheduled a meeting in Jamaica for January 1976 to discuss the topic. As usual the lines were drawn between France on the one hand, urging a system of stable but adjustable parities similar to that which characterized the European Snake, and the United States on the other, opposing any revival of the stable exchange rate system it had sponsored three decades earlier at Bretton Woods. American officials continued to insist that the floating exchange rate system was working, and seemed in no hurry to reach any agreement to stabilize world currencies.

The end of unique U.S. veto power within the IMF

The final issue of the 1975 IMF meetings concerned how to allocate quotas and voting rights as IMF resources were increased by one-third, from $29 billion to $39 billion. OPEC would obviously be entitled to increase its equity ownership of IMF stock by virtue of its enhanced role in world finance. But U.S. officials sought to persuade OPEC to contribute to the IMF and the World Bank without gaining voting rights in keeping with its contribution. To a large extent this strategy worked: OPEC members contributed enough money to the World Bank's "soft loan" affiliate, the International Development Association (IDA), to give them a one-third vote, but they received only a 15 per cent vote in the World Bank proper, and a 10 per cent vote in the IMF (the latter representing a doubling of their modest earlier credit quotas, but still far below their actual weight in world trade and payments). Voting rights in these organizations were based on capital subscriptions, not on government purchases of World Bank bonds (of which OPEC members bought $377 million during 1972–74), contributions to the IMF Oil Facility and so forth. Instead of purchasing equity ownership in the IMF and the World Bank as other members had done, OPEC was asked to (and did) enter through the back door.

The second U.S. objective in reallocating quotas was to maintain its veto power within the IMF. If America could not ram through its own plans to fund the dollar overhang, at least it could block foreign monetary strategy. This required that it maintain its veto power over IMF actions so that no change in the world financial system could occur under IMF auspices that did not directly serve U.S. interests. Its own quota was falling dangerously near the 20 per cent level required to block major fund decisions. In May 1975 Under Secretary of the Treasury Jack Bennett announced that "the United States was willing to accept a reduction from the present 22.95 per cent of the total to 22.42 per cent, but was resisting suggestions 'by Europeans and the I.M.F. staff' for a drop to 'the range of 19.5 per cent.' "[13] A compromise was reached by which the U.S. quota would fall to about 20 per cent, but the proportion of total IMF votes needed to veto any decision would be reduced to only 15 per cent.

Henceforth nearly any bloc of countries can veto IMF decisions. This implies that future transformation of the international financial system will have to occur largely outside the IMF as long as national groupings or regions find their own economic interests to differ from that of other regions. OPEC's 10 per cent vote in the IMF will probably enable it to round up enough support from other countries to block any change in IMF rules to which it objects. Third World countries can unite to veto any given legislative package. As a result the IMF is becoming as impotent as the United Nations in effecting meaningful change in the world. Monetary diplomacy is reverting to regionalism and nationalism for the first time since World War II.

U.S. strategy to hook OPEC on the Treasury-bill standard

The fourfold increase in oil prices transformed the oil-export-ing countries into the world's major international savers as the balance of payments of industrial Europe and Japan moved $40 billion into deficit in 1974 vis-à-vis OPEC, $20 billion in 1975 and about $20 billion again in 1976. This paved the way for a massive shift in investment capital from the industrial nations to OPEC. From the American vantage point the emerging "petrodollar problem" was how to siphon off OPEC's higher export earnings by "recycling" them back to the United States (and, to a lesser extent, to other industrial nations). By becoming world creditors, OPEC governments supplanted Europe and Japan as the richest lodes of potential exploitation through the Treasury-bill stan-dard.

In past epochs the problem of the terms of trade shifting in favor of raw-materials exporters had been avoided by foreign control over their economies, both by the international minerals cartel and by colonial domination backed by the threat of armed force. Now that these paths were closed, OPEC was to be con-fronted with more subtlety. Oil-producing countries could easily be permitted to run a trade surplus on the condition that the resulting petrodollars were recycled to governments and central banks in the industrial nations, much as Europe and Japan had recycled their surplus dollars by buying U.S. Treasury bills. Bal-ancing their international payments in this way would also help the industrial nations finance their domestic budget deficits. Thus, the higher oil prices paid by oil consumers would end up in their own central banks, i.e., would be cycled through OPEC treasuries back to governments in the industrial nations to finance their domestic and international spending.

To be sure, this would entail growing indebtedness of the industrial nations to OPEC. But under inflationary conditions the purchasing power of OPEC-held bank claims on foreign central banks (as well as bank deposits and investments generally) might deteriorate nearly as fast as new debts were being piled up. The key was to provide oil exporters with no secure store of value for their international savings.

Here again the U.S. Government found itself at odds with

Europe, especially France. In October 1974 Giscard d'Estaing announced that France would not accede to plans for confrontation with the oil-exporting countries. Rather, he suggested that "the first problem is to find what type of guarantee could be provided to the oil-exporting countries regarding the protection of their revenue, in other words, the problem of indexing the price of oil [and implicitly, petrodollars] to a number of reference points." The previous month the Common Market had been reported to be "considering a bond issue, to be guaranteed by all member states, that would be offered to oil-producing countries." Treasury Secretary William Simon acknowledged that the U.S. Government "had not ruled out the possibility of gold-backed bonds if demand for gold by Americans should exceed expectations," but his concern was not with protecting Arab interests. Rather, he was speculating that the price of gold might be forced to so high a level that OPEC would lose by the indexing scheme. For if the oil exporters tied their oil to gold at, say, $300 per ounce, and the price subsequently fell to $150 per ounce, they would have to reduce their oil export prices by one-half.

America sought to transfer the burden of financing its balance-of-payments deficit (and if possible its federal budget deficit too) onto the shoulders of OPEC. Oil exporters were accumulating dollars even in excess of their bilateral trade surplus with the United States, as Europe, Japan and many Third World countries paid for their oil in dollars—the very dollars previously held in the form of U.S. Treasury bills. Thus, it became essential to convince OPEC governments to maintain their petrodollars in Treasury bills so as to absorb those which Europe and Japan were selling out of their international monetary reserves. Treasury Secretary Simon traveled to the Middle East to coax Arab nations to buy U.S. Government securities. He also sought to foreclose any other use for OPEC's balance-of-payments surpluses. He warned European banks not to accept more than their existing $15 billion in liquid commercial bank deposits, leaving OPEC governments with little option (he hoped) but to invest their surplus funds in U.S. Treasury securities. (Their investment in private industry was also discouraged.) He held conversations with Saudi Arabian officials about their nation "investing some of its potentially huge supply of dollars in special Treasury issues that have been available for years to foreign central banks gener-

ally," that is to say, the nonmarketable securities such as had
been bought by the German Government to finance U.S. military
occupation costs. (So far the Treasury had issued $26 billion of
these special securities, some $20 billion to Germany.) Saudi
Arabia expressed a willingness to hold some of its surplus funds
in this manner if the value of these securities could be indexed
to world industrial export prices or to the price of gold (i.e., if
they could be "guaranteed" by the U.S. monetary gold stock),
but this proposal was flatly rejected. It was perceived that in
practice Mr. Simon's proposal would mean "that foreign monetary authorities [would] finance part or all of the government's
budget deficit" much as central banks in the industrial nations
had been doing since 1968. And indeed, on June 8, 1974 the
United States and Saudi Arabia signed a military and economic
agreement including a provision for the two countries to "consider cooperation in the field of finance." Mr. Simon suggested
"that the Saudis purchase from $8 to $10 billion in special nonmarketable Treasury securities this year."[14]

A problem obviously existed in the fact that the United States
actively supported the Arab countries' military rival, Israel. As
one Arab spokesman put matters, "It is ironic that while the
Israeli Premier, Yitzhak Rabin, asks the United States for some
$5 billion in military aid, Treasury Secretary William E. Simon
travels to the Arab world and unabashedly asks the Arabs to
invest $10 billion in America—to help the United States help
Israel!"[15] But the Arabs did just this.

As long as OPEC could be persuaded to hold its petrodollars
in Treasury bills rather than investing them in capital goods to
modernize its economies or in ownership of foreign industry, the
level of world oil prices would not adversely affect the United
States. What OPEC earned through higher oil prices would be
channeled back to the U.S. Treasury in what was very nearly a
process of forced saving. The Treasury-bill standard might remain intact thanks to this unforeseen turn of events that enabled
Europe and Japan to reduce their Treasury-bill holdings by transferring the U.S. Government debt to OPEC.

CHAPTER 9

Closing the Open Door
to World Investment

While the industrial nations sought ways to effectively "sterilize" OPEC's petrodollars by recycling them to their own central banks, OPEC governments had plans of their own. Their first priority was to replace their dwindling natural endowments of petroleum and natural gas with growing industrial and agricultural sectors. Sheik Yamani of Saudi Arabia announced in January 1974: "In the future we won't sell our oil for dollars. We will sell only to those who will give us technology and industrialization." A major portion of the Middle East's oil revenues would be spent on capital goods to create a vast industrial infrastructure.

Saudi Arabia's $144 billion five-year plan called for immigration of 700,000 technicians, managers, teachers and workers to provide enough labor to build housing, pave highways, electrify towns, expand port capacity almost threefold, multiply cement production tenfold, and erect oil refineries, petrochemical plants and facilities for other heavy industry.[1] Iran's five-year plan called for $70 billion in similar types of investment (with a somewhat heavier military bias, to be sure), while Kuwait and the Arab emirates (Abu Dhabi, etc.) had plans of nearly equal magnitude. The Shah of Iran announced that within a generation his country would achieve an economic status equal to that enjoyed by Germany in 1974, and would rank as the fifth major world power. During 1974 he contracted with French firms for $6 billion in capital goods to create a forty-mile-long subway in Teheran, a color TV network, steel and automotive plants, and two nuclear power plants.

Regarding his nation's increased oil revenues, the Shah announced, "We are going to invest and spend the whole thing in

111

our country. . . . Why should we lose the purchasing power of our oil which is going to be depleted and finished in 30 years time if we continue to use it in the way we are? I suggest we use it for petrochemical purposes, for medical purposes, making protein out of it . . . and then we have this stuff last 300 years instead." He also forecast a major move toward protectionism for domestic Middle Eastern industries, particularly in the petrochemical area, by stating, "I will sell you aspirins . . . proteins. I won't sell you crude oil." He announced his intention to transform the world's comparative cost structure to the advantage of the Middle East: "We have two good reasons for building up a motor industry. One is that no country in the world could produce steel at the price that we can because we have iron ore and natural gas, and through that we can produce steel at half the price that you [Westerners] can." Furthermore, within a decade Iran's population would top 45 million, requiring massive industrial facilities to employ it. The Shah granted that Iran needed skilled labor, and that until such time as the country could develop or attract a skilled labor force, "we might very well invest abroad."[2] To aid the nation's development he also sought to buy foreign firms outright, the classical response of trade-surplus nations.

The industrial nations were not too happy with this entrance of the Third World into the arena of international investment. The more OPEC spent on capital infrastructure to accelerate its own agricultural and industrial development, the less the OPEC governments would have left for recycling to governments in the industrial nations, and the higher the price of capital goods would climb in these nations. OPEC arms purchases were welcomed, for this connoted profitable business for a war industry operating below capacity. Furthermore, arms did not help countries to produce goods or enable OPEC to compete in world markets with industrial exporters. But purchase of capital goods threatened greater economic self-sufficiency, hence independence from the industrial nations—and, at a point, prospective competition. OPEC's use of its financial resources was therefore to be constrained if possible. In principle, Third World countries were to produce the oil and other raw materials needed by the industrial nations to maintain their own established production patterns and prosperity, but not to supplant imports from the oil-deficit nations. Certainly Europe, North America and Japan had little desire to become industrial customers for their erstwhile hewers of wood and drawers of water.

As it became apparent that industrial purchases by the oil-exporting countries would provide massive profit opportunities for Western firms, OPEC sought major ownership shares in these companies. Its interest was concentrated on firms and industries that could play major roles as suppliers and managers of industrialization programs in key sectors such as steel, petrochemicals and transport.

When OPEC government agencies or private financiers invested in such companies it was effectively to help them participate in Middle Eastern growth. Sale of partial ownership of European, American or Japanese firms to OPEC thus implied improved sales prospects as well as financial resources for these companies. Still, OPEC domination was not altogether welcome. A German economist suggested channeling OPEC direct investments in his country into marzipan factories, and the French government installed controls requiring "prior notification of, and formal application for, major share acquisitions." (These controls originally were prepared to qualify the terms on which U.S. takeovers might be made, but were not implemented until threat of OPEC purchase of companies became a reality.) When a large bloc of Mercedes-Benz stock came onto the market in 1975, Helmut Schmidt urged German banks to purchase it so that it would not fall into Iranian hands (at a time when Kuwait had already bought into the firm the previous year). Nonetheless, Iran purchased 25.01 per cent of Krupp, enough to give it veto power in company decisions. It also invested $1 billion to develop French uranium enrichment capacity as part of an advance payment toward two Iranian nuclear power stations.[3]

OPEC investors were blocked from making similar acquisitions in the United States and Japan. U.S. officials opposed the purchase of more than 5 per cent interest in viable firms in heavy industries such as U.S. Steel or General Motors, armaments companies such as Grumman, or in major U.S. raw-materials or natural resource companies. America became the most adamant advocate against OPEC takeovers. Government officials sought to attract petrodollars but to deny OPEC investors any say in the management of corporations they might invest in or help finance. Along these lines Treasury Secretary Shultz suggested "consideration of a new kind of multi-national joint venture—a type of mutual fund, as it were—which would employ expert investment management to channel OPEC funds into a diversity of profitable investment outlets in the consuming countries. The investing nations . . . would 'maintain control over some basic decisions concerning the volume and distribution of the funds,' " but could not determine the company-by-company allocation of these funds.[4] One is reminded of Britain's experience in the nineteenth century when its investors financed U.S. railroads, agriculture and other basic industries only to see their holdings manipulated, embezzled or otherwise wasted by the stock market manipulations of Jay Gould and other great robber barons. Perhaps a similar tactic could be used on the Arabs. It would be less politically sensitive than outright nationalization for it would be construed as the workings of the free investment market!

George Ball echoed Secretary Shultz's line of reasoning when he suggested that OPEC countries participate on a fifty-fifty basis in a "Fund or Bank for Capital Recycling" so that they might "place their surplus funds at the disposal of the West in order to bolster the Western economies and (to a lesser extent) those of the poorer developing countries." (The other half of the funds would come from the United States, the European Common Market and Japan.) The following month a group of international economists led by Robert Roosa and the heads of Iran's Development Bank and Japan's Overseas Economic Cooperation Fund published an article in *Foreign Affairs* asserting that the prospective OPEC balance-of-payments surplus would be so large (about $600 billion during 1975–79) that any aid or dollar recycling they would provide to oil-consuming nations must "be only slightly distinguishable from grants." The authors suggested two funds to use up OPEC's petrodollar surpluses. The first was an "OPEC Fund for Government Securities" which would "purchase only special direct issues of various governments" in the industrial nations, with provisions for "orderly redemption features" so that OPEC governments could not liquidate their investments at their own convenience. An "OPEC Investment Trust" would be established for equity investment in American, European and Japanese firms, but OPEC would not be able to use its investment as an instrument for control. The directors of the investment trust "should agree that voting shares in companies will be exercised by management [of these companies] with a view solely to protecting the value of the investment," as if OPEC were comprised of widows and orphans rather than of governments with strategic economic interests. The fund would thus serve explicitly as "a buffer against the direct holding of voting stocks by OPEC governments," as if mere earnings rather than control represented the sole OPEC concern. "In the interests of the oil-consuming countries," the article continued lugubriously, "no trust should hold shares in any company which would bring the known total holding of such shares by OPEC governments or their agencies above, say, 10 per cent of the total outstanding. . . . The trusts should undertake to buy or sell shares (or debentures) in amounts above, say, $1 million (or the equivalent in other currencies) only with the knowledge of the company."[5] OPEC was thus to dissipate its funds by spreading them around, not focus them into instruments of control. (One can readily imagine the derision American investors would have expressed if Europe had insisted that the United States spread surplus dollars throughout European industry in the 1940s and 1950s in such a manner, instead of buying control of specific foreign firms with a view toward promoting the investment strategy of the head offices of U.S. multinational firms.)

One-time Nixon aide William Safire suggested such tactics as charging *negative* interest "on short-term cartel deposits in U.S. banks coupled with a minimum time for deposit, such as six months. The oil cartel's billions must rest somewhere safe; we should charge for safekeeping rather than let them play havoc with our banking system." He also suggested "armaments with strings attached" such as insisting that OPEC governments buy Treasury bills in proportion to their arms purchases, and that "investment restrictions" be imposed inasmuch as OPEC had, in his opinion, little option but to invest in the United States.[6]

Americans debated whether or not to permit direct Arab investment in U.S. firms. For decades U.S. investors had purchased control of such industries in other countries, with sharp U.S. Government reaction against all foreign attempts to stem this investment takeover. Now that the process threatened to reverse itself the American government stepped in rapidly to prevent its evolution along lines not strictly in accord with what it held to be the national interest. Federal officials announced their willingness to see OPEC investment in near-bankrupt companies such as Pan American World Airways, Chrysler, government-regulated industries such as railroads or other tottering sectors, or some of the consumer-goods and "breakfast cereal" companies. Federal Reserve Board Chairman Arthur Burns suggested that oil-country investments "should be confined to such nonsensitive companies as Quaker Oats and Coca Cola." But investment in more important industries was strictly forbidden.

The Federal Reserve Bank of St. Louis pointed out that, "so long as our industry produces all the goods and services that we are willing to purchase, why should we be so concerned about ownership? If foreign ownership is undesirable from a political point of view, or from a strategic point of view during a war, foreign owners could be controlled by legal sanctions." Indeed, in 1974 Congress enacted the Foreign Investment Study Act requiring the Secretaries of Commerce and Treasury to conduct studies of foreign direct and portfolio investment in the United States. "U.S. Treasury officials said that the new Congress will introduce and perhaps enact 'draconian' measures to block Arab acquisition of American corporations or land," leaving only U.S. Treasury securities open to them to purchase with their surplus funds.[7]

John J. McCloy, first head of the World Bank and former chairman of the Chase National Bank, made an interesting suggestion: "Why not let the Arabs buy up all the big Western corporations —GM, Imperial Chemical and so forth. Then we'll expropriate them. Without compensation, of course." Lest his remarks be taken in a jocular vein, he repeated this proposal in testimony before the Senate Foreign Relations Committee on Multinational Corporations. "Let them [the oil-exporting countries] come in, then nationalize them. The Arabs learned that." (He revealed some degree of prejudice in the matter by acknowledging that he had represented about twenty-three oil companies since the 1960s, and that he had sought special exemption from U.S. anti-trust legislation to enable them "to bargain collectively with the petroleum-producing states . . . to prevent those nations from playing off one company against the other to drive up the price of oil again and again.")[8] Former advocates of free markets and an Open Door to world investment quickly changed their stripes now that oil-exporting countries were in a position to do what America had been doing all along.

Kissinger acknowledged that "a manageable minority interest [in U.S. firms] would be in our interest," but added, "There are some industrial segments we would not want to be dominated by potentially hostile investors." He endorsed the creation of a U.S. Congressional agency to "monitor" foreign direct investment in the United States. An emerging congressional coalition was described "as being composed of pro-Israeli legislators and conservatives. One top Administration official expects them to put about 40 bills into the legislative hopper to block or slow investment in the U.S. by oil-producing countries." One senator's aide said, "The problem is that, although we have always been free-traders, the scale of the potential investment here is so vast that we will have to write an entirely new set of rules." Yet another bureaucrat warned, "If the United States continues to buy high-priced foreign oil, within 30 years the foreign oil countries will be able to buy everything in the United States. . . . In the next three decades the OPEC nations will accumulate enough reserves to buy the top 500 companies in the United States, and have enough left over to buy anything else anyone in the U.S. still owns."[9]

Strong public opposition arose when two Arab millionaires sought to buy banks in San Jose, California and Pontiac, Michigan. In March 1975 Senators Jacob Javits of New York and Harrison Williams of New Jersey sought to amend the Securities Exchange Act of 1934 so as to bar "foreign investors who engage in boycotts or other discriminatory practices from buying more than 5 per cent of a U.S. company," and to freeze and sell all assets already owned in excess of the magic 5 per cent level. (The discrimination in question was a reference to the Arab boycott of Israel, analogous to the American boycotts of Cuba, China and Rhodesia.) In addition the proposed legislation required that "any foreign investor seeking to acquire 5 per cent or more of a United States company must give 30 days' notice" to the Securities and Exchange Commission and recommended that the President be given authority to bar, "on grounds of national interest, any foreign investment exceeding 5 per cent ownership of any domestic company with assets of more than $1 million." This strategy obliged the United States to block almost all foreign investment without discrimination. Under Secretary of the Treasury Jack Bennett observed that "the U.S. already has curbs on various types of foreign investment, including airlines, communications, atomic energy and in federal mineral lands. But the controls are dispersed among a number of federal agencies."[10] This suggested creation of a new office to coordinate U.S. investment restrictions.

After Kuwait and Iran were forbidden to buy into Lockheed and Grumman or into major nondefense industries, OPEC spokesmen indicated that this would become a key issue at the upcoming North-South meeting (formally called the Council for International Economic Cooperation, or CIEC) to convene in Paris in December 1975.

Treasury Under Secretary Gerald Parsky traveled to the Middle East in 1975 and got the oil-exporting countries to curtail their investment in the United States. He announced that Iran had indicated an intention to invest in companies "which are in a position to help it expand its domestic industrial base through access to foreign products, increased technology, manpower skills and resources. I don't believe Iran will be interested in investing in real estate or highly speculative ventures." The Kuwaitis and other Arabs were "exploring the entire spectrum from common stock to real estate," but he "would be surprised if Saudi Arabia invested more than 10 per cent in a particular country and more than 5 per cent in a particular company," a judgment that indicated considerable U.S. pressure on the Saudis. Mr. Parsky estimated that in 1974 OPEC had invested less than $1 billion in the U.S. private sector, an indication of the success of U.S. political barriers to them.[11] (The threat of U.S. expropriation of OPEC assets, particularly under conditions of military hostility, also induced oil-exporters to concentrate their investments in Europe.)

Meanwhile both advocates and opponents of free and unregulated international investment conjured up images of a new era in which multinational corporations would determine the international application of technology, and the pattern of world trade and payments generally, in accordance with the principle of international profit maximization. Governments were held to be unable to act in accordance with their own long-term economic or political objectives where they diverged from those of the large multinational firms.

Advocates of private enterprise asserted that corporations tended to be run more efficiently than governments, and that they should therefore dictate economic policies. Proponents of government planning criticized business priorities and practices. Both groups held that governments were being overwhelmed by the magnitude of worldwide private finance capital. A widely publicized Congressional study argued that the liquid assets of multinational firms were deranging national exchange rates and perpetuating the worldwide currency instability by causing numerous revaluations and devaluations. Investment managers were described as allocating technology according to corporate profit objectives unrelated to national planning priorities, and evading national tax policies by manipulating intrafirm transfer prices. For better or worse the direction of world economic development, technology and balance-of-payments flows would seemingly elude the guiding hand of governments.

This was the thesis of a popular 1974 book by Richard Barnet and Ronald Müller entitled *Global Reach: The Power of Multinational Corporations*. As one reviewer, Eliot Janeway, summarized its argument, "The efficiency of the multinationals . . . is the measure of the threat they pose to take over from the duly constituted civil authorities in jurisdictions the world over. The profitability Barnet and Müller attribute to the multinationals is cited as proof that they know what they are doing and that they are doing what works." But the reviewer was quick to perceive that this was only the first phase of the multinational saga: the very threat of this development materializing had triggered a nationalistic reaction abroad "subjecting the various national arms of the multinationals to crackdowns restricting their operations, freezing their profitability, taxing their resources, and, as in the case of the big oil companies, expropriating their assets. . . . Any resemblance between any of them and a functioning octopus is rapidly becoming a blurred memory. They are falling apart as power entities and profit vehicles. . . . In country after country—and by no means in just the oil-producing countries—the foreign subsidiaries of the multinationals are being taken over into protective custody by governments left holding the bag with the bust their boom invited. . . . On November 28 [1974] Chancellor [Helmut] Schmidt clamped a 'code of good behavior' on 14 American multinationals and committed them to the protective custody of Krupp."[12]

The idealized image of multinationals neglected to consider

the political and institutional setting in which they operated, and the fact that foreign affiliates of multinational firms are legally resident citizens of their host countries. Ironically, economists chose to formulate a theory about multinational control over the direction of world economic development at the precise moment that the process began to deteriorate. (This is one more example of how the analysis of historic processes tends to be formulated at the end of these processes, generally when new ones are already under way). To be sure, the theory voiced by Barnet and Müller was not disinterested: it was suggested explicitly to urge a nationalist program of U.S. Government regulation over the foreign activities of American corporations, essentially the system of controls advocated by the AFL-CIO.

In the face of attempts by industrial nations to mobilize the foreign-investment activities of their firms to serve specifically national ends, it would have been surprising had the raw-materials exporting countries not sought to develop their own countervailing power. Foreign-owned firms were destined to fall under the sway of the first government that chose to regulate them, and the United States had taken the lead in initiating regulatory action in the 1960s, followed soon after by governments in other industrial nations. The world's richest nations all had achieved industrialization in the nineteenth and early twentieth centuries by regulating their domestic economies. Why should today's Third World countries not follow suit?

Host-country governments therefore began to regulate foreign investment within their boundaries. A general outline of their position was set forth in a 1974 United Nations study of "whether a set of institutions and devices can be worked out which will guide the multinational corporations' exercise of power and introduce some form of accountability to the international community into their activities."[13] Competition over regulatory powers as between host-country and home-office governments was under way, and multinational corporations had become the battleground.

CHAPTER 10

The Ending of U.S. Foreign Aid

Only rarely is foreign aid a gift in today's world. "Humanitarian" assistance in the form of emergency food and medical relief for victims of earthquakes, drought, floods or other natural disasters represents less than 2 per cent of American overseas aid. Most U.S. aid is military in nature, comprising logistical support and arms credit, plus back-up aid to countries of strategic military interest to the United States, e.g., Southeast Asia before 1973, countries that face communist neighbors, and those such as Spain and Turkey which provide America with military bases. Aid is extended mainly to contain communism by securing foreign adherence to U.S.-backed treaty organizations such as SEATO, CENTO and NATO, and to oppose domestic communist movements by propping up incumbent regimes, including some of the world's most reactionary governments: South Korea under Park, Iran under the Shah, Greece under the colonels, and dictatorships in Chile and Brazil. Such aid is thus an extension of America's national security programs.

Most nonmilitary U.S. aid directly or indirectly is made up of export credits. Both bilateral U.S. aid and that extended through the World Bank and other multilateral institutions are designed to support foreign demand for U.S. products. Aid lending is usually extended on easier terms than can be arranged through commercial channels (i.e., it has longer repayment periods and a number of years of grace at the outset). U.S. bilateral aid prior to 1973 was dominated by food sales to Third World countries under Public Law 480, enacted two decades earlier as part of the Agricultural Trade and Development Act (which developed America's export capacity, not foreign agricultural production). PL-480 enabled the United States to dispose of its otherwise unsalable farm surpluses and to transport these surpluses in U.S.-flag ships for whose high-cost services world demand was slack. But the motive for American food aid dissolved once the nation was able to sell its surplus crops for hard currency to the Soviet Union.

If the function of foreign aid is to promote the government's economic and military self-interest, why is it called aid at all? The answer is simply because it sounds good: it is a euphemism. Statistically, any government-financed export credit is counted as "aid" so long as it is extended to or through another government, or through an international consortium such as the World Bank. All nonmilitary aid-lending falls under the rubric of "development aid" whether or not it actually contributes to the development of the aid-borrowing country. "Development aid" sounds much more altruistic than "export credits" or "cost of securing foreign diplomatic and military support for U.S. objectives." Idealists usually have a rude awakening when they examine the workings and tactics of U.S. foreign aid in practice.

To be sure, intergovernmental credits differ in some basic ways from commercial loans. The latter usually are extended only for projects that will generate an income sufficient to repay them with interest. Countries—or at least, specific projects for which the loans are granted—must be judged "creditworthy" in order to qualify for commercial bank loans and other private-sector credits. By contrast, intergovernmental lending is not contingent upon the aid-borrower's ability to repay. Much of it is extended to the poorest and least creditworthy countries such as India and Bangladesh. It is nonetheless extended in the form of loans. If the aid-borrowing country cannot repay, it can usually reschedule its debt by offering some other form of *quid pro quo:* acquiescence in a world division of labor that is not in its interest; provision of military base rights, support for U.S. positions in world diplomacy, and, in general, opposition to communism at home and abroad.

Since 1973 the aid-borrowing countries have not been very eager to perform these functions, which has diminished America's interest in extending further aid. In addition, Congress and the executive branch began to disagree about an appropriate national defense philosophy. Congress opposes military aid that might lead to American involvement in a new Vietnam situation (e.g., in Angola or elsewhere in Africa), or that would prop up the type of nondemocratic regimes supported in the past.

In short, U.S. foreign aid is being wound down because it no longer serves the broad functions that characterized it prior to 1973: (1) to extend or mask military support, (2) to dispose of domestic agricultural surpluses in exchange for "soft" foreign currencies and to build up foreign dependency on U.S. food exports, (3) to tap the resources of payments-surplus nations by channeling their aid programs through the World Bank and regional banks whose lending and investment policies have reflected U.S. objectives, and (4) to sustain the existing division of labor between industrial and Third World countries. Since 1973 these objectives have been rejected both by the U.S. Congress and by foreign governments.

Foreign aid's contribution to the U.S. balance of payments

During the early 1960s, as Cold War expenditures drained the U.S. balance of payments, American nonmilitary aid was granted only if it were spent in the United States. Since 1962 it has been extended only on the condition that it not displace American commercial exports and commercial financing. Only commodities such as grain that could not be sold abroad on commercial terms, and services such as U.S.-flag shipping (whose costs far surpassed those of non-U.S.-flag carriers) for which there was no strong world market, were subsidized by U.S. foreign aid. Upon delivery of these exports, aid-borrowing countries turned over to the State Department's Agency for International Development (AID) an equivalent value of their domestic currencies, which the State Department, the Defense Department and other federal agencies spent for their operations abroad. No commercial exports were displaced, nor did U.S. aid contribute to a payments outflow. In balance-of-payments terms this aid was initially a wash transaction: an export credit canceled out the aid loan. Over time the U.S. balance of payments benefited as foreign governments began to repay their aid borrowings in dollars. In recent years U.S. bilateral foreign aid programs have contributed an average of $1.9 billion annually to the U.S. balance of payments (Table 10.1).

By 1973, however, foreign currencies acquired via earlier PL-480 programs reached so high a level that further accumulation seemed pointless. (Indeed, most of India's aid debt was simply

TABLE 10.1

Foreign Aid in the U.S. Balance of Payments, 1960–76

(millions of dollars)

	Total Net Effect	New Grants and Other Capital Outflows	Spent in United States	Net Balance-of-Payments Cost	Net Interest Received on Official Aid-Lending*	Net Repayment of Principal*
1960	$ (300)	$ (3,617)	$ 2,492	$ (1,125)	$ 279	$ 546
1961	(329)	(4,329)	3,185	(1,144)	307	508
1962	(186)	(4,555)	3,512	(1,042)	357	499
1963	13	(4,794)	3,981	(813)	351	475
1964	40	(4,614)	3,922	(691)	288	443
1965	70	(4,527)	3,774	(753)	326	497
1966	319	(4,655)	3,921	(734)	412	641
1967	537	(5,238)	4,511	(726)	467	796
1968	903	(5,093)	4,452	(641)	569	975
1969	1,145	(4,838)	4,104	(734)	732	1,147
1970	1,329	(4,935)	4,248	(687)	715	1,301
1971	1,199	(6,042)	5,160	(881)	624	1,456
1972	1,166	(5,827)	4,718	(1,110)	613	1,663
1973	1,617	(7,178)	6,190	(998)	657	1,958
1974	792	(9,905)	8,537	(1,368)	905	1,255
1975	1,917	(8,792)	7,523	(1,270)	1,025	2,162
1976	1,971	(10,007)	8,261	(1,746)	1,199	2,418
Cumulative, 1960–76	$12,203	$(98,946)	$82,491	$(16,463)	$9,826	$18,740

*Balance-of-payments basis, excluding debt service financed by new U.S. bilateral aid-lending.

Source: U.S. Department of Commerce, Office of Business Economics, *Survey of Current Business*, Table 5 (published quarterly). Cross totals may not justify due to rounding.

wiped off the books.) Structural balance-of-payments deficits suffered by aid-borrowing countries had deteriorated so far by 1973 that these countries were unable to repay the United States, becoming a source of diplomatic aggravation rather than friendship. Therefore, if foreign aid were to continue yielding a dollar inflow for the U.S. Government, other nations would have to provide the funding.

Multilateralizing U.S. aid programs

By extending foreign aid through multilateral organizations such as the World Bank, the U.S. Government tapped foreign resources by what U.S. officials called "burden sharing." Multilateral aid used foreign funds to finance essentially U.S.-oriented policies. It was extended largely to help foreign countries develop their export sectors and thus hold down the price of raw materials. The World Bank helped finance massive foreign purchases of U.S. capital goods and consulting services, and borrowed funds in payments-surplus nations to invest in the United States, its head office.

As the National Advisory Council observed, "U.S. political goals are in varying degrees dependent on strengthening friendly governments important to the United States. Channeling aid through the international development lending institutions (IDLIs) rather than through bilateral programs reduces our flexibility to direct funds chiefly to countries of highest priority to the United States at any point in time; these institutions are not intended to serve the political goals of any one country, and their funding comes from many countries. However, because of a broad similarity of objectives, the IDLIs have in fact carried out a pattern of lending that is generally consistent with U.S. interests. The large recipients of such lending have also been large recipients of U.S. bilateral assistance. . . . Korea, the Republic of China, Thailand, the Philippines, and Indonesia—all countries with close ties to the United States—are the major recipients of Asian Development Bank (ADB) funds. Furthermore, the ADB is the only IDLI currently lending to the countries of Indochina. . . . The international development lending institutions have proven to be an effective instrument for reducing the U.S. share of the burden of providing development assistance. . . . The

United States thus gets a direct 'multiplier effect' only in multilateral lending."[1]

It was hardly surprising that these multilateral loans were consistent with U.S. aims, for the U.S. Government enjoyed veto power over all aid funneled through the World Bank. Furthermore, most of the loan operations of these institutions were financed by funds raised in payments-surplus nations—at first Germany, Japan, and Switzerland, and after 1973 the oil-exporting countries. Not only were these funds used in large part to buy U.S. exports financed by these multilateral aid programs, but the World Bank, its soft-loan affiliate the International Development Association (IDA), and its sister regional organizations, the ADB and the Inter-American Development Bank (IDB), held their bor-

TABLE 10.2

Net Contribution of the World Bank Group to the U.S. Balance of Payments
[Excluding short-term capital]

(millions of dollars)

	Total	World Bank[a]	IDA[a]	IDB	ADB[b]
1966	$ 602	$ 538	$ n.a.	$ 64	$ –
1967	300	294	n.a.	7	(1)
1968	87	138	(84)	22	11
1969	342	365	(4)	(14)	(5)
1970	454	576	(36)	(54)	(32)
1971	(233)	(43)	19	(177)	(32)
1972	467	416	(25)	54	22
1973	587	273	(50)	253	111
1974	534	456	14	(25)	89
1975	(2,119)	(1,526)	(322)	(288)	17
1976	(1,144)	(849)	(295)	n.a.	n.a.
Inception through 1976	$ 559	$1,600	$(948)	$(273)	$180

[a]Fiscal year basis.
[b]Including Special Fund.

Source: National Advisory Council on International Monetary and Financial Policies, *International Finance: Annual Report to the President and to Congress: July 1, 1975–June 30, 1976* (Washington, D.C.: 1977), House Doc. 95–67, Tables E-6, F-4, H-5, H-6, I-7 and I-10.

rowed funds on deposit with U.S. banks or invested them in U.S. Treasury securities, providing savings for America's faltering capital markets. World Bank programs contributed some $456 million to the U.S. balance of payments in fiscal 1974, largely through OPEC bond subscriptions. For 1973 (the most recent year for which figures are available) the ADB yielded $3.3 billion (Table 10.2). Since its inception in 1945 the World Bank has contributed some $2.4 billion to the U.S. balance of payments, much of it by investing its working capital in U.S. Government securities in recent years. The foreign aid process thus became part of the U.S. Treasury-bill standard of world finance.

Despite these financial benefits, Congress balked at financing further World Bank Group programs after 1973. Prior to that time, countries had been obliged to pursue policies supported by the U.S. Government if they hoped to get their aid requests to the World Bank Group passed without U.S. veto. But now foreign countries were beginning to act in their own self-interest regardless of U.S. wishes.

In 1974 Treasury Secretary George Shultz questioned whether U.S. interest lay in adding to World Bank funds in view of Third World rejection of private-sector investment. "Every sovereign nation has, of course, the right to regulate the terms and conditions under which private investment is admitted or to reject it entirely. When such capital is rejected, we find it difficult to understand that official donors should be asked to fill the gap." Why should World Bank resources be made available to Third World countries if this would only enable them to become independent of U.S. and European multinational firms? U.S. bilateral aid and/or multinational aid might well be used to induce Third World countries to maintain an open door to foreign investment, complementing rather than substituting for private appropriation of their raw-materials resources. But it was not to be used to help these countries become economically independent. "Moreover," Mr. Shultz added, "we do not find it reasonable that a nation taking confiscatory steps toward investment that it has already accepted from abroad should anticipate official assistance, bilateral or multilateral."[2] Essentially the same policy had been voiced by the Eisenhower administration in witholding aid from Iran in 1953 until such time as the Shah's coup d'état reversed Mossadegh's policies. U.S. representatives similarly vetoed World Bank credits to Chile under the Allende government.

In the case of the Asian Development Bank, Congress dawdled for five years before putting up the first U.S. share of $50 million —which it finally did in 1973—and did not subscribe to a second $50 million installment. Furthermore, it scaled down by $50 million the original U.S. commitment to provide $200 million to the ADB's "Special Fund" (to finance its "soft loan" program). The ADB's 1973–74 increase of $2 billion in capital funding occurred without U.S. participation, reducing U.S. voting power from 16 to 8 per cent. And yet the bank purchased over $100 million in long-term U.S. assets, in addition to financing about $10 million in U.S. exports.[3] (The Inter-American Development Bank purchased some $197 million of long-term U.S. assets in 1973, mainly certificates of deposit in U.S. banks.)

An important element of the World Bank Group's operations was its 1974 sale to OPEC of some $2.3 billion in bonds, more than two-thirds of the Group's total bond sales in that year. OPEC governments held a mere 4.5 per cent of the World Bank's voting rights, having originally subscribed to only $100 million of its capital. Had they financed their World Bank participation by capital subscriptions rather than bond purchases, their 1974 purchases by themselves would have given them a 75 per cent voting share in the World Bank.

And yet some U.S. spokesmen considered even this seemingly beneficial aspect of World Bank financing to be ambiguous in serving U.S. world interests. To be sure, it raised funds from OPEC and other payments-surplus regions and spent or invested them in the United States. But it also provided higher interest rates than U.S. Treasury bills, thereby undercutting the Treasury-bill standard. "In effect," the *New York Times* summarized the American position, "the oil-producing countries are asking the stronger industrial countries to take the risks involved in lending OPEC's surplus earnings to the less-creditworthy nations. The United States has been asking the oil producers to share these risks by investing in or lending directly to the countries that buy their oil, particularly the developing countries."[4] But OPEC preferred to invest in the World Bank. The U.S. position was that if OPEC wanted to lend its funds to Third World countries, it should do so on a bilateral basis rather than through the IMF and

World Bank. Thus, if OPEC's bilateral aid to Third World countries (e.g., to India or Bangladesh) went sour, OPEC governments would be cast in the role of rich Shylocks trying to collect
their debts (a position which the U.S. Government already found
quite uncomfortable).

Secretary Kissinger urged that the IDLIs extend loans to help
countries achieve energy independence and thus put downward
pressure on the price of world oil exports. He suggested that the
IMF borrow $25 billion from the oil-exporting countries through
the sixteen-nation International Energy Agency, and lend the
proceeds to consumer nations to finance the development of
energy independence. But he opposed these institutions financing the importation of oil from OPEC, thereby supporting its
world price while providing OPEC governments with creditworthy investment vehicles.

At best, oil-deficit Third World countries were to become in-
termediaries in "a triangular relationship in which OPEC members channel part of their surpluses to the poor countries, which
in turn use them to import from the industrial countries"[5] (the
United States, Britain, etc.). The Committee on Economic Development, a Washington-based research organization, recommended joint actions by OPEC and the Organization for Economic Cooperation and Development (OECD) to channel more
aid to the poorest nations while simultaneously channeling financial payments to the industrial nations from OPEC members.

Growing congressional disillusionment with
U.S. foreign aid

One of the earliest examples of congressional disenchantment
with foreign aid occurred in the case of India. The subcontinent
seemed unable to help itself and ungrateful for what it received
from abroad. Foreign aid left the masses untouched as some 230
million Indians reportedly lived on less than $60 per year while
wealthy landlords kept a stranglehold on the nation's agricultural
economy. In keeping with orthodox Western economic thinking,
India neglected its labor-intensive agriculture to develop its
heavy industry. For over a decade per capita agricultural output
had been declining. One Indian observed, "Our ideology dictated, while common sense deplored, that we invest in basic

heavy industries instead of agriculture and consumer goods."
Another noted that "the share of agriculture in successive [Five-
Year] plans has dwindled from 31.4 per cent in the first plan
(1951–56) to 20.7 per cent in the fourth (1969–74). It has been
slashed further in the annual plan for 1974–75." However noble
the U.S. desire to help feed India's masses might be, the effort
was countereffective. But it took India's explosion of its first
atomic device to shock the Western world into realizing that
increasing billions of dollars were being devoted to arms, weaponry and heavy industry, less and less to agricultural development. Food-aid was merely subsidizing the nation's militarism
and backwardness. Finally, Indira Gandhi's 1975 coup and her
subsequent suspension of democratic institutions dissolved foreign sympathy for the government. Aid to India was reduced—
and India responded by moving closer and closer to Soviet
Russia.[6]

Congress began to recognize that foreign aid had systematically impaired foreign countries' ability to feed themselves by
persuading (and enabling) governments to refrain from pursuing
agricultural protectionism and land reform, or otherwise "inter-
fering" with existing market structures. Such aid financed a rising
stream of food imports by countries whose domestic agriculture
was not modernized and whose raw-materials exports were unable to cover the cost of feeding their populations with foreign
food (the "Chile syndrome"). This type of foreign aid kept those
governments in power that were willing to produce for export
rather than to pursue domestic economic diversification and self-
sufficiency. Indeed, by providing compensation over and above
that supplied by market forces, it had induced many Third World
regimes to export a rising volume of minerals and plantation
crops in the face of deteriorating terms of trade. The National
Advisory Council described the U.S.: "The United States supports IDLI efforts to expand and strengthen the role of market
forces as the most effective means of allocating resources, developing outward-looking trading economies, strengthening the
role of private enterprise and promoting the creation of economies with trade and investment patterns compatible with the
economies of the industrialized countries."[7]

Meanwhile, Congress blocked aid to Southeast Asia during
America's final years of military involvement there, and then
suspended or scaled down aid to Greece, Turkey, Spain, South

Korea and other countries whose foreign and domestic policies did not meet with its approval. A major course of antagonism between the executive branch and Congress occurred over Turkey, which had been receiving aid in large part to secure its adherence to NATO. The U.S. Air Force base at Incerlik was the biggest in Europe, dominating NATO air strength from Germany to the Middle East. America's defense support facilities in Turkey included an electronic surveillance system extending along the Soviet border, as well as nuclear warheads and delivery systems under U.S. control. These were all important considerations to the Secretary of State. But Congress objected to Turkey's occupation of Cyprus following Greece's attempt to annex the island (whose population was both Greek and Turkish in heritage). Congress also objected to Turkey's cultivation of the opium poppy. In 1971 the U.S. Government had persuaded Turkey to stop harvesting poppies in return for American aid of $5 million annually. The result was a world shortage of legal opium derivatives (e.g., morphine), which led the U.S. Army to begin growing opium in the southern states of America. Turkey found itself losing some $7 million in foreign exchange and terminated its agreement with the United States.[8]

On September 25, 1974 the House of Representatives voted to cut off all military aid to Turkey until it made substantial progress toward reaching a settlement with the Greek Cypriots and stopped cultivating opium. Partly in response to the politically active Greek lobby in Washington, Congress suspended a $250 million allocation for forty F-14 Phantom jets, $60 million in low-cost sales of war-surplus materials, and $50 million in military grants.

Another antipathy was emerging within the U.S. Government as the State Department sought to use the foreign-aid program to support Asian and Latin American "anticommunist" dictatorships from Vietnam to Chile over mounting Congressional opposition. The Foreign Assistance Act of 1974 included a "Sense of Congress" amendment that obliged the President, "except in extraordinary circumstances," to reduce significantly, or even to terminate, security assistance to "any government which engages in a consistent pattern of gross violations of internationally recognized human rights." If military assistance was proposed for any government in "gross violation," the President was obliged to "advise the Congress of the extraordinary circum-

stance necessitating the assistance." This seemed to bar U.S. aid
to South Korea, Taiwan, the Philippines, Indonesia, Brazil, Chile,
Iran and other repressive dictatorships in the American camp.

In November 1975 the Ford administration refused to comply
with this congressional mandate. The State Department con-
tended that "so many nations around the world engage in such
violations that there was 'no adequate objective way' to distinguish which countries were more reprehensible than others.
Thus, no nations were cited. . . . Mr. Kissinger rejected the
country-by-country draft on the ground that since all but a relative handful of countries committed human-rights violations, it
served no useful purpose to specify for criticism American allies
and friends."[9] In an attempt to depoliticize American aid, and to
deter Kissinger from using PL-480 "as an alternative means of
supporting such nations as Chile, Egypt, South Korea and South
Vietnam," support under the Foreign Assistance Act was cut
back.

On December 30, 1974 President Ford signed into law a new
foreign-aid bill that contained an amendment sponsored by Senator Humphrey stipulating that "no more than 30 per cent of the
food aid provided under Public Law 480 could be given to countries not classified by the United Nations as 'most seriously
affected' by food shortages and financial circumstances. There
were only thirty such countries, and they did not include South
Vietnam, South Korea or Egypt. Given an overall food-aid program of $900 million, this limited "political" aid to only $300
million. However, Kissinger had earmarked some $475 million
for political aid. He had promised $150 million to South Vietnam
alone, plus $124 million to South Korea, $65 million to Chile,
$43 million to Indonesia, and $88 million to Egypt. Congress cut
Chile's appropriation in half, refused to grant any aid to Indonesia, knocked down food aid to South Korea by nearly $100
million, and cut back Egypt's allocation to $53 million.

Secretary Kissinger sought to circumvent the spirit of these
restrictions by suggesting that the category of food aid to South
Vietnam be shifted from "political" to "humanitarian." If the
wording of the congressional amendment forbade a given policy,
why not simply change the definition of the words used to suit the
purpose at hand? Senator Humphrey announced that he would
play ball in view of his desire "to increase the food aid program

to the hungriest areas, such as India, Bangladesh and North Africa." He was "willing to bargain on the status of the Saigon Government to obtain this. If the President gives us a more liberal over-all program he can have more liberal treatment on definitions." The overall U.S. aid program would be increased to provide more political aid to Indochina and South Korea if this would be accompanied by an increase in aid to the Indian sub-continent. Also, aid for Saigon was linked to further aid to Israel (which enjoyed strong support among liberal congressmen and senators). Accord was finally reached when the Ford administration increased its PL-480 package by two-thirds, from $900 million to $1.5 billion. This had the effect of increasing humanitarian aid for India from $53 million to $131 million, and that for Bangladesh from $56 million to $149 million.[10]

Congressional opposition to U.S. aid has developed from two sides of the political spectrum. Internationalist-minded liberals have accused it of not helping foreign countries develop and even of retarding their growth in food-producing capacity. Neo-isolationists have become disillusioned with the failure of foreign aid to secure the gratitude of aid recipients such as India and other Third World countries taking anti-U.S. positions in the United Nations and other world forums.

U.S. public opinion was already turning against the Third World when the non-aligned nations voted to admit China into the United Nations and then danced in the aisles when they won —and followed this up by voting to grant observer status to the Palestine Liberation Organization and to condemn Zionism as a form of racism. The United States therefore chose not to participate in a new U.N. fund formed in December 1974 to aid countries in crisis. John Scali, U.S. ambassador to the United Nations, assailed the emerging Third World bloc as a "tyranny of the majority." The United States announced its preference for "direct aid by the United States or other countries, or through existing machinery," rather than extending aid through the United Nations where it could not veto or otherwise control it.[11] If it was not able to use aid to steer the course of foreign development (or lack thereof) and foreign diplomacy, then there seemed to be little national motive for continued aid-lending.

CHAPTER 11

America's Steel Quotas Herald a New Protectionism

When the General Agreement on Tariffs and Trade (GATT) was established in 1951, national tariffs represented the major barriers to world trade. In the postwar years of rising incomes and relatively full employment, the world was well able to afford the cost of moving toward freer trade. Foreign trade seemed to lead to a more efficient allocation of labor as each country produced what it seemed to be best at producing. World economic interdependence seemed politically desirable on the ground that commercial ties were a force for peace. International commerce and payments were sufficiently in balance that the payments deficits of Third World countries could be financed by their World War II currency and gold accumulations, by international loans and, where absolutely necessary to support existing trade patterns, by foreign aid. Thus, no urgent pressure for protectionism stemmed from balance-of-payments problems. Largely under U.S. leadership a series of tariff-cutting agreements was negotiated within GATT, the most recent being the Kennedy Round completed in 1967.

However, free trade principles could not withstand the inflationary pressures of 1973 and their balance-of-payments consequences. Government after government faced currency fluctuations, trade instability, spreading unemployment and underused productive capacity. Many began to impose wage and price controls. Italy, Finland and Portugal imposed a series of import restrictions under GATT's balance-of-payments "escape clause" (Article XII). Regulation of domestic economic processes and foreign trade logically went together. International bank credit and foreign aid were curtailed out of fear that countries could not afford to pay back loans designed to finance much higher importations of food, energy and industrial manufactures. What was left of the open world economy envisioned in 1945 began to close up rapidly.

The United States was the first to perceive the extent to which free trade principles must go by the board in this new environment, and it acted rapidly on this awareness. Since the early 1960s it had suspended free trade principles whenever these were not in its economic interests. In fact it had never joined GATT as a full treaty member, but was merely a participating observer. Any agreement made by trade officials representing the executive branch of government was subject to congressional rejection. For instance, Congress refused to ratify the 1967 agreement to move away from the American Selling Price method of tariff valuation, which was supposed to have been the capstone of the Kennedy Round.

Throughout the 1960s the United States sought to negotiate quota agreements outside of GATT to assure its exporters a fixed proportion of the food markets of European and other countries, including Third World recipients of PL-480 food aid. In 1970–71 it demanded "voluntary" export quotas on Far Eastern textile products, threatening even tighter U.S. restrictions on textiles and footwear if foreign manufacturers did not acquiesce. These demands, followed by America's 1973 export embargoes on food and other commodities, made it clear that if and when domestic U.S. shortages threatened, the United States would ignore contracts, treaties or foreign needs. Foreign demand for American products was treated as a residual function to be satisfied only after U.S. needs were met.

American officials recognized that any nation pursuing free trade principles, in a world where governments of other countries were financing, subsidizing or otherwise regulating their commerce, made its foreign trade a derivative function of foreign regulations. The U.S. strategy was to act first, to render the trade patterns of foreign countries a function of its own trade controls. For the United States specifically, the aim of domestic full employment—in a world where U.S. productivity growth lagged behind that of nearly all foreign countries—called for tightened import controls to restrict competition from abroad. This was the rationale underlying the Trade Act of 1974, signed into law by President Ford on January 3, 1975.

The new legislation gave personal authority to the President to impose import quotas whenever imports were a "substantial cause of serious injury" to U.S. industry and employment. The Trade Act made virtually no distinction between industries suffering from recession conditions and those suffering from import competition. Presidential authority to levy import quotas and otherwise protect American industry, reasoned the National Advisory Council on International Monetary and Financial Policies, was "of special importance given the changes in trade flows anticipated from the liberalization to be achieved through the Multilateral Trade Negotiations,"[1] that is, the scheduled Tokyo Round of tariff reductions within GATT. Other countries might pursue free trade so as to improve export opportunities for U.S. firms—as long as these exports did not create U.S. supply shortages—but the United States would import more goods only when this did not threaten employment in established industries or prevent establishment of new industries such as synthetic fuels deemed to be in the national interest.

Requests for import quotas under the Trade Act were soon filed by the shoe industry, automakers and manufacturers of "iron blue" (ferrocyanide), as well as by producers of agricultural commodities such as asparagus and mushrooms. All were turned down by President Ford. But matters changed in August 1975 when the specialty steel industry applied to the U.S. International Trade Commission for quota protection. The hearings which followed on stainless and tool steel were the most elaborate conducted in any industry to date.

The specialty steel industry seemed to be waging an uphill battle when it applied for quota protection. American steelmakers had difficulty demonstrating that imports rather than the recession or the new antipollution requirements were responsible for the declining employment and output suffered by American steelmakers. Additions to U.S. steel capacity had been quite modest in recent years. Much of the industry's investment had been to meet new air and water pollution regulations. The United States already was burdened with more antiquated factories than most foreign countries, and the antipollution regulations had only aggravated matters. A number of obsolescent steel mills had been phased out altogether.

Unemployment in the specialty steel industry reached 40 per

cent in 1975, although this resulted mainly from the economy's severe recession. Capital spending projections indicated that the nation's steel capacity probably would not grow by the three million tons per year required to keep pace with estimated growth in domestic demand. Import quotas were thus almost certain to raise prices. This was defended by the chairman of U.S. Steel, E. B. Speer, who argued that "the price of steel would have to rise about $100 a ton [or about 40 per cent] from current levels to justify investment" in new plants. In fact, by the time the Trade Commission acted in January 1976 domestic steel mills were approaching capacity operations even though the steel-using capital goods and construction sectors of the economy were only in the early stages of recovery from the 1974–75 recession. It seemed likely that demand for stainless and tool steel would soon outstrip output as it had as recently as 1974.

Stainless and tool steel imports in 1975 amounted to 154,000 tons, or 18 per cent of the U.S. market. In the first three months of 1976 they fell to 16 per cent of the market, the lowest share in eight years (down from 22 per cent in the first quarter of 1975). Not only were domestic specialty steel shipments up by 10 per cent, steel companies had raised prices across the board while warning that a new round of scarcity might develop.

The Trade Commission nonetheless recommended a unilateral import quota of 147,000 tons annually, slightly less than actual recession-level 1974–75 imports. This called for a substantial reduction in foreign steel sales to the United States at a time when demand was rising. U.S. trade officials argued that despite the Republican administration's nominal support of free-trade principles, President Ford "would bring on a Congressional override under the new trade act rules and solve nothing" if he rejected the Trade Commission's recommendation. They pointed out that "the law required Mr. Ford to announce he would impose quotas unless the major exporters of specialty steels to the United States . . . accepted 'orderly marketing agreements,' which also would limit their exports." President Ford hinted in May at a 150,000 ton quota based on 1972–74 import volume, with some adjustment to be made if domestic steel shortages developed. Foreign suppliers were given until mid-June to reach an "orderly marketing agreement."

On June 7, 1976, on the eve of Ohio's presidential primary,

President Ford announced in Middleton, Ohio, that he had signed documents establishing import quotas on specialty steels as the first application of the Trade Act of 1974. Middleton was the home of Armco Steel Corporation, one of the nation's largest specialty steel manufacturers. Mr. Ford's action may have helped him win local votes (he carried the Ohio Republican primary handily against his rival, Ronald Reagan), but it was reminiscent of President Nixon's announcement of textile quotas six years earlier, when the United States secured "voluntary" trade-limiting agreements from Far Eastern textile producers.

America's system of quotas that had been levied since World War II on food and oil imports to support their domestic prices at higher-than-world levels was now extended into the area of industrial manufacturers. Since the early 1950s the United States had defended the legality of maintaining its agricultural and mineral quotas on the ground that they had been enacted prior to the formation of GATT, and hence were permitted under the "grandfather" clause. But this could not be claimed for its new quotas on industrial imports. Furthermore, the U.S. balance of payments was moving into surplus, so that there was no basis for quotas under the GATT balance-of-payments escape clause. For that matter, there was no basis in international law for the U.S. Trade Act.

U.S. trade negotiators used the Trade Commission's decision as a lever to try to persuade Sweden, the European Community and Japan to "voluntarily" restrict their sales of specialty steels to the United States. When America had extracted similar textile agreements from Far Eastern exporters in 1970, Europeans had expressed the fear that they might culminate in controls on world steel trade—partly by diverting surplus Japanese steel production from the American market to Europe. Now these fears were coming true.

Sweden, which accounted for 40 per cent of U.S. specialty steel imports in 1974 (and for whom the United States was its major customer), rejected U.S. demands out of hand: it had never yet entered into "voluntary" trade restraints and preferred not to set a precedent. The European Community also rejected the U.S. proposal, pointing out that its specialty steel exports to the United States actually had declined in 1975.

In 1970 Europe had merely grumbled that the Americans were

violating GATT's trade principles, but because they were not directly threatened they had no legal recourse under GATT rules. The new U.S. move triggered much more than a verbal wave of ill will, it set off an Atlantic trade war as Europe retaliated. Article XIX of GATT allows any member country "to impose restrictions, increase tariffs or apply any other trade measures to limit imports threatening injury to domestic producers." However, this could not be done on a discriminatory basis, so that in protecting itself against American trade attacks Europe would have to hit other exporters besides the United States. At the very least a repetition of the glass-and-chicken Atlantic trade war of 1963 seemed to be brewing.

U.S. trade negotiators concentrated on the Japanese, whose specialty steel exports to the United States had shown the most rapid growth. Japanese trade representatives had visited the United States in May to discuss "the percentage share to be allotted to Japan of total U.S. specialty steel imports under the proposed limits and the question of whether or not Japan will demand compensation for the restraints." The problem was that if the United States allocated import quotas based on the 1972–74 period, Japan's share of the U.S. import market would be rolled back to 37 per cent.

U.S. officials had reasons of their own for wishing to give the Japanese a larger quota. Because Japan supplied over 50 per cent of the nation's specialty steel imports in 1975, thereby accounting for a "significant" share of the U.S. market, it followed "under U.S. trade law [that] the President can assign quotas whenever a significant share of the import market is subject to voluntary restraints." Thus, "on the basis of the Japanese agreement . . . President Ford may legally apply unilateral quotas against the EC, Sweden, and other specialty steel suppliers."[2] Japan's acquiescence fulfilled the conditions of U.S. law, although the principles of international law and GATT were violated by the American import quotas.

The U.S.-Japanese agreement made it virtually impossible for private firms to conduct normal business without cartels. It in fact forced creation of a 21-firm Japanese cartel to control specialty steel exports. At least one American asked, "When will we realize that for a country which treats cartels as illegal per se, it is anomalous to insist on cartelization as a condition for trade?"[3] Europe concluded that Japan had effectively placed itself in the American trade sphere and let it be known that further tariff reductions in favor of Japanese and other Far Eastern products were compromised by the prospect of these countries dumping in Europe those products which they had agreed not to sell in U.S. markets. Within a month of the Japanese-American steel agreements the European Community's commissioner in charge of Internal Markets and the Customs Union, Finn Olav Gundelach, estimated Japan's 1976 trade surplus with Europe at over $4 billion and insisted that "nontariff barriers must be eliminated within a reasonable time to avoid restrictive retaliation." Warning the Japanese of a rising protectionist mood in those parts of Europe beset by unemployment, he told the press, "I think there is not much time before the eruption point is reached."[4]

Meanwhile, Europe's steel industries joined into two cartels. The first and largest comprised the steel industries of Germany, Holland and Luxembourg and accounted for over half of EEC steel output. French and Belgian producers were quick to react against what they feared was a resurgence of German nationalism: they joined to form a countervailing cartel "to monitor investments more closely and set up machinery for fixing production quotas and minimum price guidelines to shield the effects of any new recession."[5] The Common Market's machinery at Brussels was being mobilized to constrain German self-assertion. This posed the question of whether Europe would fight within its own borders or make common ground against foreign steelmakers. World steel trade was fragmenting, and governments were intervening to play their most intensive roles since the 1930s.

The so-called Tokyo Round of tariff reductions under GATT was being prepared at the very time that these steel-quota agreements were being negotiated. The Tokyo Round now seemed dead. Of what use were tariff reductions if the world's largest trading nation, the United States, erected nontariff barriers to achieve the same protectionist effect as import duties? Furthermore, Japan itself was in the middle of delicate tariff negotiations with Europe concerning the rapid growth in its exports to the European Community. The latter's trade representatives were able to argue that, inasmuch as Japan had agreed to trade-restriction quotas with the United States at Europe's expense, Europe need feel little compunction in maintaining its trade barriers against Japan. About the only results that seemed likely to come out of any further world trade talks were in the area of shipbuilding and tanker rates, as an intergovernmental cartel was being created to regulate tanker prices.

Meanwhile, Japan's agreement with the United States had vastly complicated its relations with Europe, the major party injured by Japan's having enabled America to impose import quotas on all countries supplying stainless steel to its market. In November the European Community again insisted that Japan reduce its exports to Europe generally so as to reduce its massive balance-of-payments surplus with Europe. If Japan did not agree to curtail its exports "voluntarily" the EC threatened to impose its own set of import restrictions on Japanese products by November 25, 1976. Japan, however, realized that if it gave in to Europe it would have to do the same with the United States and other customers, especially if the products it diverted from the European market began to flood the United States. Prime Minister Miki was in the midst of an electoral campaign and could only promise Europe that Japan would increase its imports of processed food from the European Community.

Meanwhile, Japanese steel exports to the United States for October were 62 per cent over their level a year earlier. And yet even this was not sufficient to prevent U.S. steel companies from raising their prices by 6 per cent. The Ford administration renewed its offensive against the Japanese. American steelmakers claimed that Japan's agreement to limit its steel exports to Europe constituted a cartel arrangement which violated U.S. antitrust statutes. The American steel industry was not even claiming that it was being injured by unemployment in view of the strong level of steel prices. It requested a "fair" price level to support new capital investment, which required higher unit profits in the face of rather stagnant growth in sales during the continued economic recession. As the *Journal of Commerce* described America's trade hypocrisy: "In some measure, at least, the Japanese-European agreements are logical offshoots of the type of 'voluntary agreements' the United States pioneered as early as the 1950s. The agreement under which Japanese mills agreed to restrict their exports of cotton piece goods to the American market was a landmark. . . . Once Japan restrained her exports of cotton goods to the United States, her producers concentrated on other markets which shortly found themselves as discommoded as the American producers had been. This is what American steel producers now claim with respect to the Japanese-European steel arrangement."[6] America's restrictions on Japanese exports caused cartel reverberations from Japan to Europe—and then America denounced these forced arrangements as being in violation of American laissez faire principles. The entire world seemed to be in a no-win situation vis-à-vis the United States.

Nor did America stop with textiles and steel. It demanded that Japan curtail its color TV exports to the United States. The Japanese finally decided to draw the line, realizing that if they did not, a domino effect might be set in motion curtailing one industrial sector after another. American TV sales and profits were up sharply, and the Japanese claimed "that their television receivers up to 19 inches just happened to meet demand for smaller sets for individual use at a time when domestic manufacturers in the U.S. and other countries were concentrating only on screens of 21 and 25 inches. They add, however, that their color TV sets are of higher quality than those produced [in America] and have received top-ranking evaluations in consumer magazines."[7] As in the case of compact cars, foreign companies seemed to have successfully fought the self-defeating American principle that bigger is better and in greater demand. American consumers chose to buy smaller foreign TV sets, cars and other products, and the U.S. Government responded by seeking to impose import quotas so that Americans would have to pay as much for these products as for larger, bulkier American models. Virtually all pretense of supporting free trade was dead as the United States turned to isolationist policies in industry to complement its already established protectionism in agriculture, energy and minerals.

CHAPTER 12

The Ending of Laissez Faire

In 1945 both American and foreign officials recognized that a worldwide move toward laissez faire could not depend on existing market mechanisms alone to link international trade with "even" economic development at stable prices and rates of growth. For the less developed countries in particular, a number of intergovernmental institutions would be necessary to ensure that foreign trade patterns dovetailed into long-term development needs. The IMF was to provide short-term financing while the World Bank was to extend long-term infrastructure loans. A third creation, the International Trade Organization (ITO) was proposed in 1945 to coordinate tariff reductions and commodity agreements. The principles of this projected organization were spelled out in Havana in 1948.

Although major pressure for the ITO had come from U.S. officials, a rising tide of protectionism from American industries led to its collapse in 1949 when Congress refused to sanction U.S. membership. Four years had passed since the return to peace and the United States decided that to link world commodity trade with Third World development objectives was too costly a luxury for the American economy to support. Resources would be provided to raw-materials monocultures not by trade but through foreign aid, with all its strings attached.

Being a prospective United Nations agency, the ITO was to give one vote to each member country. This meant that it would be dominated by countries that supplied products to the United States, not by America or other industrial nations. Because the projected ITO would have no capitalization and would make no direct loans, there was no way for the United States to secure veto power over its decisions. By creating such an institution America would thus turn over control of its world trade prices to foreign countries that probably would act together to support their export prices, at a direct cost to American (as well as European and Japanese) consumers. On the other hand, a line of much less political resistance beckoned. Tariff-cutting authority could be (and was) centered within GATT (the General Agreement on Tariffs and Trade), an agency established within the stillborn ITO. World commodity agreements could be (and were) negotiated outside of any single world forum, on an ad hoc basis among the major commodity-producing and consuming governments. Such agreements limited themselves to purely operational matters such as determining maximum and minimum target prices for wheat, coffee and other commodities, with no explicit or implicit connection to the overall development process of commodity-exporting countries. The resulting system of laissez faire clearly worked in America's economic interests. Why then rock the boat by creating an ITO?

One of the arms of the ITO was to have been a stockpile mechanism. "To integrate the stabilization and adjustment programs of separate commodity agreements," wrote the economic adviser Alvin Hansen in 1945, "it would be desirable to set up . . . an International Commodity Corporation designed to buy, store and sell international raw materials and to act as a buffer in the raw-materials market. In the event that a deflation of raw-materials prices were impending, the Corporation should make large purchases of storable raw materials. It would permit the free play of market-price forces within upper and lower price ranges for each commodity. . . . These upper and lower limits should be the subject of continuous study by the Corporation and should be adjusted from time to time according to fundamental trends of demand and supply."[1] It seemed inevitable that if less developed countries were to dominate the ITO's voting by their simple weight of numbers, they would use the stockpile mechanism to support their export prices. It also seemed highly likely that they would press for special exemption from free trade principles, and demand numerous favors from the industrial nations. Better to let matters drop so as to prevent such a forum from developing. In effect the U.S. Government raw-materials stockpile acted to support world prices after 1952, and in the 1960s sold its accumulated metals and minerals to exert downward price pressure on copper and other commodities in short supply.

Not until 1964 did Third World pressure to link trade and

development issues lead to creation of the United Nations Conference on Trade and Development (UNCTAD). America's opposition to the new organization was made evident in its veto of
nine of the fifteen general principles, and four of its specific
principles. (Table 12.1.) The United States alone vetoed the general principles of sovereign equality of nations, acceleration of
growth and narrowing of income gaps, increased export earnings
for Third World countries regardless of their political system,
and use of funds freed by general disarmament to aid Third
World countries. America was also alone in vetoing the special
principle calling for international disposal of surpluses in accordance with international rules. (It feared that foreign countries
would gain control over PL-480 food aid, the world's largest
surplus-disposal program in the 1960s.) As part of its opposition
to communist and other statist regimes the United States also
vetoed the UNCTAD principle against discrimination by socioeconomic system. It vetoed the principle of freedom to dispose
of natural resources in the national interest, and also vetoed
trade preferences for less developed countries and extension of
foreign aid without political or military strings. It opposed UNC-
TAD sponsorship of compensatory financing for countries suffering from deteriorating terms of trade. In short, of all the industrial nations the United States took the hardest line toward Third
World countries (followed by Britain, Australia, Canada and Germany).

By the 1970s American attitudes had hardened further. If
Third World countries needed to raise more funds to cover their
trade and payments deficits, they should borrow from the IMF's
compensatory financing facility rather than join in export agreements to increase their raw-materials prices. Inasmuch as IMF
borrowing had to be repaid in time, with interest, and was strictly
limited in amount, Third World countries would enjoy only a
short-term respite. They would remain on a credit string as their
foreign debt was suspended over their heads like a sword of
Damocles. In short, if world trade issues were to be linked with
international finance and development, American officials
wanted this to occur on terms that would specifically benefit the
U.S. economy.

In January 1975 the Ford administration sponsored trade legislation to extend generalized Third World tariff preferences

TABLE 12.1

UNCTAD General Principles—Voting Patterns

General Principles

1. Sovereign equality of nations.
2. Against discrimination by socioeconomic system.
3. Freedom to trade and dispose of natural resources in the national interest.
4. Acceleration of growth, narrowing of income gaps.
5. In the international division of labor, developed countries will help less developed countries.
6. To increase the export earnings of less developed countries, regardless of their political system.
7. International arrangements for market access, at remunerative prices for primary products.
8. Trade preferences and non-reciprocity permitted less developed countries.
9. Regional groupings should not harm outsiders.
10. Encouragement of regional groupings and integration.
11. Increasing aid without political or military strings.
12. Resources freed by disarmament are to be used to aid less developed countries.
13. To permit transit trade for land-locked countries.
14. Complete decolonization necessary.
15. Recognition of differences in stages of development

	1	2	3	4	5	6	7	8	9	10	11	12	13	14	15	Total V	Total A
United States	V	V	V	V	A	V	V	V	–	–	V	V	–	A	–	9	2
Britain	A	A	V	A	A	–	V	V	–	–	V	A	–	V	–	5	5
Australia	–	A	V	A	A	–	V	V	–	–	V	A	–	V	–	5	4
Canada	–	V	V	A	A	–	V	V	–	–	A	A	–	A	A	4	6
Germany	–	V	A	A	A	–	A	A	A	–	V	A	–	A	–	2	8
Netherlands	–	A	A	A	A	–	A	A	A	–	A	A	–	A	–	0	10
Belgium	–	–	A	A	A	–	A	A	A	–	A	A	–	A	–	0	9
Italy	–	–	A	A	A	–	A	A	A	–	A	A	–	A	–	0	9
France	–	–	A	A	A	–	A	A	A	–	A	–	–	A	–	0	8
Japan	–	–	A	A	–	–	A	A	–	A	A	A	–	–	A	0	8
U.S.S.R.	–	–	–	–	–	–	–	–	–	–	–	A	–	–	–	0	1

V: Negative vote   A: Abstention   –: Positive vote

Source: UNCTAD Final Act (June 16, 1964).

UNCTAD Special Principles—Voting Patterns

Special Principles

1. Setting targets for trade expansion.
2. Need for industrialization and for modernization of agriculture.
3. Trade preferences. [No action taken.]
4. Right to protect infant industries.
5. Domestic support prices should not stimulate uneconomic production.
6. Developed countries should help less developed countries in cases of commodity substitution.
7. Compensatory financing of worsening terms of trade.
8. Surplus disposal by international rules.
9. Opposition to dumping.
10. Technical assistance.
11. Assistance, more multilateral aid, easier terms for repayment, e.g., in local currency or in commodities.
12. Action to promote invisible earnings of less developed countries.
13. Multilateral trade and payments arrangements among less developed countries.

	1	2	3	4	5	6	7	8	9	10	11	12	13	Total V	Total A
United States	V	–	No action taken	A	A	–	V	V	A	–	A	V	A	4	5
Britain	A	–		–	–	–	V	A	A	–	A	V	–	2	4
Australia	A	–		–	A	–	V	A	A	–	A	–	A	1	6
Canada	V	–		–	A	–	V	A	A	–	A	A	A	2	6
Germany	A	–		–	A	–	V	–	–	–	A	V	–	2	3
Netherlands	A	–		–	A	–	A	–	–	–	A	A	–	0	5
Belgium	–	–		–	A	–	A	–	–	–	A	A	–	0	4
Italy	–	–		–	A	–	A	–	–	–	A	A	–	0	4
France	–	–		–	A	–	A	A	–	–	A	A	–	0	5
Japan	A	–		–	A	–	V	–	–	–	A	A	A	1	5
U.S.S.R.	–	–		–	–	–	A	–	–	–	–	–	–	0	1

V: Negative vote A: Abstention –: Positive vote

Source: UNCTAD Final Act (June 16, 1964).

only to countries that refrained from joining OPEC or other
raw-materials export organizations not blessed by the U.S. Government. This strategy seemed to deter Mexico from joining
OPEC, but the move was not without diplomatic cost. Latin
American officials argued that "if the United States discriminates
against petroleum-producing countries today, it could easily dis-
criminate later against exporters of coffee, bauxite or other products that take part in producer cartels. . . . Both Ecuador and
Venezuela have said they will not attend the meeting of [West-
ern] hemisphere foreign ministers unless the United States
modifies the clause denying them tariff preferences."[2] The U.S.
Government had offered foreign aid ostensibly to help these
countries develop during the 1950s and 1960s. Now that their
leading group, the oil-exporting countries, were actually making
major advances, Washington came down hard against their development plans.

Limited Third World trade preferences were put into effect by
the United States in January 1976. The administration soon received over forty requests from U.S. firms or trade associations
to withdraw preferences for ferroalloys, baseballs, plywood,
naphthols, leather wearing apparel, flashlights, vinyl "squeeze"
toys, eyeglass lenses and frames, candles, model trains and air-
planes, turpentine and wheelbarrows. These protests led an in-
teragency committee called the Trade Policy Review Group to
withdraw prefinished plywood from the preferences list and restore the 20 per cent import duty as imports from Taiwan,
Singapore and the Philippines undersold U.S. products.[3]

By the time the Fourth Meeting of UNCTAD was held in
Nairobi, Kenya, in May 1976, positions had hardened between
Third World countries and the industrial nations. Within the
industrial nations themselves a further split set the "hard liners"
—the United States and West Germany, followed by England and
Japan—against countries more willing to reach accommodation
with the Third World. Representatives of the Third World entered the conference asking for intergovernmental stockpile purchases of $6 billion to support the price of 17 raw materials at
target levels indexed to a market basket of 89 industrial products.
The industrial nations opposed the indexing principle, but were
willing to discuss stockpile accumulations on terms designed to
secure certainty of short-term supply for themselves. It was in

this setting that Kissinger unveiled a plan to create an International Resources Bank (IRB) that had been discussed among the U.S. and foreign governments for over a year. In its general outlines the Kissinger proposal harked back to the ITO stockpile proposals made three decades earlier. But it was also designed to tackle some specific problems of the 1970s: it was to create a kind of investment guarantee fund to insure renewed private-sector investment in Third World raw-materials development. The industrial nations would bear part of the cost of purchasing and storing Third World commodities, in exchange for the stockpile providing supply assurances in the event of a Third World commodity boycott. Once put in place it would be held over the market as a source of supply to hold down price rises for world raw materials.

The proposed IRB was to function as a World Bank affiliate. Its $1 billion in funding was to finance raw-materials development in Third World countries. "For many countries," Kissinger asserted, "private capital flows are, and will continue to be, the principal form of development finance." The IRB would safeguard private investment in Third World resources by minimizing political risks: IRB-financed mineral production would enjoy "guarantees of both investor and host-nation performance in accordance with conditions established in the project agreement." Assistant Treasury Secretary Gerald Parsky described the proposed bank and its bonds as providing "a guarantee for private investment" in Third World countries rather than "a substitute for it." The IRB would relieve "the fear of expropriation and nationalization" by guaranteeing companies a "full recovery" of investment losses resulting from political takeovers of their holdings. It thus would act as an insurance pool somewhat akin to the Overseas Private Investment Corporation within the U.S. Government.

The IRB's resources of $1 billion would be used to insure its bond issues, "which could be secured by a specific commodity" or "be retired through delivery of a specific commodity," say, copper. Third World governments would receive funds from the bank as prepayment for future mineral shipments, much as farmers sold their crops on the "futures" market in industrial nations in order to secure certainty of sale of their future output at a known price. The bank's advances—and in turn, its bonds—

would be retired by host-country commodity repayments to the bank. In effect, it would take a lien on production and be paid out of the sales proceeds, thereby acting as an intermediary between industrial and Third World countries.[4]

Most Third World governments rejected the bank's emphasis on increasing world raw-materials output. Over the longer term this would hold down the rise in primary commodity prices rather than support them. Control of the proposed stockpiles and mineral output by the financiers—mainly the industrial nations— threatened that the raw materials would be sold in times of rising prices. The World Bank already possessed an affiliate, the International Finance Corporation (IFC) designed to provide equity capital for Third World projects. Why limit the new IRB specifically to investment in raw materials? Instead of increasing their minerals output, Third World countries wanted to earn more on their existing level of output. They wanted money from the industrial nations to spend as they chose, in particular to become free of existing trade patterns. The IRB threatened to reinforce these trade and dependency patterns.

Once the Third World countries decided to oppose the Kissinger proposal and tallied the votes informally, nearly ninety were able to abstain from the official UNCTAD voting in an effort to minimize their already strained relations with the United States. The IRB proposal was defeated by only 33 to 31, in large part by the fourteen communist countries attending the conference. This seemed to infuriate U.S. officials all the more.

Even before the IRB vote, American representatives urged the European Community to withdraw its position paper conceding that "discussion of a comprehensive commodity fund should move forward within two years." Only toward the end of the conference did the United States join Europe in recognizing that Third World representatives were sincere in threatening an absolute commercial break with the industrial nations on a go-it-alone basis if no concrete progress was made at Nairobi. On May 24 the UNCTAD delegates announced that the conference was "hopelessly deadlocked over major issues to restructure the global economy." Seven OPEC governments were among the nineteen Third World countries sending UNCTAD a message saying that "failure to achieve 'substantial results' at Nairobi could jeopardize the Paris talks on oil prices." This spurred Kissinger to urge

West German officials at least to agree to call a future conference to discuss proposals for a world commodity stockpile to be funded after "four or five individual commodity agreements had been worked out and seen to be functioning successfully for several years." The industrial nations made it clear that this was not to be taken as a sign that they had agreed to the Third World's proposals, merely that they were willing to discuss them in more concrete detail than before. A French-sponsored compromise was finally adopted which called for creation of buffer stockpiles for ten raw materials accounting for about three-fourths of the Third World's non-oil commodity exports: cocoa, copper, cotton, hard fibers, iron ore, jute, rubber, sugar, tea and tin. The Netherlands Minister of Economic Cooperation, Jan Pronk, spoke on behalf of sixteen industrial nations including the Common Market (except West Germany and England), Scandinavia, Spain and Portugal, Austria, Turkey, Switzerland and Canada, pledging to develop a "true and comprehensive" commodity program by March 1977. Slowly but certainly, domination over world raw materials production was passing out of the hands of large private-sector companies into those of host-country governments.[5]

Belatedly, the world seemed to be moving toward the type of international commodity agreements that the United States had come to oppose by the late 1940s when it became apparent that its trade objectives simply were not those of the less developed countries. The principle of Third World control over its foreign trade could no longer be held back. As the *Journal of Commerce* editorialized, "The United States must now cope with a political move by the OPEC group to win a commanding position of leadership in the third world, as reflected in the big majority of small powers that invariably voted against the United States in the United Nations General Assembly." Indeed, Kissinger's agreement to create a world food and raw-materials stockpile "stirred throughout the third world . . . a vision of numerous commodity cartels, of fixed prices, buffer stocks and something approaching the ill-fated plan that Congress killed before birth in 1948. That was to have been the International Trade Organization as conceived under the so-called Havana Charter. It would have been the International Monetary Fund of the commodities world, and probably a good deal more. . . . it would probably have done less damage if launched 27 years ago than anything that can reasonably be expected to emerge from future talks with OPEC and other third world nations now."[6] The commodity cartels envisioned in the industrial nations were designed merely to stabilize world prices at their low recession levels of 1976, not to improve the terms of trade of Third World countries.

The UNCTAD conference made clear to U.S. officials that neither America nor other industrial nations could gain control of any new international trade organization. OPEC governments seemed prepared to provide balance-of-payments resources to Third World countries as part of a common strategy to seek general economic independence from the industrial nations. All that was left to the United States was its domination of the IMF, the World Bank, and the world financial system in which U.S. commercial banks and their overseas branches played a leading role. Perhaps world trade patterns could be controlled through the system of international credit creation, by providing loans to Third World countries and payments-deficit industrial nations only on terms which served U.S. national interests. These interests would be determined by the head of the Federal Reserve Board, the Secretary of the Treasury, and the U.S. delegates to the IMF and World Bank.

A key ploy would be to insist that any country which discovered new oil or other raw materials would give private firms in the industrial nations a major share of ownership and management. For instance, when England's balance of payments collapsed in 1976, despite the fact that its North Sea oil was just coming onstream, the IMF refused to extend credits until the British government raised funds by selling 20 per cent of its oil resources to foreign investors. An even more pronounced financial leverage was used against Mexico, which also suffered a major run on its currency and subsequent devaluation despite major oil discoveries by the state oil company Pemex (Petroleos Mexicanos). Pemex sought to borrow some $15 billion in world financial markets during 1977–82 to develop its oil to a level surpassing Venezuela's rate of production. In February 1977 it opened discussions with U.S. banks to put together a consortium to extend the needed credit, as well as funds to enable Mexico to service its $20 billion in foreign debts. While these negotiations were under way Arthur Burns delivered a major speech urging U.S.

commercial banks not to make further loans to Third World countries unless these credits were extended as part of IMF packages. If U.S. commercial banks extended credits to Third World countries on their own, Dr. Burns warned, they could not expect the Federal Reserve Board or the U.S. Government to bail them out in case of default. Furthermore, the FRB's bank examiners might classify commercial bank exposure in Third World countries as "problem loans," thereby creating liquidity and balance-sheet problems for international banks participating in loan consortia on their own.

In 1976 the IMF had insisted that Mexico adopt an "austerity program" in order to qualify for IMF credits, and that it halt its move toward large-scale land reform. True to form, the austerity program created a political and social crisis within Mexico which only aggravated the capital flight that the IMF credits were designed to counteract.[7] Resources extended by the IMF and the world commercial banking system seemed likely to be denied countries that did not adopt "reasonable economic programs," i.e., those which would tend to perpetuate the inequities of the postwar economic order. But now there was one major difference: under the postwar economic order the control of world trade and finance had been exerted ostensibly through "free market" mechanisms. True, behind these mechanisms stood the invisible hand of foreign aid and other world diplomatic levers, but at least the semblance of market operations was maintained. Now the pretence of atomistic market forces was dropped altogether in the face of countervailing government power being asserted by Third World countries. These countries had run up a foreign debt of more than $200 billion, largely to private commercial banks. The rollover of these credits henceforth was to become a function of U.S. Federal Reserve regulation and U.S. Treasury policy as expressed through American delegates to the IMF and World Bank. The American government quite visibly superseded private multinational corporations in seeking to control the allocation of world financial resources, hence the direction of physical investment and trade. In this respect America itself became part of the New International Economic Order.

Outlook for trade policy under the Democrats

Early indications are that the incoming Carter administration will become increasingly protectionist in an attempt to transfer U.S. unemployment and recession to foreign economies. The first tests came in March, when the Customs Court of the U.S. International Trade Commission ruled in favor of higher tariffs on shoe and electronics imports.

Imports accounted for more than half of U.S. shoe purchases in 1976, and of these imports South Korea and Taiwan supplied over half (doubling their 1974 sales volume). Foreign TV sets accounted for two-thirds of the U.S. market. Although tariff increases on these imports would be illegal under GATT rules, the new administration used the court rulings as a lever to obtain a series of foreign "voluntary" export quotas: it offered not to charge higher tariffs if foreign governments would impose upon themselves "Orderly Marketing Agreements" based on fixed shares of the U.S. market.

President Carter's special trade representative, former Democratic Party chairman Robert Strauss, warned Korea and Taiwan that the 1974 Trade Act directed the United States to levy higher tariffs on their shoe exports if they did not reach amicable agreement to limit their sales to the United States (after the pattern of rubber footware and textiles three years earlier, and stainless steel in 1976). This stance enabled the president to pursue the substance of protectionism while striking a free-trade pose in rejecting (for the time being) the Customs Court endorsement of higher tariffs. Furthermore, "American trade officials have observed the right to negotiate similar [export quota] agreements with the other shoe suppliers [most notably Brazil, Italy and Spain] if, as one official put it, they step up their shipments sharply as a result of the pressures put on Taiwan and South Korea."[8] Meanwhile, $300 million in government funds were budgeted for 1977 to help modernize production techniques for shoe producers and other industries threatened by rising import competition.

In mid-March the Trade Commission recommended that import duties on television sets be quintupled from 5 per cent to 25 per cent (falling gradually over five years to a permanent 15 per cent level). When President Carter met with Japanese Prime Minister Takeo Fukuda at the March 21–22 summit meetings in Washington, he suggested that Japan avoid these tariff penalties by setting "voluntary" quotas on its sales of TVs and other electronic products to the United States. But Japan refused to yield, despite Mr. Strauss's visit to Tokyo to secure Japanese adherence to the hoped-for agreement. The Japanese calculated that the prospect of GATT condemnation would deter the United States from actually increasing its tariffs, a move that would destroy any hope for the already lagging Tokyo round of trade negotiations. Furthermore, if the United States actually levied higher tariffs, Japan would qualify for countervailing trade penalties against the United States, but it would not qualify if its export quotas were "voluntary."[9]

On April 12 the Customs Court escalated the tariff war by voting to levy special anti-dumping duties on Japanese television sets, on the somewhat dubious ground that Japan's electronics exports were exempt from the consumer-goods tax levied on its domestic sales. A year earlier Treasury Secretary William Simon had rejected a petition to impose higher duties on Japanese radios and TV sets, asserting that Japan's tax rebate on export sales did not constitute a bounty or grant under international or American tariff law. But Zenith sued the U.S. Government to obtain the higher tariff protection offered under the 1974 Trade Act, which specified that foreign tax rebates were indeed liable to countervailing U.S. duties if they provided either direct or indirect export benefits. The Customs Court agreed, and U.S. electronics importers were obliged to post bonds on their inventories against possible duties of 40 per cent being levied at some future date.

The Japanese Embassy in Washington decried the new ruling, and pointed out that "The decision disregards the established international rule that the exemption of export products from internal taxes such as the commodity tax in Japan does not constitute a countervailable subsidy, as is clearly stipulated in relevant regulations of the General Agreement on Tariffs and Trade." Even the U.S. Treasury publicly deplored the Trade Commission's judgment, acknowledging that it would pave the way for a host of U.S. claims against all European Community exports inasmuch as the EEC's value-added tax (VAT) was not levied on export sales.[10]

The $1.5 billion in Japanese electronics exports which rode in the balance of the Customs Court ruling was substantially overshadowed by the $5.5 billion in U.S. auto imports threatened by President Carter's energy conservation program, his first major domestic political fight. In fact, the president used his energy program as a vehicle to bolster American auto-makers' share of the domestic market: although nine out of the ten most fuel-efficient car makes in the United States were imported, he proposed to limit full price rebates (on cars meeting the government's fuel-efficiency ratios) to U.S.-made cars and those imported from American-owned affiliates in Windsor, Ontario (just across the river from Detroit). Foreign-made cars were to receive no rebate at all under the original drafts of the energy program, but at the last minute modest rebates were offered to European and Japanese manufacturers on the condition that they impose "voluntary" export quotas on their sales to the United States. President Carter's new Assistant Secretary of the Treasury for International Affairs, C. Fred Bergsten (a Carter alumnus from the Trilateral Commission), told reporters that auto-exporting countries would have to share in the "costs" of the U.S. energy program, apparently by suffering unemployment in their own industries so that American employment could be buoyed. After all, he pointed out, Congress "would hardly be likely to approve a Treasury 'subsidy' of foreign car imports" in the face of substantial unemployment in Detroit. However, smaller rebates for foreign-made autos would render the United States liable to foreign reprisals under GATT rules. Dr. Bergsten suggested that "full rebates might be paid on a prescribed annual level of imports, based, say, on actual deliveries in [the recession years] of 1975 or 1976, but imports beyond that would get smaller [if any] rebates."

Europe and Japan were thus caught in a pincer movement between the executive and legislative branches of the U.S. Government. The executive branch found it handy to argue that under the American Constitution it could not commit the United States in world tariff, foreign aid or international financial negotiations. What it offered foreign countries, Congress might withhold. Furthermore, if foreign countries did not acquiesce in executive branch proposals for export quotas, Congress would probably enact even more damaging protectionist legislation in keeping with stiff Trade Commission recommendations.

The new Chairman of the Council of Economic Advisers, Charles Schultze, acknowledged that the auto-rebate proposal was creating severe problems within GATT, but stressed that "all these things were carefully considered and debated" and had received broad support throughout the new Democratic administration. He concluded laconically that "Bob Strauss, the President's special trade representative, has his work cut out for him." Mr. Strauss set off for Europe to suggest that West Germany, Japan, Italy, France, Sweden and Britain impose "voluntary" export quotas as to the number of cars qualifying for the rebates, holding out the threat that they might receive no rebates at all if they did not establish such quotas.[11] (Under the Trade Act of 1974 only Japan and West Germany, or any other group of countries representing 50 per cent of U.S. car imports would have to agree to quotas in order for the new administration to impose quotas on other countries.)

The fact that foreign auto-makers were to be prevented from increasing their share of the U.S. market seemed to make it difficult for the U.S. gasoline conservation program to succeed, given Detroit's difficulties in meeting the government's fuel-efficiency guidelines (not to mention its pollution regulations). This suggested that the energy program's primary concern was not with fuel efficiency as much as with increasing U.S. automotive employment—along with its complement, foreign unemployment. (The alternative was for overseas car manufacturers to establish U.S. plants to employ American labor, so that their products would cease to be imports but would become domestic output.)

Inevitably, the new wave of American protectionism spurred similar moves abroad. Italy's Prime Minister Giulio Andreotti urged special anti-dumping protection against U.S. and Japanese petrochemical exports, as well as a "European selling price" system of customs valuation to match the American Selling Price (ASP) system on which U.S. tariffs were based. Now that the U.S. dollar was falling in value, Europe moved to prevent American exporters from getting a cost advantage through monetary means rather than through increasing productivity. Under the Andreotti plan European tariffs would be set on the basis of European prices rather than on the (lower) import value, thereby raising EC protectionism to the levels existing in the United

States and elsewhere. (This move occurred at the same time that President Carter's energy message called for sharp increases in the price of natural-gas feedstocks to petrochemical companies. Thus, U.S. exports of petrochemicals and manmade fibers faced problems both on the domestic supply side and the overseas demand side.)[12]

Were these trade developments "right" or "wrong"? They were inevitable, given the new chronic recession conditions. The Carter administration recognized that renewed American prosperity required a higher level of capital investment to increase productivity and employ more labor. This implied that a larger proportion of the nation's income had to be channeled into capital formation rather than spent on consumer goods, used for speculative or other unproductive purposes, or paid to foreigners. Under the depressed economic conditions that still marked the U.S. economy in early 1977, new investment and modernization of existing plants required a larger cash flow—a kind of super-profit—and hence higher unit prices in the face of slack sales volume. "If you can't sell more, charge more" had become the motto of steelmakers during the Nixon-Ford administration, and there seemed little reason to change it now that the Democrats had returned to office.

Higher unit prices for corporate output in general required tariff or quota protection so that foreigners would not earn for themselves the added income resulting from higher domestic prices. In the absence of quotas, foreign producers would undersell American firms to increase their share of the American market. (For many decades America's system of agricultural and petroleum price supports had required tight import quotas to maintain U.S. farm and oil-industry incomes at higher-than-world levels.) This explains the insistence by U.S. officials that foreign countries establish fixed and permanent market shares for all major trade categories, beginning with steel, textiles, electronic goods and shoes, and extending into the realm of international services such as air travel. Meanwhile, America pressed for reciprocal fixed shares of foreign markets for wheat, soybeans, computers and other leading products.

All this was just the opposite of what postwar One Worldism had promised. The world economy originally was supposed to be integrated by growing trade and price advantages as nations depended on each other's specialized industries for a widening range of products, while gradually phasing out their own domestic sectors whose output was not as low-priced as could be obtained through imports. But with the onset of general world recession each government moved to bolster its domestic employment wherever possible. This stifled further growth in world trade. It involved giving up lower-priced imports, but it also kept domestic labor off the unemployment and welfare rolls. The costs from free trade had come to surpass its costs. For many decades imports and exports had grown much more rapidly than domestic economic output. But now that fixed international market shares were being negotiated, growth in world trade was limited to growth in domestic demand, which was itself held down as resources began to be transferred more to the investment sector than to the consumer-goods sector.

The world economy was being divided into monopolized market shares to a degree undreamed of by prewar economists. It was becoming a bed of Procrustes in which competitive power and sales patterns were becoming less and less a function of price and efficiency, more and more a function of negotiated intergovernmental agreements. What was left of competitive market forces seemed to be confined to the domestic economy, and even this was being increasingly partitioned. Price and productivity competition was certainly being phased out of the international economy.

How long could the new system last before one country (or set of countries) gained substantial productivity advantages, leading to political pressures to renegotiate foreign market shares? To what extent could world price and productivity levels diverge without dislodging exchange rates further? Where could Japan and South Korea turn to earn the foreign exchange to pay for their energy imports, now that they were being closed off from the U.S. market and blocked from making up the difference in added sales to Europe? The answer was anyone's guess. But one thing was obvious: the agreements being put in place could be maintained without renewed economic and political antagonisms only in a world devoid of technological change and shifting international efficiency, a state of affairs that had not characterized the world economy and its technology since the Middle Ages (if then).

Closed off from the U.S. and European markets, Japan and South Korea (along with Taiwan) faced the prospect of having to retool their export industries to produce the type of factories and turnkey projects desired by the Middle Eastern countries that supplied their oil. This type of investment required substantial movement of labor across national boundaries to construct a new Middle Eastern infrastructure. Only those parts of the world whose domestic economies and export revenues were growing rapidly could avoid pressures to partition their economies on the basis of regulated market shares.

It seems impossible for government planners to anticipate every ramification of their actions. Quotas designed to prevent further growth in Far Eastern shoe imports had the immediate effect of reducing foreign demand for American exports of shoe-making machinery. It also had a pressing financial effect: South Korea, Brazil, Italy and other exporters of commodities now being regulated by U.S. trade officials were also substantial debtors to U.S. banks, the U.S. Government, and to other foreigners. How were they to service their rapidly growing debts without being able to raise the funds by growth in exports? This opened the prospect of their arguing to their American creditors as follows: "We fully intended to repay you when we borrowed funds from your banks and government agencies. However, your loan evaluations of our economies was based on the then-current outlook for our exports, which are highly competitive in world markets and in your economy specifically. Now that our firms are being denied the ability to earn the foreign exchange we need to service our debts to you, these debts must be held in abeyance —including their interest charges. For it is certainly unfair of you to deny us the ability to repay you, and then continue charging us interest." Alternatively, these countries could continue borrowing from U.S. banks to finance their imports with paper credit rather than with their own exports. But this type of international lending is now being brought much more within the sway of the IMF and its stabilization programs, which impose domestic austerity on countries qualifying for IMF loans. This is as politically untenable abroad as are recession conditions in the United States. Hence, reduction in the rate of growth in imports from debtor countries will tend to create a widening range of problems, requiring increasing settlements at the intergovernmental level and thus a growing regulation and rigidification of the world economy. Growth in world trade and international investment will be confined largely to the OPEC economies and those of other raw-materials exporters as the industrial nations steer their foreign policy increasingly in view of domestic economic and political considerations. It is to cope with this emerging situation that the New International Economic Order is primarily designed, being itself a system of countervailing intergovernmental power.

PART III

The New International
Economic Order

CHAPTER 13

Basic Objectives

> The participants agreed that the present crisis in
> the world system was neither a 'normal' eco-
> nomic recession nor the result of the oil prob-
> lem. It in fact marked the gradual crumbling of
> an old order in which a group of rich nations
> constituting the developed centre continuously
> expanded by the use of energy and raw materi-
> als provided by the poor nations at the periph-
> ery at cheap prices. The increase in the price of
> oil by OPEC could therefore be seen as a part of
> the struggle of the Third World to obtain a bet-
> ter deal from the world order.
>
> —Communiqué of the Karachi Conference,
>   January 10, 1975

America's systematic abuse of the world order in the 1960s,
when it forced upon its allies a double standard in international
finance, trade, aid and investment, led foreign countries to press
for a New International Economic Order. Their moves in this
direction have led the United States to become even more self-
centered, self-righteous and autarchic. A spiral of mutual disenchantment, confrontation and antagonism has thus been set in
motion, consolidating the world's new regional divisions.

Each party feels itself aggrieved. Europe and Japan complain
that the fruits of their export prosperity have been passed on to
the U.S. Treasury via their central banks. Third World countries
complain that they have had no surplus to dispose of at all, and
have in fact fallen further and further into debt while their natural
resources have been depleted. Americans reply that Europe and
the Third World have been consuming U.S. aid and military

165

resources for years and are therefore paying back a moral debt.

Because different nations and regions have distinct economic and political interests, the slogan of a New International Economic Order has become somewhat of a catch-phrase that covers a multitude of programs and alliances. The term was first popularized by French diplomats seeking to supplant the dollar standard with a gold-based European currency system. It was subsequently taken up by Third World spokesmen in reference to improving their terms of trade so as to finance their long-term development and economic diversification. All proponents of a New International Economic Order are seeking economic, political and military independence on the basis of regional consolidation and long-term economic planning. In other words, they are seeking what America has aimed at for itself all along. Their domestic resource allocation and international diplomacy are no longer being determined by merely short-term objectives in the context of dependence on distant regions for economic essentials. The Eastern Hemisphere is seeking to become independent of the Western Hemisphere, while within each hemisphere the South is seeking economic independence from the North. The new economic ideology thus focuses on regional self-sufficiency and long-term capital formation. These objectives require statist policies, intergovernmental coordination and regional integration within a framework of economic independence from the United States and its Treasury-bill standard, its new wave of commercial protectionism, its self-centered foreign-aid philosophy and its tampering with the domestic political affairs of foreign countries.

Third World countries are reexamining their philosophy of international trade and development and are setting out to accomplish what they did not seek three decades ago: to transform and modernize their economies on a thoroughgoing basis. They intend to secure the benefits of advanced technology in all aspects of their lives, not merely in their export sectors. Their concept of interdependence—which has connoted, in essence, dependency—is being replaced by the goal of self-sufficiency. This requires regional consolidation so as to secure the necessary economies of scale required to make economic independence practical in terms of modern-day technology. It is also necessary to provide agricultural-industrial balance so as to wind down international food dependency.

These principles of broad regional objectives superseding simple nationalism apply to Europe fully as much as to the Third World. No single EEC nation can maintain its currency parity in the face of renewed dollar outflows and destabilizing currency speculation. In fact, no nation can secure its economic independence in the face of U.S. domination of international finance and investment. Nor can foreign countries ensure their domestic employment and prosperity in the face of America's new protectionism—unless they begin to "go it alone" together and shift their trade patterns away from the United States. Together, the Common Market countries may form an effective world force. Through a long and often painful process its members are therefore beginning to agree to abide by majority rule in key areas, giving up their national authority in the process of asserting a distinctly European position.

Regional consolidation is occurring within five broad geopolitical blocs: (1) the resurgent Mediterranean triangle comprising Europe, the Near East and Africa (and some of Europe's former Pacific Ocean and Caribbean colonies), (2) the Western Hemisphere dollar areas including the United States, Canada and Latin America, (3) Japan and Southeast Asia, (4) Soviet Russia and its Comecon satellites, and (5) China. Each of these regions is characterized by a broad range of complementary products enabling approximate self-sufficiency to be secured in industry, food production and raw materials. Long historical relationships (originally of a colonial nature) have established trade and investment linkages within each of these regions.

This new regional system is as far removed from the pre-World War II system of nationalism as it is from the One Worldism preached in the early postwar years. Prior to World War II self-sufficiency was conceived on the basis of nation-states, sometimes associated with colonial systems. After the war it became obvious that this goal could no longer succeed. At that time the major alternative seemed to be a general system of world independence, subject to the splitting off of the communist economies. (Yugoslavia was the first gray area in this world division, followed by China.) There followed a cracking within the Western Alliance as the European Common Market, acting as an expanding regional entity, grew to rival the U.S. economy. Today, the New International Economic Order is being designed to create a full-blown countervailing force as Europe, noncommunist Asia and Africa seek to become independent of the United States.

The major obstacle to regional confederation is that which led to the formation of regional blocs in the first place—potential exploitation of one nation (or set of nations) by another, and specifically of the raw-materials exporters by the industrial nations. A North-South *contretemps* thus exists within each of the major regional groupings over the terms of trade, investment and the financing of payments imbalances as between (1) industrial Europe and the raw-materials exporters of OPEC and Africa, (2) the United States vis-à-vis Latin America and Canada, and (3) industrial Japan and resource-rich Asia. Extension of the European Snake, the dollar and the yen to create a Eurocurrency area, a dollar area and a yen area, respectively, is thus linked to the question of trade and investment relations within each of these areas.

These North-South tensions have been mirrored within the Comecon nations. Soviet Russia has succeeded in exploiting industrial Eastern Europe by demanding highly favorable terms of trade for its raw-materials exports. It also has tapped Eastern Europe's financial surpluses by means of the ruble area in much the same way that America has tapped the central bank surpluses of industrial Europe and Japan. (The fifth major region, China, is nearly autonomous except for its discretionary trade and investment.)

Because today's North-South rivalries are occurring within the context of an interhemispheric split, a subsidiary rivalry may also develop within the Third World among Latin America, Africa and Southeast Asia. For instance, if African countries accept European trade preferences, they will disqualify themselves from those made available to Third World countries by the United States. America for its part is unwilling to extend trade preferences to countries joining OPEC or other intergovernmental organizations designed to support the price of raw-materials. By the same token, Europe has shown itself willing to support the export prices of its former colonies through the Youande and Lomé conventions and subsequent trade agreements, but is not willing to extend these benefits to non-associated (e.g., Latin American) countries. Thus, countries that choose to adhere to one or another of the emerging regional blocs will be cut off from generalized worldwide tariff preferences, sealing the world economic fracture along regional lines.

A primary goal of the New International Economic Order is to constrain any single nation or region from unilaterally exploiting others. "The rules and balances on which the old economic order was built cannot and, what is more, should not be restored in their existing form," asserted Giscard d'Estaing in Zaire in 1975. "Equilibrating means returning to situations of equilibrium that should themselves result in the implementation of a procedure for limited adjustments."[1] What is required is a system of checks and balances that will prevent a recurrence of the problems that have arisen over the past three decades, not merely an ad hoc solution that will lead to new instabilities. This new economic system will have to operate on the intergovernmental plane.

Only a few years ago many observers were forecasting that the course of world economic evolution would be determined by multinational firms alone. Their very size, as measured by their sales volume, was larger than the gross national product of many countries. But in today's new battleground between Third World and industrial nations these firms find themselves with little voice or leverage. Their new strategy lies in selling their raw-materials holdings back to host-country governments on as favorable terms as possible.

Orthodox laissez faire theory postulated that the private sector, acting by itself, would prevent balance-of-payments disequilibrium. Payments imbalance supposedly led to inflation and higher interest rates, slower domestic economic growth, and hence lower imports (and higher exports) until equilibrium was restored. In practice this failed to happen. International inflationary pressures were conveyed abroad during the 1960s while suspension of gold convertibility enabled key-currency countries to draw freely on the resources of other nations while communicating their own inflation abroad. A kind of neo-imperialism was established based on international finance rather than on international trade, and operating via central banks rather than private corporate investment. The solution to this problem must also be found at the intergovernmental, central-bank level.

Other economic models were breaking down as well, and with them the policies based on these models. The great industrial expansion occurring within the industrial North during 1961–73 was fueled at first by relatively low-priced raw materials—thereby preventing the South from participating in this economic development—and subsequently by the vast increases in international dollar reserves stemming from America's Cold War spending. The terms of trade between North and South thus evolved in just the opposite way from that required for them to equilibrate wage rates and living standards. Incomes and productive powers became polarized between the integrated industrial economies and the raw-materials exporting dual economies. The Third World's share of world commerce fell from 30 per cent at the peak of the Korean War boom in 1950, to 17.5 per cent in 1972, despite its increasing dependency on food imports and other essentials, and despite its rising volume of raw materials exports.

Meanwhile there was an increasingly fictitious aspect to the North's pseudo-prosperity. The culmination of this process was the so-called stagflation of 1974–75, when a high rate of inflation in the industrial nations was coupled with high unemployment and low levels of economic output. The very possibility of this coincidence of events was denied by orthodox economic theory. It created once-and-for-all changes, both within the industrial North and in the area of North-South negotiations. During this process the private sector's supposedly invisible hands were pushed increasingly by those of government. It began to appear that only governments are in a position to resolve the problems they have helped create, with a highly visible hand operating from above.

In the face of these tendencies market-oriented economics relating world prices simply to supply and demand conditions must fall by the wayside. Political considerations are leading governments in both Third World and industrial nations to regulate and manipulate market forces to serve their own national or regional self-interest. Increasing economic statism in the form of protectionist trade and financial policies leads to government regulation of domestic economic affairs as well. This implies a general centralization of political power. In most countries intergovernmental negotiations are overriding private-sector foreign trade, strengthening the executive branch of government at the expense of the legislative branch. The world is thus seeing the end of a transitory laissez faire interlude which emanated from

England at the time of its Industrial Revolution and reëmerged to determine the course of world affairs during 1945–73.

These issues have pitted Eastern against Western Hemisphere, a reemerging Old World against a conservative New World, that is, a New World seeking to preserve the pre-Vietnam status quo. The Western Alliance is dividing on the basis of new nuclei. Europe and Asia are urging the creation of new monetary and trade arrangements to replace the IMF, the World Bank and GATT, which were established—and subsequently abused—by the U.S. Government. Central banks within the emerging blocs are forming regional currency relationships. The world economy thus faces the prospect of a number of currencies, such as the U.S. dollar, the Japanese yen, the Comecon ruble, and a Eurocurrency based on the EC Snake. Intraregional agreements are also being extended to cover trade, investment, immigration and technology transfer.

Americans must recognize that foreign countries are pursuing the same ideals of economic independence that their own government has always insisted upon in international negotiations. Development of the New International Economic Order does connote the end of America's unique foreign-fed affluence that it has come to enjoy in recent years. But the longer it seeks to retard the emergence of this new economics, the more isolated it will become. The nation therefore faces two choices: it can either participate in the new order as a joint architect, relinquishing the particular advantages which it gained from World War II, or it can struggle against this emerging order, and perhaps continue for several years to finance its government debt by borrowing abroad while dictating special trade "agreements" in its own interest. But the longer it seeks to maintain exploitative trade, payments and investment relationships with foreign countries, the deeper the break will be when it occurs, as occur it must.

Neither U.S. officials nor those of other nations intend the new system to be accidental. Each set of officials is seeking to design the new system so as to benefit their own particular nations or regional grouping of nations.

The essence of nationhood, hence also of regional, supranational strategy, is for governments to seek the greatest degree of autonomy from foreign economic, political and military constraints. To the degree that political rivalry is a more vital con-

TABLE 13.1

Postwar International Economic Order, 1945–73

World economy regulated by "free market forces" shaped by large multinational firms and U.S. foreign aid.

Imports of manufactured products by the industrial nations determined mainly by price competition. Growth in imports and world trade therefore outstrips the rate of domestic economic growth.

Foreign aid provided by industrial nations (subject to U.S. veto) to Third World countries primarily to develop their export sectors or to subsidize their food dependency.

World trade develops patterns of dependency by encouraging Third World food deficits and industrial nation raw-materials deficits.

Private firms from industrial nations invest freely abroad and, in particular, acquire control of Third World raw materials.

Third World exports priced at their low-cost margin, with export income used mainly to purchase consumable essentials.

Multinationals transfer their profits to their home countries, thereby concentrating the world's saving and investment functions in the industrial nations.

Foreign-fed industrial affluence in the United States, Europe and Japan provides the base for consumer affluence. Low prices for raw materials provide low per capita incomes in Third World countries. In Soviet bloc, governments dictate minimal increase in living standards and invest excess productive capacity in weaponry.

Brain drain from Third World to the industrial nations.

Commodities exported by private sector for dollars and sterling.

Fixed currencies, with the U.S. dollar (i.e., Treasury bill) serving as the standard of value.

Trade imbalance between countries settled in intergovernmental credits.

World divided into satellites of either Russia or the United States.

Legislative (parliamentary) branch of government has major role; abundant range for party politics.

Major spokesmen today: Henry Kissinger, Helmut Schmidt, Pat Moynihan, Robert McNamara, Herman Kahn, *New York Times, The Public Interest, Commentary.*

TABLE 13.1 (*cont.*)

New International Economic Order, 1973–

World economy regulated by governments acting in their national self-interest.

Industrial imports increasingly regulated by quota agreements based on fixed market shares. Growth in imports therefore held down to the rate of growth in domestic demand.

OPEC provides aid to Third World for development of regional self-sufficiency, especially in agriculture, primarily using European technology.

Third World goal of self-sufficiency reduces world trade in essentials and encourages industrial nations to develop their own resources.

Governments regulate foreign investment and control their own raw-materials resources.

Third World exports priced at their high-cost margin and traded for technology and equipment to produce essentials.

Multinationals are bought out or taxed, transferring profits to host countries, thereby concentrating world saving and investment functions in Third World countries.

Profits from raw materials provide higher living standards in Third World countries. In the industrial nations, loss of high profits radically shifts priorities, calling for increased government intervention to manage domestic economy under austerity conditions. Soviet Union maintains minimal growth in living standards and invests excess productive capacity in arms.

Emigration of skilled labor from industrial nations to help develop and educate Third World countries.

Commodities bartered by governments, often motivated by diplomatic ends.

Regional-bloc currencies float against one another, with only the European Snake tied loosely to gold for purposes of intra-European settlement.

Trade imbalance between regions settled in gold or stock in private firms.

World divided into five major regions, comprising separate nations confederating for purposes of world diplomacy and economics.

Executive branch dominates governments in a crisis atmosphere. This, and coalition government, reduces the role of party politics.

Major spokesmen: Giscard d'Estaing, Houri Boumedienne, Shah of Iran, Sheik Yamani.

sideration than economic efficiency, the objective of self-sufficiency takes precedence over participation in a division of world labor and production, its associated pattern of commercial dependency, and the general philosophy of One Worldism. National security norms thus become counterposed to economic norms, the economy of self-sufficiency to that of the open world marketplace. This is the problem now facing the United States in the field of energy: it must choose between seeking energy independence at a relatively costly price, or remaining largely dependent upon OPEC for oil. A similar choice now faces Europe and the Near East with respect to agricultural commodities, arms, capital goods and other key products, as well as creation of a regional financial system to supplant the U.S. Treasury-bill standard.

To date, American diplomats seem to be either blind to the far-reaching economic transformation represented by the new regional statism, or to believe that they can readily break up the new tendencies. Yet there is every indication that the spread of technological and social modernity to the Middle East, Africa and other Third World areas will match the impact of the industrial revolutions in today's developed economies. The first industrial revolution inspired liberal economic philosophy in England and France. The foundation laid by John Locke in the 1690s was largely completed by Adam Smith in 1776. Liberal ideology gave birth to classical economics at a time when steam-powered large-scale factory production was just coming into wide application. The second industrial revolution—that which occurred in America, continental Europe and Japan—gave birth to modern political and social-economic philosophies. "Sociology" as defined by Auguste Comte in France—and elaborated in Germany and the United States on the basis of technological optimism and class collaboration (but international economic conflict)—became counterposed to Marxism with its own historical view of economic evolution and class conflict growing out of British economic experience. Both these philosophies sought to integrate technology, economics and social relations into single disciplines, which found their heyday in the years preceding World War I. They also formed the ideological basis for the diverging forms of nationalism and economic protectionism pursued by most countries during this period. Today's cracking of international relations inevitably will be associated with a similar set of new ideological forms, rationalizations and justifications. The following chapters will attempt to outline the foundation of these new perspectives.

CHAPTER 14

World Financial Reform

> It is up to the international community not to reform . . . a monetary system which has ceased to exist, but to draw up a new monetary order.
>
> —Valéry Giscard d'Estaing,
> June 7, 1973

Without international financial reform to create an alternative to the U.S. Treasury-bill standard, whatever payments-surplus countries earn through increased net exports will continue to accrue to the United States as these countries hold their international reserves in Treasury bills. Domestic or intraregional trade and investment can be financed by existing national currencies, but world commerce requires a world monetary standard not associated with national debt.

One way of avoiding the transformation of trade and payments instability into intergovernmental debt is to retain the present regime of floating currencies. But this lacks the stability necessary for long-term government and private sector planning and threatens to lead either to a chaos of national currencies of shifting worth, or to restoration of the dollar. Another alternative is for regional entities outside the United States to create their own currency systems. Inasmuch as currency is based on debt, and specifically government debt to finance economic, political, social and military programs, it presupposes political integration (or at least coordination) with foreign governments accepting this debt money. This foundation of money upon government debt explains why it first developed in the international sphere in the form of key currencies issued by single governments—first England and subsequently the United States—at a time when their balance of payments was in surplus and their currencies were highly desirable.

The European Community is now trying to create a common currency in the form of its own government debt. But which governments will derive the money-issuing benefits? What will be the offsetting assets? Where will the proceeds of European currency debt be spent, and on what? These questions must be answered before European monetary integration can become a reality.

The major problem in establishing a key currency is to get one nation's debt accepted by other governments. The world has learned from America's abuses of the system, and a number of conditions would now have to be imposed. Only the United States, Europe (possibly with OPEC), the Soviet Union and China are in a position to create an international currency, that is, an intergovernmental credit system that will be accepted by other governments. All these regions hold major gold reserves, and all but Europe are current gold producers. (Although lacking major gold reserves, Japan may be able to gain limited acceptance of the yen among Asian countries.)

The currency (or group of currencies) and hence debt used for international financial reserves must be relatively stable in purchasing power. To prevent its value being eroded by price inflation, its international parity must be indexed. The alternative is to index world trade itself on a commodity-by-commodity basis, which is almost a reversion to barter. If financial instruments vary in purchasing power more than commodities themselves, commodities (or denomination of debts in terms of commodities) will take the place of money—just as gold took the place of national monies for long periods of time.

Governments must believe that international currency debts will be honored by the debtor (key-currency) country or countries. The closer the trading countries are to political federation, the greater will be this security. Conversely, the more politically antagonistic creditors and debtors become, the greater is the risk of nonpayment. (The Soviet Union held its dollars in European commercial banks in the 1950s precisely to avoid this political risk.)

The national currency must be widely used in third-party transactions. A convertible Soviet ruble, for instance, could not become a world trading vehicle until such time as many countries desired rubles in order to purchase Soviet or other Comecon exports. Countries running trade surpluses with the Comecon countries would then have a motive for accumulating their currency: it would be a marketable asset whose world demand would be a function of Comecon's export surplus.

To the extent that the above conditions are not simultaneously satisfied, intergovernmental claims may exist only within politically associated regions. Conversely, to hold or invest in the currency-debt of a nation or regional grouping of nations not politically associated with the creditor central bank is tantamount to financing an alien diplomacy. To be sure the United States is striving for just such a system. It hopes to continue financing its world spending with the resources of politically rival powers. It would like to use Arabian petrodollar investments in U.S. Treasury bills to extend arms credits to Iran or Israel, or to finance domestic military or foreign aid programs to countries which OPEC itself would not choose to finance directly. But this is precisely why the Treasury-bill standard is being repudiated by the world's creditor nations.

In short, without a Eurocurrency there is no alternative to the dollar, and without gold (or some other form of asset money yet to be accepted) there is no alternative to national currencies and debt-money serving international functions for which they have shown themselves to be ill-suited. Classical economic theory ignores this problem by assuming that all international payments tend perpetually to be in balance, so that foreign trade is essentially barter. "The basic tenet of the theory of international trade," observes Terence McCarthy, "to whatever school of economics the theoretician may belong, is that money is neutral. As one economist has summed it, 'The first of the major simplifying assumptions [of classical trade theory] is often referred to as the neutrality of money. . . . We deal with a pure barter economy in which monetary magnitudes have no influence on relative prices. The only function that money performs is to set the absolute price level.' " But money ceased to be neutral with the advent of massive payments imbalances and floating exchange rates. "Unstable money is aggressive money, used aggressively. . . . The paradox emerges that, because of the nonneutrality of money in today's *de facto* world, the equivalent of the neutrality of money in international trade can be accomplished in one of only two ways. The first is by actualizing the pure barter implicit in the theory of international trade, i.e., by removing money from the transaction of trading product for product. The second way is to confine trade among nations to multi-nation blocs characterized by a common currency or, what is almost the same thing, possessed of a common central bank of issue, and to specify in advance what quantities of what products will be exchanged in each major transaction. Money would then be truly neutral."[1] Then and only then would international trade reflect the equilibrium (i.e., barter) principles simplistically assumed by classical trade theory.

Whatever the new form of international money turns out to be, it must serve the three basic monetary functions, i.e., it must provide a stable measure of value, a satisfactory medium of exchange, and a store of value. When currencies were no longer convertible into gold and began to float, several attempts were made to find some other form of stability. An early approximation was the IMF's SDR, a composite of sixteen of the world's major trading currencies. The U.S. dollar represented one-third of its weight, and EEC currencies accounted for 33 per cent. In early 1975 the oil-exporting countries linked their currencies and oil prices to SDRs. Iran began the process with its rial on February 12, followed by Saudi Arabia with its riyal on March 14, Kuwait with its dinar on March 17, and then Qatar. Algeria wanted to price OPEC oil in SDRs as of July 1, but Venezuela and Saudi Arabia persuaded the organization to wait until October 1 because of its earlier promise to hold the price of its oil stable (in terms of unstable dollars) until that date. As of June, it seemed that SDR pricing might increase world oil prices by about 3 per cent (or 30¢ per barrel), inasmuch as the value of one SDR had risen from $1.20 to $1.25 since the preceding October.[2]

In May the International Air Transport Association announced that in the autumn all international air fares would be priced in SDRs rather than in dollars. In June the Guyana Bauxite Company sounded out foreign customers concerning a move to a "composite unit" comprising four equally weighted currencies (the U.S. dollar, the pound sterling, the German mark and the Swiss franc). As an alternative, an EEC Unit of Account was proposed that would be based exclusively on the European Snake.[3]

Similar attempts were made to find a suitable store of value for international savings. For years the Middle East had sought some form of bond whose capital value would be adjusted on the basis of a price index or a terms-of-trade index. The Journal of Commerce suggested that "the time may even come when the U.S. Treasury, in selling its securities to foreign investors, official or private, may have to give the investors an option of being paid on the basis of SDRs. This would take some of the 'profit' out of selling dollar securities abroad at a dollar exchange rate which has fallen badly by the time the securities mature."[4]

If not SDRs, then perhaps some market basket of industrial export prices might be indexed by OPEC countries. The Shah of Iran suggested "a relationship . . . between the prices of . . . 20 or 30 commodities and the world inflation because if we cannot link the price of oil with the price of inflation, there will not be any pressure or incentive for the industrial world to check their inflation. If they do not check their inflation, we can defend ourselves with the pricing of our oil. But who is going to suffer? The poor countries."

U.S. officials opposed such suggestions. "Asked about the Shah's proposal to link oil prices to an index of commodity prices, [Assistant Secretary of the Treasury Gerald L.] Parsky said the U.S. has talked with the Shah about such a scheme, but he added the U.S. wants to move the fixing of world prices back to the marketplace,"[5] with "marketplace" being a euphemism for turning the terms of trade in its favor and/or letting the dollar depreciate in value. Kissinger offered to discuss commodity prices on a commodity-by-commodity basis but not in terms of overall shifts in the terms of trade.

Meanwhile, France sought to lead continental Europe in developing a financial and banking mechanism to act as an alternative to the dollar as a medium of exchange and, through its cumulation of working balances, a store of value. Jean-Pierre Fourcade, Minister of the Economy and Finance, told an interviewer that he "would like the Arabs to carry out transactions in francs. We are heading for a system in which the franc and the deutsche mark, for instance, will be instruments for international settlement like the dollar; we are witnessing the end of the dominance of the dollar."[6]

The European Snake, perhaps in conjunction with a gold-backed Arab currency, might thus supplant the dollar at least in Eastern Hemisphere transactions. This implies development of a Mediterranean regional monetary institution largely outside of the IMF. "It is useless to build on ground that is sinking," declared France's Minister of Foreign Affairs Jean Sauvagnargues before the United Nations General Assembly in September 1975, "particularly when monetary settlements can spirit away the gains of a long-term policy in the space of a few weeks."

Rather than setting out to dismantle the IMF, Europe's central banks took the softer option of selling back to themselves one-sixth of the gold subscriptions they had originally turned over to the IMF in 1945. Through the Bank for International Settlements in Basel they sought to purchase part of the other one-sixth of IMF gold which was to be sold at market prices to benefit Third World countries. Europe, Africa and Asia are thus turning away from the dollar to gold to settle payments balances, to serve as a store of value (but not as a *numéraire* now that gold's value is shifting daily in terms of world currencies), and most of all as a mechanism for inducing nations to adjust their *domestic and foreign* behavior so as to live within their international means. Gold is not merely something dug out of the ground in one set of countries, sold abroad and reburied below the ground in other nations. Rather, it is a set of institutions, a compromise enabling national governments to hold their monetary resources in some form other than loans to foreign governments.

To serve the three essential monetary functions, any form of international money requires a satisfactory adjustment mechanism in world payments. The balance of payments no longer responds to the adjustment mechanisms postulated by classical laissez faire trade theory. One way to discourage governments from running payments deficits is to oblige them to finance these deficits with some kind of asset they would prefer to keep, yet can afford to part with when necessary. To date, no one has come up with a better solution than that which history has institutionalized over a period of about two thousand years: gold. All central banks currently hold, and obviously desire to keep, substantial values of this metal. For centuries, possession of gold and monetary autonomy have been nearly synonymous, for the domestic money supply has rested upon the monetary gold stock.

With the link between money and gold now severed, international economic equilibrium requires that nations be permitted to run payments deficits (i.e., draw upon foreign resources) only with the permission of the foreign payments-surplus countries concerned. Europe pressed for a general code of behavior along these lines at Bretton Woods in 1944 when it argued for the scarce-currency clause in the IMF Charter. But the United States denatured this clause on the ground that it did not want payments-surplus nations (at that time itself) to be subject to demands made by payments-deficit regions (at that time Europe). It has since become apparent that some system of mutual surveillance, and hence subordination of national monetary sovereignty to international authority, must be established. To be sure, some degree of imbalance in international payments each year is naturally to be expected. But a means must be found to prevent systematic abuse: the New International Economic Order must end the international "free lunch" enjoyed by countries settling their payments deficits merely with paper of questionable value.

Another major problem is the cumulative dollar overhang stemming from past U.S. payments deficits, along with Britain's sterling overhang and the foreign debt of Third World countries. Today's level of international debt makes one pause: America owes over $105 billion to foreign central banks, Britain's debt threatens it with international insolvency, and Third World countries owe nearly $150 billion, a sum far in excess of their ability to pay out of foreseeable net export earnings.

U.S. officials have proposed that America's foreign debt become a kind of "paper gold," to be transferred from one central bank to another to settle international payments imbalances, but not to be returned to the United States on the ground that this would reduce world monetary reserves. U.S. dollar liabilities—which represent the monetary assets of foreign central banks—would remain world assets while ceasing to be specific U.S. liabilities. America thus would enjoy a $105 billion free ride.

Nations are unable to resort to the bankruptcy laws which permit insolvent private enterprises to wipe their debt off the books when it grows beyond their capacity to repay. Apparently their only alternative to outright default or repudiation is to enter into some agreement with other governments to "fund" their debt (probably in conjunction with other debtor governments) on a take-it-or-leave-it basis. This approach has been suggested

by Chile and Algeria. "I think there is no choice but to wipe out
the debts," concluded a high Pakistani official in December 1975.
"I mean to reschedule them. That's a politer, more acceptable
way of putting it." Algeria's President Houari Boumedienne insisted in April 1974 at the Sixth Special Session of the United
Nations General Assembly that the Third World foreign-debt
burden be lightened. The strong implication was that the Third
World should at least be excused from paying interest on official
debt in view of its relative inability to pay. (Perhaps the creditor
nations could subsidize this interest by giving themselves new-
SDRs created out of the monetized debt of Third World countries.) Not only should foreign aid move from loans to outright
grants so as to stem the debt process, President Boumedienne
argued, but "we should consider the cancellation of the debt in
a great number of cases" along with refinancing the balance on
better terms and with lower interest rates.[7]

In view of Europe's prospective payments deficit vis-à-vis the
raw-materials exporting countries taken in the aggregate (i.e.,
including OPEC), its interest may lie in transforming its existing
foreign-aid grants to Third World countries into new-SDRs, and
then paying for its raw materials in this new kind of money. By
transforming Third World official debt into new-SDRs this debt
would no longer be the specific liability of the original debtor-
countries. But it would be an asset given to the original lenders
(i.e., Europe and America), to be used as a means of payment for
future raw-materials imports. The objective of this system seems
to be to get the most for nothing and to make concessions that
are not true sacrifices.

Perhaps creditor nations will permit some countries to wipe
out their debts in the interest of establishing a new international
stability and political amity. The existing debt is a product of past
instability, that is, the inability of countries to finance their current imports and other international payments with their export
proceeds. If this debt process is not to repeat itself, then greater
equilibrium must be achieved between international export earnings and import payments. (Exports and imports here refer not
only to commodities but to service transactions as well.) Some
international capital movements will take place in the form of
direct investment. But this investment will require some counter-

part in the borrowing (or host) country's ability to pay out of future earnings. The alternative is to accumulate once again a mass of unpayable international debts leading to renewed political antagonisms.

CHAPTER 15

New Aims of World Trade

> The Shah said at his news conference that he
> would like to see the whole oil business national-
> ized and then have international transactions
> conducted on a state-to-state basis.
>
> —Report of France and Iran signing a
> $4 billion barter agreement of oil
> for nuclear reactors, June 27, 1974

Today's argument over world export prices centers around
two distinct debates: first, that of a "just" price for Third World
raw materials vis-à-vis industrial products, and second, the type
of "equilibrium" supposed to be produced by world price relationships.

Third World economists believe that world trade will be balanced equitably when all countries have similar per capita incomes, productive powers and economic opportunity. (Historically, this was the rationale for laissez faire. Presumably
"automatic" international adjustment mechanisms were held to
lead naturally to this happy state of affairs.) The only way to raise
Third World incomes is to increase productive powers. The quality of labor must be upgraded through widespread education and
higher capital investment per worker. Improvement of Third
World agriculture requires modernization of rural institutions,
beginning with land tenure systems. Capital goods must be imported to transform the economic and social structure. At present, the only source of funds for these investments is export
income. Thus the starting point for this process is to improve the
terms at which raw materials exchange for industrial capital
goods. Third World spokesmen therefore view international economic stability in reference to the terms of trade—preferably

using as their base year the "golden age" of 1950–51 when the Korean War boom bid up the raw-materials export prices to peak levels.

Economists in the industrial nations tend to view world trade as being in equilibrium as long as the balance of payments is stable—especially now that their own payments positions have moved into deficit. They point out that the 1973 rise in oil prices threw their international payments into massive deficit. (American economists, however, ignore what Giscard d'Estaing was quick to acknowledge: of the "increase in the [1974] deficit of the countries without oil, the portion caused by oil is $11 billion but the portion caused by grain is $8 billion.")[1] The industrial nations are therefore seeking balance-of-payments stability in the face of higher world raw-materials prices.

Since 1973 these two concepts of international equilibrium have been in opposition to one another: improved terms of trade and evolution toward income equality for Third World countries connotes worsened balance-of-payments positions for the industrial nations. In today's economic recession, rising Third World living standards, domestic investment and economic self-sufficiency are at odds with maintenance of existing U.S. and European living standards and investment. The industrial nations must either borrow from OPEC, sell ownership of their industry, or export more capital goods, arms or other products to balance their international payments and prevent their currencies from sinking. These alternatives all involve inflationary pressures as an increased portion of U.S. and European labor and income is used to pay for higher-priced imports from OPEC and other Third World countries. To the extent that one set of countries succeeds in improving its living standards and wealth accumulation, the other set of nations must pay.

The collapse of orthodox trade theory

Today's situation is quite different from the post-World War II world in which economic growth in any one nation was presumed to increase its demand for imports from its trading partners, thereby spurring employment and incomes in the latter countries. The surplus labor and productive capacity available in the early postwar years has been used up, so that exports no longer represent the "free" resource they seemed to in 1945. Today, higher prosperity for Third World countries threatens to divert production of capital goods and other investment resources from U.S. and European economies, reducing their ability to evolve into postindustrial economies.

This new state of affairs has thrown orthodox economic theory into disarray. Since the Great Depression, economists have claimed that their expertise lies in allocating scarce resources among competing ends. This accepted view was expressed by Lionel Robbins in 1933 at the depth of the depression when resources were not free, but were not particularly scarce either. When resources really did become scarce in 1973 economists panicked and called it a crisis. The problem was that these economists—especially those working for governments in the industrial nations—did not want to recognize the fact that they would have to scale down their "ends," i.e., their economic targets. Third World countries were learning how to play the international economics game and were pricing their exports at levels justified by their relative scarcity over time, taking into account their long-term replacement costs. Orthodox price theory did not explain the structural rigidities built into the world economy since 1945. It failed to deal with the technological and institutional structures that formed the context of economic behavior. It also failed to trace the consequences of the attempt by most industrial nations to become postindustrial societies. This development required low-income countries to perform most of the world's real work, that is, produce its industrial manufactures and raw materials. The industrial nations were becoming leisure-oriented, white-collar service economies, living off their investments in Third World economies and importing the products of blue-collar labor.

This vision of a postindustrial future could hardly be reconciled with the traditional ideals of laissez faire theory and its hypothetical equilibrium mechanisms. What did it imply for the future of Third World countries, if not that they would work harder rather than share in the prosperity and leisure being enjoyed in the industrial nations. Indeed, ever since World War II gaps in incomes, productive powers and living standards have widened between Third World countries and the industrial nations. According to classical laissez faire models they were supposed to narrow in response to "automatic" market adjustment mechanisms. In 1973 this clash between theory and reality began to be settled by Third World governments intervening into the trade and development process. It had become apparent that world markets were dominated by large international firms in the industrial nations, regulated in turn by their governments. Self-serving (to the industrial nations) but seemingly "objective" market forces thus could no longer serve as arbiter of international pricing and resource allocation.

The laissez faire models that guided postwar development had presumed no cartels or governments (or as economists put it, markets were "perfect" and governments were "neutral"). Trade patterns were viewed as being somehow "natural," as if nature itself had decreed the existing productivity and cost differentials among nations and their patterns of specialization. This was in large part a carryover from nineteenth-century trade theory as elaborated by David Ricardo and John Stuart Mill, who discussed the exchange of cloth for wine in basically seventeenth-century terms. They assumed "perfect" small-scale markets, cottage industry production characterized by diminishing returns and balanced international payments. This approach hardly reflects the modern-day world of international cartels, rising productivity, balance-of-payments instability and a long legacy of national protectionism that has transformed the division of world labor over the centuries. In practice, economic momentum has been seized by the most highly protectionist economies, led by England in the seventeenth and eighteenth centuries, the United States in the nineteenth century, and followed by continental Europe, Japan and Russia. These nations all consolidated their modern industrial development when they repudiated laissez faire doctrine. By contrast, the countries which are today underdeveloped are those which have not managed market forces in their own national interests. For the past century they have been enmeshed in a colonialist and post-colonialist system that forbade its members to enact protectionist policies or even to determine the price of their exports. These countries could only export products that the industrial nations elected not to produce. In the absence of protective tariffs their domestic production patterns were determined by competitive forces shaped by economic forces determined outside their jurisdictions, i.e., by the more economically aggressive industrial nations. Third World Countries that did not manage market forces in their own national interests permitted their evolution to become warped into a monoculture syndrome.

All this is now changing. Resolution of today's conflict over world pricing is moving out of the hands of multinational firms ("the marketplace") into intergovernmental forums representing both Third World and industrial nations. The multinationals and their home-office governments are being countered by the combined weight of Third World governments administering export prices rather than leaving them to be set by "market" forces.

This new approach won its first victory when the oil-exporting countries quadrupled oil prices and announced their intention to appropriate ownership and management of their natural resources. If they now start producing steel and oil-based fertilizers for export and buy capital goods to further enhance their productive powers, the focus of world economic growth will shift toward the Middle East and other Third World areas whose investment is financed by OPEC. There will be nothing "natural" about the resulting world trade patterns: they will result from deliberate government policy.

Developing a more refined concept of "cost" for world raw materials

The concept of cost itself has been called into question in an attempt to determine a commodity's "just" world price. In addition to accepting resource-cost differentials as given and natural, economists also tend to accept existing wage differentials as a "just" element of the comparative-cost structure that gives low-income countries a competitive advantage in producing the type of goods that can be produced with low-wage labor. In fact, all international cost differentials are accepted as "just." The only issue debated by orthodox trade theory is the proper relationship between production cost and sales price, taking production costs for granted.

Commodity pricing is strongly influenced by supply and demand factors. These refer indirectly to costs in the sense that producers will stop supplying products whose price is less than their production costs (including normal profits). Matters are complicated by the fact that raw-materials producers in the industrial nations generally face higher production costs than Third World producers. The questions to be determined in international trade are therefore (1) whether the price for a commodity will be set at its high- or low-cost margin, and (2) the nature of these costs. A figure quoted frequently in the American press for the "true" or "economic" value of Saudi Arabian oil is ten cents per barrel, the cost required to pump the country's vast oil resources out of the ground. But this is like defining the value of a lathe or other industrial machine merely in terms of the labor necessary to walk into a factory and carry it out the door. What is lacking is a sense of replacement cost.

Marginalist economics (e.g., Marshallian price theory) tends to confuse resource- and capital-replacement costs with economic rents (that is, cost differentials) as both representing something for nothing. The theory argues that American and European oil producers should receive higher oil prices than Third World producers because their production costs are higher. A "just" international price structure is one which enables producers in each country to receive incomes sufficient to cover their current production costs plus normal profits. Hence, it appears "fair" to pay efficient producers less than inefficient ones so as to prevent superprofits from being reaped. (Superprofits represent "something for nothing" in terms of current expenditures on labor and capital.)

The fact remains, however, that as long as production costs differ among countries, *someone* must reap the value of these differences. Until 1973 this profit—which economists call economic rent—accrued to producers, consumers or governments in the industrial nations, not those in Third World countries. Actually, the benefits of low-cost Third World minerals can accrue to (1) industrial-nation investors whose Third World branches sell inexpensive minerals to their own refineries and distributors, and sell the products at relatively high prices (pocketing the difference), (2) governments in the industrial nations which levy tariffs approaching or equal to their production-cost differential, (3) other consumers or producers in the industrial nations fortunate enough to buy low-cost Third World minerals, (4) governments in the Third World minerals-exporting countries via export royalties or other taxes, or direct ownership of their own mineral resources, (5) Third World private-sector own-

ers of low-cost mineral resources, or (6) Third World resource-
users who buy inexpensive minerals locally and work them up
into finished products which are sold abroad at world prices, or
(7) Third World consumers of low-cost Third World products.

A major shortcoming of classical laissez faire reasoning is its
failure to consider capital replacement costs and mineral depletion. Industrial and agricultural production can continue *ad infinitum,* but exportation of minerals is an exchange of naturally
endowed capital for renewable industrial manmade capital in a
process that terminates in the exhaustion of the raw-materials
exporters.

Suppose, for instance, that a country earns foreign exchange
for its oil for twenty-five years, in the process depleting its wells.
This is like owning a bond and receiving current interest but not
recovering the principal. If an oil-exporting country spends its
export proceeds on foreign grains and other foodstuffs rather
than modernizing its agriculture so as to produce its own food,
and if it buys foreign manufactures instead of creating a domestic
industrial capacity, then its economy and living standards will
collapse once the export product is gone. Unable to sustain its
existing pace of economic activity, the population will be forced
either to drastically curtail its living standards or to emigrate.

Governments in the industrial nations have long recognized
this problem and have given their own mineral producers a tax
allowance for depletion. The purpose of this allowance was to
enable producers to replace the value of their minerals used up
in production, in the face of rising replacement costs over time
(assuming the richest mines and oil reserves to be the first ones
exploited). For many years the U.S. depletion allowance stood at
27.5 per cent of the sales revenue of direct production affiliates.
This meant that American oil and mining companies could regis-
ter $27.50 out of every $100 in sales revenue as a production
cost, and therefore pay no taxes on it. (At a 50 per cent corporate
tax rate this was the equivalent of pre-tax earnings of $55 on each
$100 of sales.) In practice, because the depletion allowance was
overly generous, its recipients were able to purchase even more
resources than were being used up in production. This depletion
allowance was granted to investors not only on their domestic
operations but also on their foreign operations: American companies in the Middle East, Venezuela and elsewhere were allowed

to deduct from their U.S. income taxes a sum calculated to enable them to repurchase equal or rising volumes of resources elsewhere as they used up the resources of their host countries.

This capital-replacement function was denied to the oil-exporting economies themselves. Multinational oil companies set aside no part of their income to provide for the needs of these countries once their minerals were gone. Third World countries have been—and are still being—urged to sell their oil for merely its carrying charges up and out of the wells and across the sea. It seems that their lot in history is to use up their resources and then quietly expire from the scene, or ideally never to rise up from their nomadic way of life in the first place.

Only since 1973 have oil exporters come to view the price of their oil (and other depletable resources) in terms of the costs required to sustain their economies after their mineral reserves are exhausted. In effect they have begun to exchange one form of capital—their natural mineral endowment—for industrial and agricultural capital by moving to secure a higher proportion of the ultimate price paid for their minerals in the industrial nations. As Alfred Marshall observed at the turn of the century, governments are wont to tax economic rents, or in this case the gains from trade resulting from differential production costs. To date, these governments have been mainly those of the industrial nations, save for the modest royalty fees charged before 1973 by minerals-exporting countries. But Third World governments are now asserting themselves. If the United States taxes its oil imports to support energy prices at a level enabling synthetic fuels, nuclear power or solar energy to become economically competitive, Third World governments will feel justified in securing an equal price-per-BTU for their energy resources.

This does not mean that the higher export prices being asked by Third World countries will mean correspondingly higher prices to consumers in the industrial nations. Much of this difference has been taken all along by the international minerals cartel and industrial-nation governments. Thus Mahbub ul Haq points out that "OPEC never raised the price of oil to the consumer in the Western world but merely asked for a higher share in the price he was already paying. Even before the price increase of November 1973, the final consumer in Europe was paying an average of $33 for every barrel of oil and oil products. Since the cost of extraction, refining, transportation and distribution was only about $5 per barrel, $28 accrued as surplus rent or profits of which the OPEC members received $2 and $26 were pocketed by the oil companies, government taxes and royalties of European countries. . . . All that the producing nations demanded was that they should be paid $8 instead of $2 out of a surplus rent of $28. And yet the OPEC action was not presented as a just struggle for a more equitable sharing of rent, which it really was, but as an unreasonable increase in the price of oil." In fact President Ford levied a $2 per barrel tax on U.S. oil imports, making it clear that supply and demand forces would sustain a price to the industrial nations even higher than they had previously paid. The Shah of Iran observed that some European countries "levy on one barrel of oil, so much tax that it is more than the government take of, for instance, my country."[2]

As for other commodities, Rene Servoise has computed that "of the $200 billion (not counting tax) the consumers at the end of the line pay for raw materials (excluding oil) imported from Third World countries, the biggest cut goes to industrial and commercial middlemen, the vast majority of them from the developed nations, while only $20 billion reaches the producer countries. The producers do not get a penny of the 'value added' by industry, science, technology and distribution. If producers swung as much weight as the developed nations, they would be taking in about $150 billion."[3] Much of this value added represents the difference between what the world minerals cartel pays Third World countries and the price it charges for these minerals in the industrial nations.

Still, the industrial nations oppose Third World goals for two major reasons. First, higher raw-materials prices will either upset their balance of payments or require greater transfers of exports (or sale of their own industrial firms) to Third World countries. Furthermore, development of domestic Third World agriculture and industry to support their own populations (rather than those in the industrial nations) will bring Third World producers into direct competition with exporters in the industrial nations. This conflict suggests several strategies and possible scenarios.

The U.S. position

From the U.S. vantage point the world economy should remain controlled by the multinationals—hence, indirectly, by itself as overseer of its large multinational firms. Third World countries should remain dependent on U.S. food and arms. Their raw-materials export prices should remain low, although U.S. raw-materials prices should be supported to ensure domestic self-sufficiency and the economic ability to break possible Third World commodity boycotts. The 1976 Economic Report of the President thus endorsed only those international agreements "which reduce excessive price swings without raising commodity prices above their long-term market trends," that is, their historically low levels. Third World raw-materials exports must be increased to help "market forces" hold down world prices as they had during the preceding quarter-century of overabundant world mineral supplies. Proposals to index Third World export prices "to changes in the price of manufactured goods . . . need to be opposed on various grounds. . . . Such arrangements tend to result in selling prices that are higher than world market forces would bring about, [and thus] impart an inflationary bias to the international economic system. Therefore, earnings stabilization schemes can better be implemented through . . . more market-oriented ways . . . and any transfer of resources to the poorer countries can better be accomplished through official aid channels."[4]

In January 1976 Assistant Secretary of the Treasury Gerald Parsky announced that the United States would not sign the recently negotiated cocoa agreement designed to support world prices, nor would it commit itself to join the sugar or coffee agreements. The cocoa agreement was rejected on the ground that its "range of minimum and maximum prices was regarded as too high, and another objection was that it sought to keep prices up by unwieldy controls over exports by producing countries." Such commodity agreements "inevitably result in higher prices to the United States and other consumers." The United States "would be willing to join a 'producer-consumer forum' to discuss problems of copper, and possibly bauxite, [but] would not join any agreement aiming at bolstering prices." If raw-materials exporters needed funds to support their balance-of-payments position, Mr. Parsky suggested, they might resort to the IMF's compensatory financing facility (borrowing from which would have to be repaid at a point, thereby adding to the Third World's foreign debt). He speculated that "if governments can set the price of copper, how long will it be before they can dictate the type, quality and quantity of copper products? Commodity agreements will increase the role and impact of government in the marketplace. Increasingly, the government will displace the role of the actual producer and consumer in setting the terms and conditions of trade."[5] Exactly! Just as had resulted from U.S. actions in the fields of textiles, specialty steels and TVs. As the international economy becomes more political, America is unwilling to be a partner in trade agreements supported in world forums by a substantial majority of small powers.

The new regionalism

The line of least resistance in resolving the conflict between balance-of-payments equilibrium for the industrial nations and improved terms of trade for Third World countries lies in regional agreements. The first such approach was taken by Europe, the Middle East and Africa to form a natural extension of the Common Market's Associate Membership system toward its historical trade and colonial relationships. European governments are seeking long-term supply assurances for raw materials and expanded markets for their industrial products. These objectives call for agreements negotiated among governments.

In April 1974 France's Minister of Foreign Affairs Michel Jobert informed the United Nations General Assembly that "France wishes, together with her partners in the European Community, to enter into a dialogue with the Arab countries, inspired by the determination to establish a long-term and mutually beneficial cooperation between two groups of states geographically close, whose common future deserves to be outlined without delay." To help coordinate the new trade relationships he suggested "an economic monitoring center under the aegis of the United Nations."[6] Pointedly, this was not an international organization in which the United States enjoyed veto power. UNCTAD, dominated by Third World countries, seemed the logical forum for coordinating international trade policy.

By 1975 the European Community was selling more to Arab countries ($17.2 billion) than to the United States ($14.9 billion). These amounts represented 12.6 per cent and 10.9 per cent of its exports, respectively. Meanwhile, Arab countries accounted for one fifth of EEC imports, worth $28.3 billion, an amount substantially in excess of the $23.2 billion worth of goods and services which Europe imported from the United States. Furthermore, Europe's exports to the Near East concentrated on capital goods and other industrial exports, whereas most of America's export growth to the region comprised arms—a much less solid foundation on which to build a long-term export relationship.

Jean-Pierre Fourcade suggested that the level of terms-of-trade aid extended by Europe to the raw-materials exporters was best determined by their capital-import requirements: "fair compensation . . . must enable the producer countries to obtain the financing required for development of their economies."[7] Bilateral aid with strings attached was to be supplanted by Third World earning power.

Toward this end the nine European Community members devised a system of "compensatory financing" to stabilize export prices for 46 associated African, Caribbean and Pacific countries. This Lomé Convention (named after the capital of Togo, at which agreement was reached) "concerns 500 million human beings, and it introduces an innovation which could well be revolutionary in its impact. The industrialized countries have undertaken to contribute to the stabilization of the income from exports of the countries associated with the EEC. The poorest countries will not have to repay this stabilization assistance, but others will be expected to do so as soon as the market permits." Simply stated, every time the price of one of 12 basic products is 7.5 per cent lower than the reference price based on the four previous years, the Community will pay the exporting countries in question the difference. The rate has been set at 2.5 per cent for the 34 least developed countries involved.

In exchange for these terms-of-trade assurances Giscard d'Estaing insisted that the Lomé Convention's Third World members "guarantee the consuming countries regular supplies under acceptable conditions."[8] These supply assurances presumably would extend to the commodities of all signatory powers, including OPEC. Industrial nations joining such an agreement would achieve certainty of supply, for which they would pay a premium. Countries not joining—possibly including the United States— would become a residual market.

Meanwhile, OPEC agreed to resolve much of the balance-of-payments problem caused by higher raw-materials prices by recycling a substantial part of its revenues to other Third World countries via the IMF Oil Facility and the numerous regional Arab development banks, and by prepaying for capital goods, arms and development-related services bought in the industrial nations. Capital formation in the industrial nations began to be refocused to accelerate exports of capital goods and related technology transfer. While Third World countries began the catching up process by investing their export surplus in creating a domestic industrial and agricultural capital base, growth in Western "postindustrial" living standards was suspended.

The Mediterranean triangle's attempt to resolve its trade and payments problems on a regional basis raised the question of whether world trade agreements could be made exclusive of the United States, or whether America had the power to block them. The first test came in 1975, when Third World and European governments established international price agreements for tin, coffee and cocoa while the United States joined only the tin agreement (and later accepted the coffee agreement reluctantly). This made possible a dual market in which the parties to the new commodity agreements (i.e., most of the Eastern Hemisphere) paid a relatively high price while the United States and other nonparties to the agreements paid lower prices—clearly an unstable situation. If tin were sold to U.S. consumers for a lower price outside the agreement, it would penalize European, Japanese and other industrial tin users whose governments chose to support Third World aims. Products made from tin in the United States would undersell similar goods produced elsewhere. With no market for Eastern Hemisphere products, demand for tin at the higher price would decline and soon the whole price agreement would become meaningless.

Regional blocs may have the best chance of equalizing world economic conditions, but this requires that their member nations join ranks and trade mainly with each other, at terms of trade designed to finance specific capital investment programs. Any

trade with other regional groupings could erode the price structure upon which their investment and income plans are based.
Thus, government control of imports and exports becomes even
more necessary.

Commodity agreements

Third World countries are joining in United Nations forums to
support higher commodity prices, using the Korean War boom
of 1950–51 as their reference point. In February 1975 in Dakar,
Senegal "110 developing countries agreed to coordinate efforts
to increase income from raw materials. One proposed method is
the creation of extensive commodity stockpiles to stabilize prices
in the face of demand and supply shifts; the oil-exporting countries were asked to provide most of the financing for such a
project." Governments would purchase their own export commodities whenever an oversupply lowered the price below some
predetermined floor, much as the U.S. Government did for many
years to support domestic farm prices. A consolidated system of
commodity stockpiles would enable one stockpile to be financed
by earnings on other stockpiles (which would buy when prices
were low and sell when prices were high so as to stabilize earnings within an agreed range). Coordination of stockpile accumulations under a single authority also would focus commodity
negotiations in a single intergovernmental agency that could set
a fixed time schedule for its initial purchase and price-support
activities.

This would help Third World countries improve their terms of
trade but would not help the industrial nations balance their
international payments. Furthermore, the United States adamantly opposed both the stockpile program and subsequent
moves toward regional cooperation. Germany and England have
leaned toward the U.S. position. In fact, by the time the Fourth
Meeting of UNCTAD was held in Nairobi, Kenya, in May 1976,
positions had hardened between Third World countries and the
industrial nations. This split was mirrored within the industrial
nations themselves between "hard liners"—the United States
and West Germany, followed by England and Japan—and nations more willing to reach an accommodation with the Third
World. The latter asked that stockpile purchases of $6 billion

support the export price of 17 raw materials, and that target prices be indexed to a market basket of 89 industrial products. The industrial nations opposed the indexing principle, at least for the time being. A French-sponsored compromise (which ultimately was adopted) called for buffer stockpiles for ten commodities that accounted for about three-fourths of the Third World's non-oil raw-materials exports: cocoa, copper, cotton, hard fibers, iron ore, jute, rubber, sugar, tea and tin. Postponed until a later date were Third World pressures for a foreign-debt moratorium, tariff concessions for Third World industrial exports, and an easing of patent restrictions limiting technology transfers to Third World countries.

The United States, West Germany and England entered the meetings opposed to any transfer of resources to Third World countries without a compensating *quid pro quo.* In fact, the four-week conference was saved only by a final emergency weekend session when it became apparent that Third World countries would not break ranks. When the industrial nations sought to form a united front against Third World governments, but were countered by a Third World threat that the North-South dialogue would break down totally and the Third World countries would attempt to "go it alone" as best they could, the industrial nations began to give ground. Although they did not commit themselves to put up (along with OPEC) the entire $6 billion requested by Third World countries, they did agree to reach settlement on the principles of joint financing by March 1977.

Why inter-governmental price agreements will work

Four reasons are often cited as to why higher prices for world raw-materials exports may not hold. One is technological: price increases for raw materials tend to induce technological breakthroughs that economize on materials use and/or development of industrial substitutes. The other three reasons concern market structure: price increases tempt producers to break rank out of greed; new producers may enter the field from outside the cartel; and a countervailing consumer cartel may be formed to confront the producer cartel. None of these events is very probable in today's circumstances.

Technological breakthroughs. It is true that synthetic rubber has replaced natural rubber, stainless steel and aluminum have replaced tin in cans, and catalytic converters have been made far more efficient in their use of platinum. But the pace of this substitution has slowed considerably in recent years and seems to have run its course in numerous areas. For instance, although the price of coffee has been supported by intergovernmental agreement and by the recent coffee blight and frost in Brazil, no coffee substitute has appeared to substantially reduce demand. No lower-cost substitute for oil looms on the immediate horizon, and the longer-term energy substitutes—nuclear and solar power, synthetic coal liquids, and so on—are many years away from being developed in large enough quantities to be competitive. Copper's early competition from aluminum has slowed since 1961, and even though copper has been phased out of many earlier uses, demand remains high for its remaining applications. Furthermore the price of aluminum will rise in coming years in keeping with higher energy costs, inasmuch as aluminum is produced as much from electricity as from bauxite. Cotton will remain a major fiber as long as much of its competition comes from petrochemicals. Several other substitutes for Third World exports are in themselves Third World products whose prices also are rising.

Producers breaking rank. "We were amused," an executive of a big commodity house said, "when OPEC was formed in 1960. We were even more amused when the copper group was created six years later. But we stopped being amused last September [1973] when both groups managed to bury their internal political differences, which we thought were too great to permit effective coordination of strategy."[9] In March 1974 the seven major bauxite producers (accounting for some 63 per cent of the world's supply) increased export prices and laid plans to take over foreign-owned bauxite properties. Three months later the four major copper-producing nations comprising CIPEC—Zambia, Chile, Peru and Zaire—met with delegations from other copper-producing countries (in addition to observers from the International Bauxite Association and an informal group of iron ore producers) to cut back production and coordinate marketing policy. On balance the oil exporters held together largely because sparsely-populated Saudi Arabia and Kuwait reduced their oil output to prevent a world oversupply.

Only rarely have countries consciously made economic sacrifices to help foreign economies. But now that the powerful binding force of ideology has entered the picture, nations like individuals may put long-term regional and national objectives above the achievement of narrow or short-term market gains. In the past, moral suasion—backed by laissez faire ideology, amply supplemented by U.S. diplomatic pressure—was a major force blocking Third World countries from improving their terms of trade by government direction of their economies. Today, the more intensely U.S. officials oppose the New International Economic Order and its state-sponsored policies, the greater the defensive pressure abroad for diplomatic and economic consolidation.

New producers entering the field. Instead of competing with existing raw-materials producers, new entrants into the field of raw-materials production have joined ranks with the established exporting associations. The most important case is that of oil, where it seems improbable that new producers will try to break OPEC's power. Norway and Britain have suggested joining OPEC when their oil comes onstream. Furthermore, Europe's North Sea output is high-cost production, as is oil production in the United States under Project Independence. Mexico's state-owned oil company made major new discoveries in 1974, but a Mexican official insisted that "the country's oil strategy is not based on massive exports. We are not going to follow Venezuela's example of unrestrained exports. Venezuela makes us think that we should keep our oil for future generations." The nation's President, Luis Echeverria Alvarez, announced that Mexico's oil reserves would be exploited in a "profoundly nationalist and anti-imperialist manner." Shortly after these developments Canada increased the export price of its oil to higher-than-OPEC levels and announced it would phase out net oil shipments to the United States in order to conserve its energy resources for future Canadian development.

Soviet Russia and China possess major oil and coal resources. However, Russia's export capacity is limited by its own domestic needs (although it may export token sums to the industrial West). China may begin to export its coal and oil to Japan, but only on political terms that pry Japan out of the U.S. diplomatic orbit. Thus, any communist-nation decision to undercut world raw-materials prices on government-to-government deals will probably be on terms that undermine America's diplomatic position.

Consumer cartels. Europe's and Japan's willingness to make their "separate peace" with Third World raw-materials exporters by dealing directly with OPEC in government-to-government negotiations dashed Kissinger's 1973 hopes to create an International Energy Agency as a consumer-country cartel. French officials endorsed world minerals agreements in oil, copper, tin and bauxite, as well as in plantation crops such as coffee and tea. Thus, Europe is unwilling to join America in creating a militant consumer cartel. In the event that it should try to do so, Third World countries apparently have gained sufficient confidence in the degree to which the industrial nations are dependent on their raw materials that they may carry through on their threat to increase prices to any attempted consumer cartel. Indeed, if Third World countries elect to interlink all of their export goods, even prices for nonessential commodities may be maintained against united consumers.

Third World governments are thus repeating the statist process carried out a century ago under protectionist-capitalist aegis in the industrial nations. Whether socialist or capitalist, dictatorships or democracies, they are using their new-found ability to dominate international market forces. A system of checks and balances is being created at the intergovernmental level. The hallmarks of international equilibrium remain payments balance, equalization of international incomes, productive powers and opportunities among nations and a growing similarity of (balanced) economic diversification. But to the extent that these goals are achieved it will be through the active hand of government rather than by what Adam Smith called the invisible hand of unregulated market forces.

CHAPTER 16

Government Regulation of International Investment

[Industrial cooperation] in the world has up to now largely been the domain of the transnational enterprises that have expanded enormously and have led to a kind of international division of labor. States however cannot let the transnationals shoulder responsibility for industrial cooperation alone.

It has now been agreed that the problems of energy, raw materials and development will be examined simultaneously . . .

—Valéry Giscard d'Estaing, August 8, 1975
Speech in Zaire on "A New International Economic Order"

New criteria to evaluate the activities of multinational firms are stemming from three major causes: (1) the superprofits earned by the multinationals, especially in the raw materials area, (2) their bribery and other illegal domestic political activities, and most of all (3) their tendency to warp host-country economies into monocultures rather than to stimulate their development and diversification. International investment is therefore coming to be viewed in terms of its long-range impact on host-country self-sufficiency and productive powers. These developmental impacts have turned out to be more important than gross export volume, contribution to GNP or yield in tax revenues.

Under international law host-country governments may regulate all investment in the national interest, providing that foreign investors are subject to the same rules as domestic investors (if any in fact exist) in their particular industries. This suggests that in years to come domestic as well as international investors face much greater regulation of their pricing, market shares and dividend payout policies. They also may face targets for their balance-of-payments contribution, production levels and domestic employment.

New rules for multinationals

Foreign investment is viewed favorably if its operations contribute to the host country's capital formation, taking into account the broad range of social factors affected by this investment and its required costs in terms of government-financed infrastructure. Investment activities are discouraged which deplete a country's resources, transfer its profits abroad, or retard domestic political evolution. In the aftermath of the Lockheed scandals in Japan, Holland and other countries, and the revelation of ITT's involvement in Chile's coup d'état (to name the two outstanding examples) the political environment was ripe for increased host-country regulation. The balance-of-payments crisis experienced by Third World countries following the massive increases in food and oil prices gave a further note of urgency to the situation. The United Nations "good conduct code" for multinational investment, drawn up in 1974, therefore called for renegotiating international minerals and plantation concessions not in host-country interests. At the 1976 UNCTAD conference in Nairobi, Third World countries insisted on a review of all foreign investment. The expropriators were being expropriated in Third World countries just as their operations were being regulated in the "national interest" in the industrial nations. The world was going either socialist or state-capitalist, beginning with the export sectors of all nations.

Firms engaged in raw-materials exploitation have become the major targets for nationalization or government "participation programs" precisely because their repatriation of earnings, dividends, depletion and depreciation funds are viewed as unreasonable leakages from the host-country economy. Henceforth the savings function and its associated investment function are to be retained in the host country.

Industrial projects generally have been left alone, as have agri-

cultural projects, although they are now getting attention. Multinational firms therefore find themselves obliged to provide host-
country governments with a rising share of the earnings and
capital recapture (i.e., depreciation and depletion) earned directly on their investment, and a growing portion of what Ricardo
termed the "gains from trade" accruing from the worldwide division of production fostered by these investments. Also, international corporations are finding themselves obliged to diversify
the range of their activities in Third World countries so as to
enable them to overcome the monoculture syndrome that has
characterized much international investment in the past.

This process is leading to a state of affairs in which international investments will take on the nature of regulated public
utilities. On the one hand, international investors may find their
riskiness of investment reduced: in exchange for their management know-how and initial financing they may be guaranteed a
definite minimum return on their capital. (This return may be
increased if firms reinvest their earnings in the host country.) But
by the same token they will find themselves constrained from
earning the uniquely high rates of return available in the past. To
the extent that host countries provide assurances against prejudi-
cial regulation or nationalization without compensation there
will obviously be less justification for abnormally high international profits that previously were viewed as "compensation for
risk." The risk will be minimized—and so will the superprofits
previously transferred abroad.

The trend toward nationalizing raw-materials investments
need not occur in a manner antagonistic to corporate or public
interests in the industrial nations. In fact, American copper companies worked closely with President Frei of Chile in drawing up
plans to "Chileanize" that nation's copper mines. The U.S. Government demonstrated that it did not oppose Chile's takeover of
Anaconda and Kennecott copper affiliates as much as the prospective shift of their marketing function away from the United
States (a shift that would threaten to deprive America of secure
copper supplies). Purchase by Venezuela, Kuwait and Saudi
Arabia of foreign-owned oil affiliates is another case indicating
that international investors can afford nationalization of their
foreign affiliates in cases where they work with host governments.
They may accept foreign government participation as part of an

overall development program with minimum stress on established world trade relationships, and in conjunction with a negotiated return on their capital investment.

The main danger to international firms lies in their being caught in a conflict of interests between home-office and host-country governments, each seeking to use them as arms of their own self-interested policies. Controls no doubt will be extended over corporate earnings, pricing and dividend remittance policies. Special tax advantages and burdens will be proposed to induce international firms to follow policies desired by home-country or host-country governments, and these policies may conflict with one another. Controls may be extended to cover third-country transactions, and hence intrafirm pricing policies, as well as hiring policies (quotas for domestic labor and management), technology transfer and diversification of investment. Some governments may go overboard in establishing balance-of-payments targets on a firm-by-firm basis, such as were applied in the 1960s by the U.S. Government in its foreign-investment control program. Whatever the strains between home-office and host-country governments, it has become apparent that international firms are not more powerful than governments. They are no longer independent entities, they have become pawns.

OPEC investment plans

Irrespective of their political systems, Arab countries are laying the groundwork for economic development based on the best technology the world has to offer. They obviously must educate their populace and upgrade health standards as a prelude to broadly based economic development. Agriculture and industry must be modernized to meet the needs of their populations. The vast size and scope of Arab development plans requires an overall coordination far beyond the ability of private firms responding to "free market forces."

OPEC's economic surpluses, which once would have lined the oil industry's pockets, have provided funds for a $144 billion five-year development plan in Saudi Arabia, a $75 billion five-year plan in Iran and investment programs of nearly equal magnitude in Kuwait and the Arab emirates (Abu Dhabi, etc.). These countries are installing the most sophisticated communications systems available, including the most up-to-date telephone and TV equipment. Their electrification program is based on the most advanced concepts. Hospitals and universities will be generally better equipped than those in the United States.

The logical place for OPEC to begin industrializing is in energy-intensive industries linked closely to oil and natural gas inputs: petrochemicals and fertilizers, oil refineries and tanker fleets to secure marketing autonomy over their oil, as well as production of aluminum and copper, iron and steel, and related heavy industries based on these inputs.

The advanced technology required for these developments must be imported. OPEC therefore is taking payment for its oil exports in the form of imported capital goods, engineering services and skilled labor. The resulting shift of net physical capital accumulation to a new area of the world promises an economic miracle rivaling that of Japan and Germany following World War II. (It is precisely these examples that OPEC governments have in mind in choosing to take their increased oil revenues in the form of productive capital rather than financial assets whose effect would be to subsidize capital accumulation abroad rather than at home.)

To be sure, OPEC governments are purchasing equity shares in foreign enterprises capable of playing key roles in their development programs. As a Saudi Arabian investment specialist explained to one American, "We're not interested simply in picking up shares at random in the stock market. We have to be allowed to participate as partners in your industry. This is of vital concern to us because this is where we consider our future lies." To some extent it makes sense for Middle Eastern countries to invest part of their oil surpluses in financing European firms and industries that seem prepared to play a major role in industrializing Third World countries. After an initial purchase of companies already located in the oil-exporting countries—such as Aramco, Kuwait Oil, and Venezuela's privately-owned oil companies—Kuwait purchased 14.6 per cent of Daimler-Benz and 14 per cent of Lonrho (the British mining, finance and industrial enterprise), Iran bought 25.01 per cent of the Krupp steel works (enough to give it veto power over all company decisions), and a group of Arab countries purchased 21 per cent of Richard Costain, Ltd., a British construction company. Iran sought to purchase Grumman in order to secure the flow of spare parts, but was turned down, as was Kuwait in the case of Lockheed. But in December 1976 Libya purchased 10 per cent of Fiat for $415 million. As the Middle East became a major new market for Japanese steel exports, and at a time when the Nippon Steel company was a leading member of a "consortium of Japanese, European and American companies currently negotiating with Saudi Arabia to build a steel mill there at a cost of about $1 billion," Kuwait purchased 1.1 per cent of Nippon Steel's shares and announced its interest in doubling its investment.[1]

Japan and most European countries have discussed imposing controls on international investment so as to maintain ownership in the hands of their own investors. Among Common Market countries only Italy has no regulations in this area. Thus, whatever gains might be offered to private-sector investors seeking to profit from sale of their companies to foreign owners, international technology transfer has become a function of government policy. Decisions are being made in terms of long-range national interest concerning the structure of production and exports, not on the basis of narrow profit motives as depicted by classical economic theory.

Participation by American companies in developing the OPEC economies has been retarded by U.S. Government opposition to OPEC ownership of more than a nominal 5 per cent share of American companies. This has precluded OPEC from participating in more than a token share of the profits made by these companies in their Middle Eastern and other Third World operations. Therefore, OPEC has been discouraged from giving contracts to these companies, being unable to share in their subsequent profits. America's repudiation of foreign investment inflows thus risks its being left out of the Third World's potential economic miracle, save to the extent that it can export arms to the Middle Eastern market.

Downstream investment in the oil industry—and its consequences for the industrial nations

Many Western observers were surprised to see OPEC invest in refineries, tanker fleets and other downstream petroleum facilities that apparently operated at or near losses throughout the world. But to the initiated, OPEC's investments proved how well they had learned from the oil companies and the extent to which they intended to replace the cartel.

The oil derivative business probably will remain concentrated in the hands of the most vertically linked companies and producer countries. Toward this end OPEC governments may desire to maintain the nominally low reported earnings on their downstream operations in order to foreclose new investors from entering the oil-products industry. (To be sure, a few oil companies that specialize in downstream operations have appeared in the picture, and tanker fleets enjoyed a temporary field day during the Arab oil embargo. But such companies have been constrained to move only in the niches and trenches left by the oil majors.) The Third World's desire to extend its raw-materials output into more finished lines thus gives it the flexibility in marketing strategy hitherto enjoyed only by the international minerals cartel.

On the one hand OPEC governments may cut the price of raw materials supplied to their own fabricating plants and other downstream operations, while supporting the price of their raw-materials exports. This would reduce the profit margin of competing plants located in the industrial nations, by holding their raw-materials costs high in the face of softening world demand (hence downward price pressure). The alternative is for Third World countries to cut their raw-materials prices to foreigners. This traditional response to softening world demand would reduce the raw-materials costs to fabricators in the more industrialized nations, increasing their profitability accordingly—and enabling them to maintain their monopoly over final industrial outlets for world raw materials.

Instead of growth in Third World economic output being focused at the raw-materials end of the economic spectrum and thrown onto world markets to depress raw-materials export prices, it will be consumed at home. Furthermore, cost disparities —and international dependency—between Third World and industrial nations may lessen as the raw-materials exporters diversify their economies, especially to increase their degree of agricultural self-sufficiency so as to avoid dependence on the food surpluses of the industrial nations. As they industrialize, and as they increase their economic self-sufficiency, they will become a growing market for their own raw materials. This will absorb the historical oversupply of minerals and plantation crops, increasing their world price accordingly. An ascending spiral of Third World capital accumulation and independence will supplant a descending spiral of resource depletion and dependency.

The prospect thus is opened for Third World countries to turn the tables on Western business practice. Instead of attempting to stabilize their export earnings by increasing their raw-materials exports (say, of iron ore) during recession conditions, they may export finished products in competition with steel fabricators and other manufacturers in the industrial nations. Instead of cutting their oil prices in recession periods they may cut the price of their plastics exports, much to the discomfiture of plastics manufacturers abroad. This threatens to aggravate the magnitude of business cycle swings in the industrial West.

The industrial nations will then face a choice as to how seriously to take their laissez faire rhetoric. If they maintain low tariffs and adhere to relatively free trade policies, they will suffer unemployment in industries that depend mainly on relatively high-cost domestic imported raw materials. (Because these industries purchase numerous inputs from other domestic firms, unemployment may spread down the line, in a kind of inversion of the Keynesian multiplier process.) Alternatively, the industrial nations may increase their tariffs and impose import quotas, claiming that their economies are being injured by low-priced industrial imports. This kind of tariff and quota confrontation may make the recent conflicts between U.S. trade officials and those of Europe and Japan look like child's play, may aggravate the break between the U.S. and Eastern Hemisphere economies —and set in motion pressures for closer integration between the U.S. and Latin American economies.

Geographic aspects of OPEC investment

In February 1974 the Shah of Iran suggested a new development fund to be "managed in close cooperation" with the World Bank and IMF, which "would receive annual contributions of from two to three billion dollars from oil-exporting countries and the major industrial countries." He was adamant that the industrial nations contribute to the fund inasmuch as they were benefiting from higher-priced agricultural exports to Third World countries just as OPEC governments were benefiting from higher world oil prices. Iran promised to buy over $1 billion worth of World Bank bonds and suggested that twelve major industrial nations join with the twelve OPEC governments to lend the World Bank $150 million each per year—for a total of $3 billion annually—at interest rates between 7 per cent and 8 per cent. The proposed fund "would be authorized to make balance-of-payments loans to developing countries unable to meet higher oil bills without either suspending other development projects or postponing payment on existing foreign debt." Thus, part of the loans made by the industrial nations would be recycled to them in payment of the past foreign-aid lending that had created so much dependency. OPEC nations would get a secure return on their investment guaranteed by the World Bank.

The Arab countries were not impressed by the Shah's proposal. Kuwait's Minister of Finance and Oil, Mr. Atiki, announced that his country, along with other Arab oil-exporting governments, would "make our contribution to the world, big or small, through our own institutions. Nobody looked at the Arabs before. Why does everybody expect us now to be the godfather? This part of the world has been neglected for centuries and its wealth has been carried away by foreigners without giving it a hand for development. The major part of our international financial aid will be put at the service of Arab countries, and to assist other Moslem countries, particularly in Africa"[2] to develop regional self-sufficiency.

In April the OPEC governments discussed a special fund to be created if and when seven of its members ratified its articles of agreement. Although the plan did not flower, during the year the Islamic Development Bank, the Islamic Solidarity Fund, and the Arab Bank for Economic Development in Africa were established. The Kuwait Fund increased its paid-in capital by $1 billion (to a total $1,350 million) and made direct loans to non-Arab countries in Africa and Asia. Other Arab aid-lending institutions include the Arab Bank for Investment and Foreign Trade, the Arab Fund for Economic and Social Development, the Arab Investment Company, the Arab Fund for Technical Assistance to Arab and African Countries, the Arab Petroleum Investment Company, the Inter-Arab Investment Guarantee Corporation and the Arab States Emergency Fund. The Special Arab Fund for

Africa started operations early in 1975, and Kuwait endorsed the Solidarity Fund proposed in August 1975 by the Lima Conference of Non-Aligned Countries (mainly to support commodity prices by financing stockpile agreements and enabling raw-materials exporters to cut back production in times of need).

Altogether, OPEC members committed some $15 billion to non-oil exporting Third World countries in 1974, followed by $11 billion in the first half of 1975. (As was the case with American foreign aid, much of this was military in nature, i.e., to support the "front-line" nations in the Arab conflict with Israel.) About half of the $4.6 billion paid out in "traditional" aid programs took the form of investment in bonds of the World Bank and its sister institutions (the African Development Bank, Asian Development Bank and the Inter-American Development Bank). But OPEC lending through these organizations was mainly of a stopgap nature, pending development of institutional structures more suited to Arab aims. "The Arab aid donors appear to regard development, and assistance for development, primarily in terms of projects which facilitate the transfer of management skills and technology, and contribute to structural change in the economics of developing countries, their own and others as well."[3] Outside of the Middle East, these development efforts focused mainly on Africa because of its abundant agricultural lands, and also because of its Moslem beliefs. Ivory Coast's finance minister Henry Konan Bedie remarked, "We intend to create not only a cultural area, but a monetary zone, which, unlike the sterling area, has not fallen apart. We are going to try to drain Arab petrodollars toward the underequipped African states." Over time the investment process promises to reach eastward toward the Moslem countries of Afghanistan, Pakistan, Indonesia, and even the Philippines.

France proposed to create a European equivalent of the U.S. Export-Import Bank to coordinate EEC exports, possibly drawing in part on Arab funds.[4] This bank would extend loans largely to increase agricultural capacity in Third World countries. Furthermore, suggested Giscard d'Estaing, "the emphasis that has been put on exportable agricultural products must not lead to neglecting the modernization of traditional food-crop production or the development of new crops necessary to improve nutrition,"[5] as had been the case with World Bank and U.S. bilateral aid. A fundamental difference in aid philosophy concerning the priority of agriculture thus split Europe and the Middle Eastern countries from the United States.

Europe's interest in the emerging countries in the Mediterranean triangle suggests a trilateral flow whereby OPEC capital is used to purchase European technology for application in neighboring Third World countries, beginning with those of North Africa. In December 1974 France's Foreign Minister Jean Sauvagnargues announced in Cairo that Saudi Arabia and other Arab governments had agreed to finance a series of French projects in Egypt, including construction of a Cairo subway system, a gas-burning power plant and a car and truck assembly plant to build Peugeot, Renault and Berliet automotives. (On the same day another French mission concluded an agreement with Iran to build a forty-mile subway system in Teheran, a color TV network, a Renault auto plant, liquefied-natural-gas tankers and a $120 million steel plant.) France's ambassador to the United States explained this emerging pattern of government-negotiated private investment and technology transfer. "I think a triangular agreement like the one between France, Iran and Senegal is well conceived and an effective form of aid to development: the [oil] producers invest capital in the non-industrialized countries and technology is sold to the latter by the industrial consumer."[6]

Companies in Germany, Britain, Switzerland and other European nations are playing a key role in an Arab plan to invest $6 billion over a five-year period to make Sudan the breadbasket of the Middle East. The Arab countries' annual grain deficit has been projected at 14 million tons by 1985, and Sudan by itself is expected to meet this target. This will provide self-sufficiency for the Arab world in foodstuffs as well as enabling Sudan to export tropical fruits and out-of-season vegetables to Europe, while maintaining its position as the world's major long-staple cotton exporter. Sudan's nearly one million square miles contain over 40 per cent of all the unused arable land in the Arab world. A recent soil survey indicates 185 million acres available in virgin soil located in "the rain-fed clay plains of central Sudan . . . flat, savannah country where mechanized farming already covers some three million acres. . . . But all the land at present under plough does not exceed 17 million acres, and that includes about four million acres under irrigation." Satellite photography may reveal further arable land of 100 million to 200 million acres in extent. "President Numeiri was therefore quick to take up the idea of 'triangle transactions' proposed by Bonn's Minister for Development Aid, according to which a European land contributes the know-how and an oil-producing country undertakes the financing of major development projects."

Saudi Arabia provided $200 million in November 1974 to establish the Sudanese Development Corporation, followed by establishment of a joint Saudi-Sudanese Authority for the Exploitation of the Red Sea Resources. The Kuwait-based Arab Fund for Economic and Social Development (AFESD) has outlined a $2 billion plan to develop Sudanese cereal, sugar and meat projects. The Kuwait Fund for Arab Economic Development (KFAED) is financing a major sugar scheme for which a British firm, Fletcher and Stewart, is building a refinery. Middle Eastern funds are also financing a $180 million project being carried out by another British firm, Lonrho Ltd., to develop the world's largest sugar project (including a powerhouse fueled by sugar-cane stalks).

The Arab Agricultural Development Organization (comprising Iraq, Syria and Jordan) plans to irrigate over one million acres of Sudan's Blue Nile province. Extension of cultivated lands is also being financed by the Kuwait and Abu Dhabi Development Banks. Other agricultural projects are being financed by the World Bank ($62 million), FAO ($40 million) and USAID ($11 million). The governments of Norway, Canada, Holland and other nations are also helping to finance development of Sudan's vast agricultural potential.

The result of such projects may be to create a twentieth-century equivalent of the Mississippi Valley development in the United States a century ago. In addition to the vast Gezira scheme lying to the south of Khartoum between the Blue and White Niles, the $170 million Rahad project is adding 30,000 irrigated acres by 1978, and the Gongoli plan will irrigate an even larger area. The White Nile scheme already has financed a canal from the main Gezira artery to irrigate 50,000 acres for cotton cultivation. The magnitude of these developments has enabled Sudan to become self-sufficient in rice and nearly so in sugar, sisal, vegetables and fruit. Wheat acreage has been quadrupled from 150,000 acres in 1972 to over 600,000 in 1975. Grain is supplanting sorghum to satisfy domestic consumption needs as export capacity is increased, and in the Gezira alone another 150,000 acres has been planted in wheat at the expense of cotton. Improved pesticides and herbicides may hold Gezira cotton output steady despite reduced cotton acreage.[7] By the 1980s Sudan will become by far the major supplier of sugar, grain and meat to the Arab world, as well as providing substantial amounts of rice, coffee, sisal, sesame and groundnuts. (It already produces nearly 90 per cent of the world's gum arabic.)

Most of these projects are concentrated in northern Sudan. Development of the rich lands in Sudan's South presupposes extension of a vast public health program, creation of an educational infrastructure, development of a massive transportation system, agricultural extension services and supporting economic structures. This type of development in turn presupposes massive state planning and coordination among the government, the domestic population, and private firms from the developed nations, as well as the Arab food customers who are putting up most of the financing. Government direction of international investment and aid flows therefore promises to become an endogenous organ of the Eastern Hemisphere economic system.

CHAPTER 17

The Future of War

The New International Economic Order introduces new constraints on the ability of America or any other industrial nation to engage in foreign wars. By moving to curtail international payments imbalance (especially war-induced payments deficits) it attacks the economic foundation of wars that might be waged by America, industrial Europe or Japan. For the sinews of war are money—domestic money supplied by taxation or government fiat, and international money raised through balance-of-payments surpluses on nonmilitary account or direct foreign loans. These options have been foreclosed by post-Vietnam developments in the world economy.

The changing international economics of war

From classical antiquity through the nineteenth century the world was often united by warfare. From the epoch of Cyrus and Alexander through the Roman Empire, the British Empire and Napoleon—followed by European colonization of Africa, Asia and Latin America—military conquest seemed to form the very foundation of geographic and economic integration.

Wars also secured foreign tributes, taxes and strategic positions. Germany won a $3 billion settlement from France in 1871 after the Franco-Prussian War, and after World War I the Allied Powers sought over $20 billion from Germany in addition to carving up its border territories and appropriating its colonies. But World War I also introduced a new element of decisive importance: the balance-of-payments costs of military conflict destroyed the international position of the belligerent powers— precisely the position that war itself was designed to strengthen. The First World War, fought basically among European powers, enmeshed all Europe in a tangle of Inter-Ally debts and reparations claims that resulted in loss of its world economic power to the United States. It also broke up the internationalism of the gold standard, fixed currency values, and *free* international payments. In short, it was more responsible than any other single factor for fracturing the world economy in the 1930s. World War II extended this process of economic destruction even further: not only did Europe's empires crumble forever, but Europe itself fell into the U.S. economic sphere by becoming indebted to its major world competitor.

Economic observers in the eighteenth and nineteenth century had argued vigorously that the attempt to create national empires had become wasteful, and that these empires did not profit the imperial power as a unit but only a narrow segment of its population (the aristocracy and munitions makers). It took somewhat longer to recognize that war itself had become economically self-defeating. Europe learned this lesson irrevocably by 1945. By the 1970s a general opposition had developed within the United States to further military involvement abroad. A sufficiently large proportion of the population had become antiwar as to render a repetition of the Vietnam experience politically and economically disastrous for any government in office. In fact, the costliness of war has become so burdensome as to convince even the most sanguine optimist of victory that military conquest is not worth the price. In today's world this price involves domestic poverty, political instability, and loss of world economic power. In fact, economic power itself rather than military strength now connotes political influence and prosperity. The traditional objective of war—seizure of foreign economic resources—has therefore become self-defeating. War involves loss of the belligerent nation's economic and diplomatic leverage in world affairs just as it stifles prosperity at home. Politically, it galvanizes foreign populations against the occupying power rather than securing adherence to its political sphere of influence.

Domestically, a nation's ability to wage war is a function of its ability to generate an economic surplus over and above civilian consumption and investment (plus nonmilitary government expenditures) in the form of munitions and related support of its armed forces. On the one hand, the vast growth of productive powers since the Industrial Revolution has enabled a given base of agricultural and industrial labor and capital to support a growing military establishment (or, alternatively, a postindustrial service society composed of other types of "unproductive" workers). On the other hand, the spread of full-employment policies prevents the building in of an arms-producing infrastructure that can be expanded or contracted at will, and makes increasingly difficult the diversion of domestic resources to military aims. Excess capacity no longer exists as it did in the Great Depression, when arms manufacturing seemed to spur economic activity. If the peacetime economy operates on a near-capacity level, the additional spending required by foreign military involvement spurs domestic inflation and creates shortages of civilian goods. Diversion of economic resources to war production threatens to aggravate inflationary pressures as governments refrain from taxing their populations and simply monetize their war spending.

War is most clearly self-defeating economically in its international consequences. Its foreign-exchange costs traditionally have involved foreign borrowing and ultimately currency depreciation. Since the Vietnam experience, the ability of one nation to borrow from others to finance its foreign wars has been drastically curtailed. In order to muster international resources, belligerent countries are driven to protectionist policies as a necessary complement to their domestic economic regimentation. Free trade, investment and finance, as well as domestic price stability, will thus become early casualties of war.

Wars no longer secure international wealth, they dissipate it. This wastefulness extends into the domestic economy as well. Wars impose domestic taxes, spur inflationary pressures that erode the value of accumulated wealth, and divert scarce productive capacity to economic overhead functions rather than more useful ends. Instead of extending the nation's diplomatic leverage in world affairs, foreign military involvement depletes its ability to grant foreign aid and trade concessions or to purchase foreign goods or resources of a nonmilitary nature. Belligerent nations become indebted not only to their arms suppliers but to foreign exporters who provide the civilian goods and services that they can no longer produce as a result of their arms production and support operations.

Before the 1960s America had enriched itself by staying out of Europe's wars. It evolved from a debtor to a creditor nation by selling arms to Europe prior to its entry into World War I. And it received most of Europe's "refugee gold" during the 1930s as the threat of renewed war led to a wholesale capital flight to the United States. After 1945, gold and balance-of-payments strength seemed a prime criterion of military capability, inasmuch as military activity absorbed international reserves like a cancer. The Cold War began to erode the U.S. balance of payments in Korea and finally broke the cosmopolitan dollar area in Vietnam. The American electorate became unwilling to sustain military involvement if this meant higher taxes, while the nation's foreign creditors withdrew their balance-of-payments support for the dollar and private investors began to fear that U.S. economic stability would crumble without taxation to finance the war on a pay-as-you-go basis.

The resulting international and domestic financial strains spurred economic rapprochement with Soviet Russia as almost the sole remaining path to achieve balance-of-payments inflows, through sale of food to Russia and a negotiated winding down of Cold War preparedness. In this respect the financial costs of war became an element working for peace.

Do these considerations mean that there will be no more war? Not necessarily. One must always hesitate to rule out war simply because it has become too costly to finance. Many believed that World War I could not last more than a few months because the Allied and Central powers would soon run out of funds (as well as physical resources). In one respect these observers were correct: the belligerent powers could not afford the war. But they carried on anyway, even at the cost of deranging and finally bankrupting their economies.

Nor can war be ruled out because it has become too awesome and terrible to contemplate. Looking back over history, practically every major new means of destruction has been viewed as a weapon to end wars. Robert Fulton's naval torpedo, the tank, the airplane and the atomic bomb all seemed to their early promotors to be means of ensuring peace by making warfare too terrible to make fighting worthwhile. But they only escalated the destructiveness of combat.

On the other hand, few people still believe the pseudo-Keynesian fallacy that war—or at least, war spending—is inevitable whenever unemployment rears its head. War spending was long represented as a means of supporting employment in the arms industries and their associated supplier industries. By supporting employment war thus seemed to support domestic living standards (much as did exports, which were also "lost" to the nation in terms of their direct use value which accrued to foreigners rather than to domestic residents). This argument can no longer be made in the wake of America's Vietnam experience. Hence, today's economic depression does not hold the threat of foreign military involvement that it might have implied a decade ago. Even for a civilian sector operating in near-recession conditions, further arms buildup would clearly erode living standards, not support them as implied by Keynesian "multiplier theory," which fails to draw any distinction whatsoever between productive versus unproductive labor, or wealth creation versus overhead.

The result is that only countries with massive balance-of-payments resources and large-scale unallocated domestic labor, capital and land resources can afford to be aggressors in modern-day wars. The economies of Europe, Japan and America have become too delicately balanced to sustain the cost of war without coming rapidly into conflict with domestic political pressures for higher living standards and increased business capital formation, and hence economic demilitarization. Ironically, only countries not fully industrialized can now afford to undertake conventional wars of aggression and occupation. Only authoritarian Third World governments enjoying massive balance-of-payments surpluses from exporting their raw materials are capable of aggressive military threats under today's economic conditions.

The changing economic technology of war

A critical development in the last decade has been the degree to which the costs of offense and military occupation have come to exceed the cost of defense in conventional (that is, nonatomic) war. It costs $10 million to build a modern fighter aircraft but as little as $10 thousand to shoot it down. This means that Soviet Russia may provide, say, African rebels with $20 million in defensive arms, whereas the United States would have to spend as much as $2 billion to attack these forces on their own ground.

Furthermore, what might have been low-intensity wars of short duration a century ago now drag out into longer-term wars that sap the strength of any aggressor nation. The technology of war now favors the guerrilla, not the heavily armed invader. Dollar for dollar, defensive antitank weaponry has far surpassed the efficiency of offensive armored divisions. Small, easily portable antiaircraft missiles inflict unsustainable costs on any power seeking to commit major air support to a military campaign. On the seas, a small submarine force can deny access to a much more expensive naval force. To be sure, conventional military strategy has evolved through the use of tanks and helicopters into highly mobile tactics in which speed of movement and psychological initiative play a major role. Third World countries hardly can match this speed or mobility. Their strategic response may be that of Mao and Ho Chi Minh, to swim like a fish in water, to simply dissolve into the general population when attacked by superior firepower, while imposing costs on the invader so high that the latter's domestic prosperity and economic growth must be sacrificed and warped to support a stalemated war effort. The lesson taught by Vietnam is that the populations of America and other industrial nations will no longer endorse conflicts and sacrifices of the Vietnam type or those which sapped the powers of France and Portugal in their ex-colonies. For this reason Europe made an accommodation that the United States made only belatedly and seems to be continually reexamining: Europe has decided to pay the price demanded by Third World countries, i.e., to pay more for its raw materials and to earn less on its direct investments in Third World countries. The alternative to this new state of affairs is a series of export embargoes in critical raw materials, embargoes that could be broken only by military invasion and occupation far beyond Europe's, or America's, means to sustain.

In short, conventional war has become too expensive for any democracy to fight without imposing the most far-reaching economic controls and centralizing all economic decision-making in the executive branch of government. If would-be laissez faire economies engage in war, it must be only that kind of war which does not entail massive balance-of-payments costs. The only type of war that meets this criterion is atomic war. But this too would terminate any democracy. Thus, the balance of terror seems to rule out atomic war while balance-of-payments instability (hence general economic controls) rules out conventional war. (Table 17.1.)

TABLE 17.1

The New Economic Characteristics of War

1. Wars no longer secure international wealth, they dissipate it.
2. The costs of offense far overshadow the costs of defense, at least in conventional nonatomic war.
3. Conventional wars are now fought by the entire populations of countries, not merely by a single layer of professional soldiers. Thus, the aggressor-occupier must face an entire mass of people, and cannot tell combatant from noncombatant, friend from foe.
4. The immense costs of offensive conventional warfare involve centralized economic control and regulation throughout the economy.
5. By forcing economic regimentation at home, wars force protectionism in international trade and investment, as well as rigid controls over international finance and foreign aid. This isolates aggressor nations within the world economy and tends to break up the world economic unit rather than to integrate it as was the case in classical wars.
6. Fighting a conventional war on foreign territory involves immense balance-of-payments costs that strip aggressor nations of their international position. They fall into foreign debt, suffer capital flight and lose their competitive position in world markets by diverting their labor and capital from productive industrial uses to military functions.
7. The electorate in democratic nations has become antiwar. Populations now realize that a choice must be made between guns and butter, and choose the latter.
8. Atomic war between superpowers (i.e., the United States and the Soviet Union) threatens total destruction of both. This has led to a policy of détente. However, this process has opened the path for war among minor powers, especially Third World countries with sufficient balance-of-payments resources to purchase foreign arms.
9. The arms trade has begun to stabilize international payments in the industrial nations, as Third World countries take partial payment for raw materials in arms. To date, the United States has been the major beneficiary of this trend.
10. Arms exports have become a major means of spreading research and development costs over a larger production volume.
11. Arms companies must also rely on domestic and foreign civilian demand for aircraft and automotives. Hence, spreading international self-reliance in aircraft, tanks and automotives will make domestic development of conventional weaponry even more expensive for the United States as its traditional share of the world arms market and associated civilian industries shrinks.
12. A tradeoff exists between military spending on superweapons and conventional arms. To the extent that a nation devotes its arms budget to conventional weaponry, it must cut back its development of atomic and outer-space weapons, particle bombs, laser weapons and other high-technology arms.

Meanwhile, Third World countries have construed U.S. disin-volvement in Southeast Asia and subsequent U.S.-Soviet détente as opening the way for their own localized wars, such as that between Turkey and Greece, and the simmering conflicts in the Middle East and Africa. Today's assurances that the United States and Soviet Russia will not go to war with one another, and that the industrial nations will not intervene directly in Third World conflicts, have released military pressures hitherto con-strained. War may have been rendered economically obsolete on the part of the industrial nations, but it is just becoming economi-cally feasible (on however temporary a basis) among selected Third World countries.

Europe's decision to integrate itself more peacefully with the economies of Africa, the Near East and Asia, and its refusal to support American adventurism in the Middle East after 1973, has completed the process that began with the dismantling of Europe's empires in 1945: its former colonialism (as well as that of Japan) based on military force has been superseded by peace-ful economic accommodation and commercial bonds based on mutual self-interest, almost irrespective of the political systems involved. Only the United States remains a military question mark. (It essentially will confine its area of operations to its own Western Hemisphere.)

Implications for Soviet-American strategies

Soviet Russia is often thought of as a military machine with an economy attached. Although its overall level of economic output is lower than that of the United States, its per capita living stan-dards and social overhead spending is so much lower that the balance available for military purposes exceeds that available to the U.S. economy. In democracies, populations have shown themselves reluctant to support a war effort at the cost of their own prosperity and living standards. Soviet Russia does not face this problem. Its research and development has therefore been channeled much more into military applications than commercial ones.

The United States, by contrast, is a democratically organized economy with a military machine attached. Its military budget may be divided into two parts: defense of its national borders (against intercontinental atomic attack from Soviet Russia), comprising mainly atomic and outer-space weaponry; and preparation for military involvement abroad, comprising mainly conventional weapons (tanks, aircraft, submarines, etc.). Given a relatively fixed share of military spending within the overall federal budget, a tradeoff exists between conventional and atomic weaponry. To the extent that America can wind down its overseas conventional war involvement within NATO, SEATO and CENTO, it can afford to devote more funds to matching Soviet Russia in the area of superweaponry, missile technology and outer space programs. Conversely, if America involves itself more in conventional wars to maintain its "global presence," it will secure its Free World allies only at the cost of weakening its own position vis-à-vis the Soviet Union. For instance, its war in Southeast Asia to support the Thieu and Lon Nol regimes in Vietnam and Cambodia was a major factor in diverting its military resources from matching Soviet Russia's gains in submarine and naval capacity, outer space technology and lasar weaponry, and its rumored progress toward linear accelerator weapons and particle bombs. Democracies must depend on congresses to allocate funds to governments, and in today's world these democracies tend to vote for higher living standards rather than foreign military involvement. Only as long as the American people believed that the economy could produce both guns and butter, only as long as U.S. living standards were increasing, did the population support Congress in its allocation of funds for war in Southeast Asia. But once it was obliged to choose between guns and butter it chose the latter and rejected war.

Meanwhile, the new economics of offense and defense have provided Soviet Russia with an opportunity to subsidize relatively inexpensive wars of national liberation. If the United States obligingly falls into the trap of repeating its Vietnam experience of supporting unpopular dictatorships by force—turning Third World populations against itself in the process—then it will be forced to divert resources from research and development of more sophisticated "exotic" superweaponry to defend the nation against possible attack from Soviet Russia. The latter's relative advantage in being able to finance new research into intercontinental and outer-space weaponry (being unburdened with the obligation to support foreign conventional wars of occupation) will be greatly enlarged.

Unlike the United States, the Soviet Union has not involved itself around the globe. Its ongoing expenditures for conventional warfare are therefore minimal. Also, it may devote its resources to special types of defensive weaponry such as compact portable antimissile, antiaircraft and antitank arms to support foreign populations in wars of "national liberation" requiring only minimal Soviet commitment. Russia's strategy is to bleed the United States in conventional wars by tying it down in Africa, Latin America or Asia in the same way as occurred in Vietnam. (In principle, America might turn the tables by bogging down the Soviet Union in foreign military involvement, but to date Russia has not responded at all in this direction.) Soviet Russia will therefore be able to wage war "on the cheap" by providing defensive antitank and antiaircraft weaponry to insurgent populations, conserving the bulk of its own defense budget for application to new space technology and related superweaponry.

To the extent that U.S. world strategists recognize this scenario and its most probable outcome, the nation need not again fall into the trap of maintaining a foreign military presence. It can disengage itself from involvement, beginning in West Germany and Korea, and it can rule out Africa and Asia altogether as spheres of vital interests. However vital foreign countries may seem, if the price of supporting pro-U.S. regimes is depletion of American economic power in the world, military involvement is simply not worth the price.

One option is for the United States to induce other nations to bear the military expenses of NATO, SEATO and CENTO. A number of senators have expressed the hope that Japan may conceivably take over the thankless task of defending the Park dictatorship in South Korea, and that Germany may pick up a growing share of NATO expenditures. But these are not likely developments in view of Japan's legacy of colonial rule over Korea, and the desire by both Japan and Germany to give commercial strength precedence over military power. American disinvolvement in Third World areas, and in the Eastern Hemisphere generally, therefore connotes a lower absolute level of Western military involvement. In particular, repressive regimes will not be able to call upon the United States at will to support their power by overt or covert means as in the past. The path will thus be opened up for foreign economic, political and social change that has been stifled for three decades.

In 1975 the Democratic Congress prevented the Kissinger administration from dragging the country into war over Angola, and President Carter has made it clear that he will not militarily support South Africa, Rhodesia, or other dictatorships. However, other industrial nations may well seek to supply arms to Third World countries on a cash basis, for such support would strengthen their own economic and balance-of-payments positions rather than deplete their resources.

The world arms trade and international payments equilibrium

Since the Middle East war the arms trade has become a vital element in balancing international payments. OPEC has spent a large portion of its increased export earnings on foreign arms, especially U.S. arms. Iran has entered into oil-for-arms barter agreements, and Saudi Arabia has discussed similar deals. This militarization of the balance of payments is yet another factor leading to increased government intervention in world trade and payments. It certainly is not subject to profit maximization or other criteria supposed to equilibrate international trade under classical adjustment mechanisms. On the other hand, America is hoping that arms exports can take the place of food exports at the major growth area in the U.S. trade balance. Iran seems dependent on scheduled purchases of U.S. arms and replacement parts for many years to come.

America's interest in maximizing arms sales to OPEC seems to conflict with its interest in minimizing oil-import prices. For instance, although many Americans rejoiced in December 1976 when Saudi Arabia and the United Arab Emirates refused to go along with Iran's demand for a dramatic increase in oil prices, it soon became apparent that an immediate effect of the OAPEC move was to reduce Iran's ability to purchase arms from the United States, or even to pay for military programs already underway. Sheik Yamani stressed that the Arabs had not held down oil prices and increased their oil output merely to be altruistic servants of U.S. interests; they hoped to encourage the incoming

Carter administration to reduce U.S. support for Israel. More important to the United States was the dampening effect on Iran's dreams of a modern-day empire: holding down world oil prices forced Iran to cut back construction of its planned air and naval base in Chahbahar on the Gulf of Oman, as well as to reduce its projected arms imports.[1]

Moderation in oil prices thus had an ambiguous impact on the U.S. trade balance: what the nation "saved" on oil imports it stood to lose on arms exports, unless it extended credit to oil-rich Iran. This would be an ironic development, to say the least: America would face the prospect of borrowing from Arab monetary agencies to extend arms credit to Iran as well as to Israel.

Irony aside, the main problem from the U.S. vantage point is that arms trade is probably too sensitive and tenuous to form a dependable foundation for a trade surplus. Nonetheless, the United States is seeking to accomplish just that. The most obvious threat comes from new entrants into the world arms market, beginning with those nations that can afford to develop their own domestic arms industries. This massive undertaking involves far more than direct government orders and subsidies. Extensive civilian linkages also are required, even for an economy as vast as that of the United States.

Military aircraft represents the foundation of modern-day arms. The volume of production required to manufacture aircraft economically is so massive as to require a parallel development of civilian aircraft production for domestic airlines plus as wide a foreign demand as possible. Both domestic and foreign civilian sales are a function of route schedules. For years, airline timetables in the United States have been more suited to aircraft manufacturers than to the airlines. The result has been a frequent overserving of cities (especially in outlying regions) by air flights with only fractional loads which are unprofitable. As world recession spread and air travel declined, air routes were cut back and airline schedules consolidated. This cast a pall over future civilian aircraft orders, and hence jeopardized the financial health of some of America's key arms companies.

Even more threatening are developments in international air transport as America faces the loss of its traditional dominance of world air routes. Britain and Japan have led the protest within the International Air Transport Association to renegotiate air routes in keeping with today's altered world circumstances. Britain has given notice that it will terminate the basic 1946 air route agreement signed with the United States unless these routes are renegotiated by June 1977. This threat has led the American government to ask U.S. airlines serving Britain for contingency plans in the event that passenger and freight services to Britain are terminated in summer 1977. Plans have been drawn up for U.S. airlines to shift their flights to Paris, Amsterdam, and even to Luxembourg.

U.S. officials argue that in view of the fact that two-thirds of the travelers between the United States and Britain are Americans, two-thirds of the air traffic "rightfully" belongs to U.S.-flag carriers. However, this line of reasoning has impaired American negotiations with Japan, which presents just the opposite traffic situation. In 1970, as the American economy fell into recession and Japan began to spend as many dollars as it could, "U.S. traffic to Japan went into a decline, while the number of Japanese citizens traveling to U.S. cities began rising sharply. Today the balance is two to one in favor of Japan. At the same time, because of restricted access to U.S. destination points, Japan Air Lines has not been able to increase its capacity to serve the growing number of its citizens who want to visit the United States. In the case of air cargo, the balance is even more heavily weighted on the side of the U.S.-flag carriers" as their air routes and schedules are out of all proportion to the nationality of freight and passengers being moved. Japan has therefore insisted on "equal opportunity" to compete with U.S. airlines in serving interior U.S. cities. "As routes now stand, U.S. airline single-plane service is available to Japan from 19 points in the United States and U.S. territories. Japan Air Lines is permitted to serve only seven U.S. points. Japan is expected to press for traffic rights to such important cities as Washington, Chicago, Seattle, Minneapolis and Portland." Japan also is insisting on "beyond rights," that is, rights to continue flights beyond their initial point of landing. Japanese officials point out that "U.S. carriers can fly to Japan and beyond to any point in the world without limitation. Japan Air Lines, at the same time, is limited by the United States in flying beyond to South American points via San Francisco and Los Angeles."[2] In an attempt to rectify this situation, Japan and Britain have coordinated their negotiations with the United States, so that the latter will probably have to yield some of its market share to either or both parties. It is difficult to see where U.S. flights to the Far East can go but through Tokyo, which is generally considered to be the equivalent of London, Paris and Rome put together so far as regional air traffic is concerned.

Most serious of all to American domination of the world aircraft market is the recent development of the British-French Concorde supersonic transport (SST). This threat explains America's refusal to let the SST land in the United States, save for minimal flights to Washington and Houston. Without major overseas flights the Concorde cannot operate on a commercial basis. This has opened the door for America's traditional stick-and-carrot strategy: it will ban most SST flights on grounds of excessive noise levels, thereby thwarting Europe's efforts to consolidate its technological lead over the United States in high-speed commercial aircraft, unless Europe lets the United States buy into the Concorde for a pro rata sum based on its research and development costs. America would then commission its own aircraft companies to build a U.S. version of the SST for sale to domestic airlines (whose demand for the plane would be supported by U.S. diplomatic pressure within IATA for extended U.S. international air routes). Commercial aircraft construction would provide the foundation for continued military production and exportation.

U.S. support of its merchant marine has similar national defense ramifications, quite above consideration of the International Longshoremen's Association's demands to hire more labor for naval construction. In some years 67 cents out of every dollar earned by U.S.-flag carriers came from government subsidy payments. The U.S. Government has spent over $5 billion since 1950 on cargo-preference subsidies (for foreign-aid shipments among others), while U.S. shipyards have enjoyed subsidies of up to 37 per cent on tanker construction. Annual government subsidies to American-flag shipping, which employs about 18,000 workers, have risen to some $14,000 per man, for a total of $250 million annually.[3] The American concept of national security thus seems to be a limitless umbrella. In both aircraft and ship construction, maintenance of America's arms-export trends requires major government intervention into the domestic air travel and shipping industries. In fact, competition in the world's most rapidly growing export markets seems likely to spur government subsidy programs in country after country—all the more so in view of the rising number of state-controlled corporations among the *Fortune* 500 largest firms of the world.

American protectionism has been strongest in the area of arms itself. In 1974 the United States and Germany had agreed on competitive trials of a new American tank against the German Leopard II, with the winner to be selected as the main battle tank for both countries in their NATO forces, which expected to pay about $10 billion for some 10,000 tanks to be purchased in the 1980s. By mid-1976, however, the United States had made it clear that even if the Leopard II should prove superior the United States would not feel obliged to adopt it. General Motors and Chrysler, suffering from the general recession in auto sales, each submitted models of their own to the U.S. Government. An earlier Congressional outcry had been triggered when the United States spent a relatively modest $30 million for Belgian machine guns at the cost of those manufactured in Maine. Matters now threatened to heat up.

Germany warned that unless the United States agreed to minimal tank standardization it would not buy the Boeing 707 air-warning and control system for the German contingent in NATO. In March, Britain refused to wait any longer: it moved to create its own Hawker-Siddeley Nimrod airborne radar defense system (using Marconi-Eliot computers instead of IBM machines). British officials acknowledged that giving the contract to its own domestic suppliers would involve higher costs, but pointed out that these costs would save over 5,000 British jobs, as well as help support the nation's troubled balance of payments. U.S. officials denounced the move, claiming that "it diminishes the whole concept of standardization," at least standardization along U.S. lines.[4] But the United States had already dashed hopes for meaningful international standardization by refusing to seriously consider adoption of European arms for its overseas military alliances.

NATO countries were balking at purchasing more American weapons, in particular F–16 fighter aircraft. The Lockheed bribery scandals in Japan and Holland also were threatening U.S. arms sales, and gave foreign lobbyists an excuse to tie up prospective purchases of U.S. arms in lengthy hearings. A case in point occurred in Switzerland, which had contracted for 72 Northrop Tiger F–5E aircraft for $500 million in April 1975. The key to the deal was a reciprocal U.S. promise to buy Swiss-made goods so that Switzerland could recoup at least $150 million over an eight-year period. In May, however, the United States awarded General Electric a $12 million order for electric motor pumps for the Clinch River nuclear project in Tennessee even though a bid submitted by Switzerland's Brown Boveri was $1 million lower. U.S. officials explained that under the "Buy American" policy foreign bids had to be at least 12 per cent lower than U.S. bids to qualify for consideration, so that Brown Boveri apparently lost out because of a sum less than $35,000. The U.S. decision made it highly questionable that any way could be found to place export orders in Switzerland, particularly in view of the upward pressures being exerted on the Swiss franc in the wake of world currency instability. A meeting was scheduled for June to discuss this problem, but the Swiss Parliament was inclined to withdraw the aircraft order unless some intergovernmental offset or barter deal could be worked out.[5]

The world economic recession altered the pattern of arms demand for the same reason that it was triggering a general move toward commercial protectionism: it became part of a make-work program to serve as an alternative to unemployment insurance and related welfare costs. If, as seemed likely, a foreign invasion of Europe would last forty-eight hours at most, then serious defense seemed almost futile. It would render NATO a charade at best—and if this were so, then why not give the arms business to home industry rather than subsidizing U.S. firms?

U.S. arms exports also were coming under fire in the Far East. American arms manufacturers were pressing Washington to sell their wares to China before the Chinese became dependent upon Western European arms. Such sales had been embargoed by the Coordinating Committee for Exports to Communist Areas (COCOM). A Japanese daily newspaper reported with some dismay that the United States was planning to term sophisticated electronic equipment, airborne early-warning aircraft, antisubmarine patrol gear, sonobuoys, phonometers and sea-bottom oil-deposit detection devices "exceptions" to the COCOM regulations.[6] This would tend to preempt Japan or South Korea from securing a foothold in the Chinese market.

In 1950 America's allies willingly committed forces armed with U.S. weaponry to United Nations operations in Korea. A decade later they agreed to supply at least token forces in Vietnam, again using American weaponry for the most part. However, after the United States insisted on monopolizing the world arms trade foreign countries began to lose interest in supporting America's world military posture. America's own military operations used arms employing American labor, carrying the research and development charges for American firms, and thus consolidating the nation's learning curve in military innovation. Now foreign countries sought to develop a similar arms-making capacity.

Prior to détente, Europe and other foreign countries had felt obliged to purchase U.S. weaponry in exchange for America bearing the cost of the nuclear deterrent. But now America seemed less likely to risk atomic confrontation with the Soviet Union over Europe, Asia or Africa. Foreign countries began to feel that they were giving too many quid for too little quo. The military balance between Europe and Soviet Russia has tilted so far in the latter's favor (without guarantee of American nuclear support) that there seems relatively little point in Europe deploying more than token forces to defend against a potential Soviet invasion that would take but a week at the longest.

Foreign countries are therefore concentrating on civilian economic development. Where creation of a domestic arms-making capacity is a national objective it takes the form of concentrating on civilian aviation and other civilian sectors with military potential as a byproduct, such as the SST aircraft, atomic reactors and hydrofoil ships. Establishment of underlying economic strength is thus viewed as taking priority over military power. To date the United States has taken a somewhat different position. When OPEC increased its oil prices, American strategists calculated that the Middle East's "absorption capacity" for civilian capital goods and consumer products was limited by the historical trends of past decades. It seemed that OPEC's balance-of-payments surpluses would have to be either invested in the West or spent on military goods. Except for a moderate flow of French and British arms, Europe was less able than America to satisfy OPEC's immediate military demand. For this very reason Europe was led to concentrate on exporting more productive, growth-oriented technology. And Japan, whose arms industry was least developed among that of all the major industrial nations, concentrated on providing entire factory complexes to OPEC.

By emphasizing arms exports America reaped the greatest initial gains in this rather concentrated area. The process seemed to be self-regenerating: the more arms U.S. firms could sell any one Middle East nation, such as Iran, the greater would be the need for corresponding arms purchases on the part of Iran's neighboring Arab oil-exporting countries. This process of arms escalation logically would culminate either in war—hence an even greater need for American arms—or in a never-ending, insatiable demand for ever newer weaponry and marginally improved models. Meanwhile, American technology was being focused on what was ultimately an economically unproductive and derivative area, that of military overhead. In today's world, offensive weaponry is rendered obsolete almost as rapidly as it is deployed. Foreign countries may counter this weaponry with increasing "cost effectiveness" by concentrating on defense or by securing military defense commitments from other nations, including the Soviet Union.

Even America's concentration on military products has not given it an unsurmountable lead in military and military-related civilian sectors. Despite the nation's dominance of the world market for fighter planes, its aircraft industry has fallen behind that of Europe since the latter has begun to produce the SST. In Latin America, Brazil is developing its own production capacity to compete with American exports of smaller commercial aircraft. U.S. firms dominate the world helicopter market but foreigners dominate that for hydrofoils. Americans retain a tenuous hold on the world tank market, but Japan and Germany lead in other automotives. Even in the field of atomic energy America faces sharp export challenges from Canada, France and Germany in peaceful applications such as nuclear reactors and refining plants. America's balance-of-payments security has thus become shaky as it concentrates on arms. Its export strategy is based on the expectation that foreign countries will continue indefinitely to devote their economic surpluses to military overhead rather than to more productive uses.

America's arms protectionism in aircraft, tanks and other weaponry, its insistence that its allies adopt U.S. arms at immense balance-of-payments costs to themselves, and its attempt to appropriate foreign arms markets and thereby to create an ongoing market for replacement parts and new weapon models suggest that it plans to balance its international payments by importing foreign industrial products and minerals while exporting relatively unproductive products—arms—that represent economic overhead to foreign nations. America is holding on to its export markets in the Middle East but may be losing its markets for civilian goods. This suggests that as foreign economies become more productive of capital goods, of consumer goods such as cars, TV sets and other electronics, and of basic materials such as stainless steel (as well as oil and other raw materials on which the United States already is dependent), American economic growth and prosperity, if it comes, will increase the nation's import dependency. Meanwhile, if the United States commits itself to agricultural goods and arms exports as its major prospective areas of export growth and trade surplus, its success will depend on foreign reluctance to become independent in domestic food and arms production. One or the other, or both, of these export categories must therefore yield over time. Long-term foreign dependence on American grain is logically a function of expected peace, whereas their arms purchases are a function of the threat of war.

To the extent that foreign countries resolve their differences and thereby minimize their prospective need for arms, or to the extent that they create an arms-making capacity of their own, the American arms market will shrink. If foreign countries seek to avoid warping their economies in a military direction such as occurred in the United States in the 1960s, American dependence on the rest of the world for nonmilitary products will be established despite all its arms-brandishing might. The nation would then find itself tilting alone at the Soviet windmill. For without the Soviet Union obligingly serving U.S. ends by threatening Europe and Asia, foreign countries will find today's level of defense spending too high and too unproductive a luxury to be tolerated by any but the most authoritarian and militaristic regimes.

To be sure, the Soviet Union may find its interest in keeping pressure on its own client regimes to purchase Soviet arms. But to the extent that these countries concentrate on relatively inexpensive defensive arms rather than offensive weaponry, to the extent that they buy antiaircraft missiles rather than aircraft, and antitank weaponry rather than tanks themselves, they may free resources for nonmilitary purposes. This would enable them to build up an economic advantage over client states in the American sphere, the fruits of whose economic growth may be channelled into the purchase of economically unproductive arms from the United States.

On the other hand, if foreign industrial nations and Third World countries begin to phase out their arms spending as being inherently wasteful, the degree to which America's economic base has become uneconomic and waste-oriented will become so great a burden as to lose the nation precisely that world power which it inherited from Europe over a half-century ago by staying out of Europe's wars. Foreign countries may now stay out of America's wars, and also out of America's sphere of arms trade. This would oblige the United States to redirect its own domestic economy to more productive, civilian ends. In this prospect lies the main danger to America's hope to base its international economic power on military exports, if not on military actions themselves. Direct military involvement abroad (with the possible exception of Latin America) is no longer a feasible policy for a full-employment industrial economy with democratic political forms such as the United States. The time may soon arrive at which concentration on arms exports is also no longer feasible as a long-term economic strategy.

CHAPTER 18

Some Implications of the New International Economic Order

> The era of cheap oil is finished . . . the era of exploitation is finished. . . . Because of the exploitation of cheap oil you had an affluent society, and then the permissive society when almost everything was free—and an abuse of liberty.
>
> —The Shah of Iran, March 7, 1974

Until fairly recently in world history the combination of gold, private investment and military power enabled industrial lead nations to dominate the world economy—as long as less developed countries pursued relatively laissez faire policies and could not or did not assert their own economic interests. This one-sided world economy no longer exists. Statism and intergovernmental planning have spread to all nations. No longer can any one set of countries manipulate the international market at will. The most important buttresses of world power in the past have crumbled. Balance-of-payments surpluses no longer connote a transfer of gold or direct ownership and control of world production by creditor nations. International investment no longer ensures high profitability now that the gains from world trade are being appropriated by host-country governments. Nor does it even ensure control over foreign trade patterns. Finally, military force itself has become a self-defeating option. The historical system of international dependency and coercion is therefore dissolving.

The principles, institutions and objectives of today's diplomacy thus have been radically transformed from those of only a

236

quarter-century ago. At that time gold represented the foundation of international power and domestic prosperity. It formed the basis of domestic money and credit, and it enabled nations to invest abroad. Without gold they were obliged to balance their international payments by succumbing to the IMF-World Bank philosophy of laissez faire/stagnation, which included an insistence that they balance their international payments by selling their resources to foreigners. This is no longer the case. For one thing, balance-of-payments surpluses and deficits are no longer settled in gold bullion, much less used to support (or contract) the domestic credit supply. The link between gold, international payments and domestic money has been severed, at least for the time being. Payments balances are settled in U.S. Treasury securities whose value depreciates steadily in the face of the U.S. and world inflation, and whose prospect of repayment (even in the form of depreciated dollars) dwindles as the debt grows. Countries are seeking to live beyond their means by borrowing as much as possible before they repudiate their debts. Central banks thus have supplanted multinational firms as the major institutions through which international economic surpluses are channeled. Trade-surplus countries are receiving only IOUs, not gold. In this situation economies aim to run trade deficits, to import more than they export. This is the consequence of the world economy changing from creditor-oriented to debtor-oriented rules, from the gold standard to the Treasury-bill standard.

In 1945, in a situation characterized by substantial surplus productive capacity, rising exports meant rising incomes and living standards. The main concern was insufficient demand rather than insufficient productive powers, and exports represented an added source of demand to support full employment. Today, as American consumption presses against the economy's productive limits (even in the near-recession conditions of early 1977) in most sectors save arms and agriculture, higher exports connote a siphoning off of scarce output, much as when American grain was sold to the Soviet Union in 1972–73. Net exports are now perceived to support foreign rather than domestic living standards, and to hold down foreign price levels while causing inflationary shortages at home. Export embargoes have therefore taken their place alongside import quotas. This is just the opposite situation from the beggar-my-neighbor export promotions of the 1930s. Today's counterpart to the export competition that existed under the gold standard is to seek as large a volume of net imports as possible, in exchange for vague promises to pay at some future date, preferably in dollars whose value has been substantially eroded by inflation and devaluation.

Instead of world raw-materials prices being set at their low-cost margin of production—what it costs impoverished Third World economies to produce them—they are being set at the high-cost margin—what it costs the industrial nations to produce them or substitutes for them. Instead of these gains from higher-priced Third World raw materials accruing to foreign-owned firms, they are being taken by their own governments. The industrial nations are no longer appropriating the fruits of world economic growth as they have done for the past three centuries. Foreign ownership is becoming divorced from foreign control. This has dried up both the motive and the means for continued overseas invest-ment. A reverse tendency has emerged: governments in the in-dustrial nations are moving to keep their capital at home (partly to develop domestic substitutes for energy and other commodi-ties they previously imported at relatively low prices), while Third World countries are becoming exporters of financial capi-tal. In this new world, industrial nations are no longer competing to invest in Third World countries but to obtain funds from OPEC. However, they are strictly limiting the forms that this prospective capital inflow from OPEC can take. America has drawn up a set of regulations prohibiting OPEC from buying major shares of its industry, so as to discourage its members from buying any other U.S. asset than Treasury bills. But there is a limit to this process. When OPEC stopped accumulating sterling balances in 1975–76, Britain was obliged to devalue the pound and to phase out sterling as a key currency. The foreign funds over which it exerted control simply dried up. This posed the prospect that other countries, including the United States, might find their currencies declining in international value unless they met the terms of payments-surplus governments (or unless their military threats or covert operations enabled them to avoid doing so).

In the past, military power was used to open up foreign export markets and private-sector investment outlets. But today nations are seeking to secure imports and to borrow from foreign central banks. War is no longer a viable means of supporting these objectives. Given its immense costs to the aggressor, the degree to which today's world interdependence renders any belligerent power highly prone to economic retaliation, and most important of all, the fact that the structure of world economic development for the immediate future is already established, what is the point of war? It is too late to prevent host countries from asserting control over their domestic resources. If war is an extension of economic diplomacy, it has become pointless and self-defeating. The world's raw-materials areas can no longer be divided and conquered by playing one off against the other. (If anything, the industrial nations are being played off against one another by their former colonies and spheres of influence.) If one oil-exporter is invaded, the rest will impose embargoes on the invader (while the threat by nations being invaded to blow up their wells and pipelines is certain to gain the diplomatic and even military support of their customers, especially Europe and Japan).

Economics textbooks may continue to depict obsolete market-oriented principles of international trade and investment, but the mechanisms portrayed belong to a past era. As businessmen yield to diplomats, and multinational firms yield to an array of competing governments establishing world prices and trade patterns among themselves, economists are being replaced by political scientists. If the relevance of economics is to be restored it must once again become political economy, and must look to deliberate government planning to achieve the ideals of world equality that "free" international markets never satisfied.

The end of laissez faire—and some ironies

Two centuries ago, when England's government was still dominated by a landed aristocracy which was often hostile to urban industry and democratic political forms, and which sought to protect its entrenched interests and revenues through the state apparatus, Britain's nascent commercial capitalism sought to dismantle state power itself. England's protectionist Corn Laws and colonial Navigation Acts had accomplished their purpose of enabling England to overtake its continental rivals. Urban industrialists, and many workers, urged a policy of free trade to supplant the centralized mercantilism whose gains accrued mainly to the non-industrial aristocracy. (Marx himself urged the Chartists—

the progressive workers' groups of the mid-nineteenth century—
to support free trade on this ground.) Free trade for England
could secure lower-priced food and other raw materials, although this would reduce their incomes of British landowners by
holding down their domestic crop prices. A prime objective of
England's free trade movement was thus to feed British laborers
and supply British industrialists with less expensive foreign grain
and other raw materials.

Another major aim of Britain's move toward free trade was to
provide "reciprocity" to other governments so as to induce them
to lower their own tariffs. Britain thus used the repeal of its own
protective tariffs in the 1840s to induce America and other countries not to erect industrial tariff systems of their own. The United
States and other countries responded as hoped: they enacted
free-trade "revenue" tariffs levied mainly on luxury imports, not
on basic industrial manufactures. This permitted British manufacturers to undersell foreign producers, so that England remained the "workshop of the world" and consolidated its industrial advantage and learning curves. Free trade thus worked to
integrate the international economy under British leadership.
The expansive forces of industrial capitalism were centered in a
single nation. The world became England's oyster—until other
countries replaced free trade with national protectionism to fos-
ter their own industrial development.

Countries have long viewed their foreign policy as an extension of their domestic economic development and interests. British mercantilism was a strategy to promote domestic profits,
hence sales and employment, by forbidding foreign competition
in the home and colonial markets. British free trade was an ex-
pression of its export-oriented industry once it had secured an
international competitive advantage. Foreign policy was thus adjusted to new domestic conditions, and economic ideology followed suit.

Meanwhile, the political imperatives of waging a flexible economic diplomacy concentrated political power in the executive
branch of government. Over half a century ago the political theorist Paul Reinsch observed in his book *World Politics:*

It is claimed . . . that in foreign affairs the nation should stand as one
man, that policies once entered upon by the Government should not be

repudiated, and that criticism should be avoided as weakening the influence of the nation abroad. . . . It is evident that when the most important concerns of a nation are thus withdrawn from the field of party difference, party government itself must grow weak, as dealing no longer with vital affairs. . . . Thus, as the importance of the executive is enhanced, that of the legislative is lowered, and parliamentary action is looked down upon as the futile and irritating activity of unpractical critics. If the government measures are to be adopted inevitably, why not dispense with the irritating delay of parliamentary discussion?

Commenting on this passage, John Hobson observed that because foreign affairs fell naturally to the executive branch of government, it could not be "controlled directly or effectively by the will of the people. This subordination of the legislative to the executive, and the concentration of executive power in an autocracy, are necessary consequences of the predominance of foreign over domestic politics. . . . So the Cabinet absorbs the powers of the House, while the Cabinet itself has been deliberately and consciously expanded in size so as to promote the concentration of real power in an informal but very real 'inner Cabinet,' retaining some slight selective elasticity, but virtually consisting of the Prime Minister and the Foreign and Colonial Secretaries [Hobson is speaking here of England] and the Chancellor of the Exchequer."[1]

As early as two centuries ago, at the time of the American Revolution, similar feelings were voiced within England by Whigs seeking to dissuade their government from pursuing an active foreign policy. Today, every nation's foreign policy must be active to the extent that it must respond to events abroad that affect exports and the terms of trade, and thus bear directly on domestic economic activity, employment and investment. This entails building up the sphere of the executive branch of the government at the foreign-policy margin, making the Secretary of State (or his counterpart) the most powerful member of the Cabinet in the United States and in other countries. The Secretary of the Treasury deals largely with international finance, especially as growth in the money supply is determined by the course of international capital flows and the disposition of intergovernmental debts. The Secretary of Agriculture becomes increasingly concerned with establishing long-term sales or purchase agreements at the intergovernmental level, the Secretary of Commerce makes similar arrangements for industrial commodities and investments, and the Secretary of Defense occupies himself with the international arms trade. As the political balance shifts from the legislative to the executive branch of government, appointed officials supplant elected legislators as the key decision makers.

It has been asserted at least since the time of de Tocqueville that democracy cannot wage war or successful foreign policy in competition with more centralized, nondemocratic political systems. It is claimed that the legislative branch cannot be trusted with delicate negotiations over foreign policy and American military commitments requiring confidentiality or objectivity, and that diplomacy therefore must be left to the executive branch. This view implies that the only way for America to remain a democracy in today's world is to forego its foreign policy and foreign military commitments. Either its world strategy must become inward-looking and neo-isolationist, or its political structure must become more centralized. Indeed, since the start of the Vietnam War, the growth of foreign policy considerations has visibly worked to disenfranchise the American electorate by reducing the role of Congress in national decision making.

Third World countries face a different situation. For centuries, ex-colonies and other less developed areas were prevented from pursuing statist economic policies, in particular those of a protectionist nature, to help them break out of their dependency on the industrial nations. Their government spending was concentrated on providing an infrastructure to facilitate the exportation of raw materials and labor-intensive products, which were sold to industrial nations whose own resource allocation was established by a long history of state protection and subsidies. Although the nonindustrialized countries have historically had relatively weak foreign policies, their domestic politics have been highly centralized. This has been largely to prevent the type of economic and political evolution that has characterized today's industrial nations. Third World statism and dictatorships have preserved an otherwise untenable domestic status quo that has benefited their landed agricultural and commercial aristocracy—the very classes that gave way to urban industrialization in today's advanced nations. For many years these oppressive Third World regimes held on to power largely by means of revenues derived from exporting depletable resources. They were supported both overtly and covertly by the United States and other industrial nations eager to see them continue these export-oriented policies. However sincerely policy-makers in the industrial nations hoped that Third World countries might improve their lot, they were not willing to put this hope above their own self-interest in seeing these countries remain hewers of wood and drawers of water. As long as their own wealth was being supported by the Third World's warped pattern of economic growth and international dependency, foreign policy in the industrial nations could easily remain relaxed and secondary to domestic concerns. Prosperity and political freedom in the industrial nations thus seemed to rest partly on dictatorships in countries supplying inexpensive raw materials and plantation products.

Meanwhile, domestic police and armies helped preserve the status quo responsible for the Third World's lack of economic and democratic growth. Antiprogressive regimes were supported by foreign weaponry whose costs often absorbed most of the country's net export revenues, and by foreign covert operations intended to abort moves toward meaningful economic reform and political self-determination.

Every action has an equal and opposite reaction. The time inevitably came when the Third World's underdevelopment, which resulted largely from its export-oriented policies pursued at the expense of domestic modernization, led to economic and political reforms. China, Cuba, Vietnam and a number of African countries experienced socialist revolutions leading to protectionist regimes. More recently, even monarchies or military dictatorships in Peru, Sudan, Saudi Arabia, Iran and other countries worked to broaden their economic base just as intently as the more-feared socialist regimes. Failure to develop domestic agricultural resources threatens to limit the tenure of any regime unable to pull its nation out of rural poverty, no matter how great its domestic repression or foreign support. In this lies the implicit domestic radicalism of the New International Economic Order.

It seems likely that as the Third World uses more of its resources for domestic development, instead of exporting them to subsidize the industrial nations and their growing "postindustrial" consumer economies, the latters' political apparatus can no longer afford to merely let things be. Governments in the industrial nations must either accept a declining standard of living,

increase their own domestic wealth-producing powers, or reestablish their international diplomacy in an attempt to secure from
abroad what they cannot produce at home. As Third World statism aims at broadly-based agricultural modernization and industrial development, and as foreign trade and investment become
more problematic for the industrial nations, the latter will be—
and already are being—obliged to become more statist themselves. In America this is taking the form of a new isolationism.
In Europe it is taking the form of a much closer economic and
political integration with the Near East and Africa.

If laissez faire is dead internationally, it is dead at home as well.
As all national governments assert their authority in the areas of
foreign trade and investment, this regulatory process necessarily
extends itself into domestic economic life. One might expect the
political parties most prepared for this development to be socialist or communist. However, two problems confront today's political left. Given a shrinking net economic surplus with which to
increase living standards, statist parties coming into office may
find themselves obliged to preside, however reluctantly, over
stringent economic policies. To be sure, communist movements
in nonindustrialized countries have pursued investment-oriented
rather than consumption-oriented programs since the Soviet
Union set the pattern in 1917. However, socialist movements in
the more industrialized nations have generally urged higher consumption standards at the expense of investment and business
profits. For socialist parties in these nations to wield statist policies in the service of capital accumulation and growth in productive powers is to promote an objective traditionally associated
with conservative parties. Meanwhile, political parties representing private enterprise find themselves obliged to become increasingly statist as they regulate market forces, prices, foreign trade
and incomes in what they construe to be their national interest.
For better or worse, the world seems destined to experience
more statist forms whose objectives will concentrate on capital
formation rather than on improving consumption standards—
save in the low-income Third World countries where improved
living standards and higher productive powers tend to go together. In this situation "left-wing" and "right-wing" labels become almost meaningless in terms of their economic programs
(although they retain their political significance).

Free trade tended to give the lion's share of economic benefits to lead nations as long as these nations owned and controlled the world's export industries and were alone in protecting and subsidizing their own key economic sectors. Today each country wants to secure for itself a larger proportion of the gains from international trade, and is asserting control of its domestic economy as well as its foreign trade so as to promote this objective. The single nation that stood to gain most from free trade under the postwar economic order was the United States, which itself took the lead in restoring protectionist policies in the 1960s, hardly setting an example for those countries it hoped might maintain a more laissez faire position. Protectionism thus spread from the very center of the world economy until finally, in 1973, it reached the Third World periphery. Cartels and counter-cartels are now being proposed by each set of countries, the industrial nations and the Third World, in a setting of economic and geographic realignment.

Unlike the case with earlier forms of statism, the world has outgrown narrow nationalism. If statism's traditional objectives are to be achieved, be they higher rates of capital accumulation or higher consumption standards, they presuppose broad regional integration to secure the basic economies of scale required for modern-day technology. Also, foreign regions must act rapidly, and as a single unit, to counter the deftness of American or Soviet foreign policy. However, socialist parties throughout the world have opposed this transcendence of political nationalism. (One may trace this tendency back to their voting for World War I war credits, an act that effectively broke the internationalism hitherto espoused.) In country after country, beginning with Stalin's victory over Trotsky in 1923, and his subsequent mobilization of the Third International under Zinoviev as a specifically nationalist instrument of Soviet Russia, communist and socialist parties have been highly nationalistic. In 1945 the British Labour Party refused to join with its continental European counterparts to create a broadly based European socialism. The problem from British eyes was that international socialism connoted the end of specifically British (that is, national) socialism. Despite the prominent role played by individual European socialists such as Monnet, the European Common Market was formed under conservative rather than socialist governments. Thus, today's tendency toward statism has been quite independent of socialism, both in its regionalism as opposed to nationalism, and in its focus on capital accumulation and growth of productive powers rather than on higher living standards. World politics seems to have come up against a technological-economic imperative that cuts across traditional political lines.

It seems ironic that the recent gains in Communist Party strength abroad have worked to benefit the United States in some unanticipated ways. Communist gains in Italy, Spain, France and other European countries have induced a capital flight to the United States similar to that which occurred in the 1930s. At that time European investors sought a haven from fascism and the impending war. Today they are once again seeking diversification against political risk. The recent move by Volkswagen to establish an automotive assembly plant in Ohio seems due largely to a fear of rising communist influence in Europe. Further communist gains abroad may trigger continued speculative flows into dollar assets, thereby supporting the U.S. stock market, the U.S. balance of payments and the nearly depleted American savings function. On the other hand, if communism recedes abroad, if it turns out to have passed its zenith in Italy and Portugal, European investors will have less need to turn to America as a more favorable business climate.

Impact on the United States of the New International Economic Order

America's double standard in international finance and trade created a unique degree of domestic affluence during 1945–73. In foreign trade Americans enjoyed low raw-materials import prices in the face of rising export prices for their industrial products and grains. For energy alone the pre-1973 price savings on imports approximated $25 billion annually. Oil, considered by many economists to be the ultimate economic input, was selling at only $2.50 per barrel—less than one-fourth its post-1973 price. America's terms-of-trade savings on imported copper, aluminum, iron ore and other primary commodities amounted to perhaps another $10 billion. These gains were secured largely through U.S. ownership of foreign mining and oil companies, which often enabled Americans to pay substantially less than going world prices for their raw materials. For instance, during the world economic boom of 1966–68, Chilean copper was sold to customers of American-owned mines in Chile at the so-called "producer's price" of 34¢ per pound, while the free-market London Metal Exchange price reached nearly three times this level (98¢ per pound). This kind of exploitation is coming to an end as foreign governments take over the marketing of their raw materials. (Only as world economic recovery absorbs the current raw-materials surplus can one tell how far the emerging price level will surpass that in effect prior to 1973.) Foreign dependence on American grain exports provided a further $10 billion terms-of-trade advantage as crop-export prices quadruped following the Russian grain sale. All together, these trade advantages amounted to some $45 billion per year by the time this state of affairs ended in the closing months of 1973.

U.S. foreign investments remitted some $58 billion in profits during 1958–73, most of it from oil- and mineral-producing branches in Third World countries. This helped concentrate the international savings function in the United States as American firms transferred to the United States the profits, depreciation, depletion, interest charges and other costs associated with foreign raw-materials production and transport. (European firms also participated in this process.) By 1973 these remitted earnings on U.S. overseas raw-materials investment were running at an annual rate of about $5 billion.

The U.S. Government used foreign-aid programs to improve its balance of payments by contributing to the World Bank, the Asian Development Bank and the Inter-American Development Bank only on the condition that their operations resulted in net payments inflows to the United States—in sharp contrast to the aid philosophy of many other nations, and to the "free market" philosophy of economic "efficiency" that U.S. officials have cited as a reason for not joining world commodity agreements. Repayments of interest and principal on its foreign-aid lending amounted to some $20 billion during 1960–73, while the World Bank and its associated regional banks contributed a further $7 billion. By 1973 America's foreign aid programs were responsible for a $1.6 billion annual balance-of-payments contribution.

Finally, foreign central banks were recycling America's balance-of-payments deficits by purchasing Treasury securities, thereby helping to finance the growth in America's federal debt. During 1958–73 this amounted to some $58 billion, including $4.7 billion during 1972, the last full year in which the process was operative.

These international trade, investment and financial processes funded an unparalleled American prosperity during the 1960s and early 1970s. In the years 1974 and 1975 alone, the U.S. Government borrowed $3 billion and $8 billion respectively from foreign central banks, while American firms remitted $10 billion and $6 billion, respectively, in profits, and America's aid-protectionism contributed a net balance-of-payments inflow of $800 million and $1.9 billion (plus a further $1.9 billion stemming from World Bank Group programs). In 1976 foreign central banks invested $18 billion more in Treasury bills and other U.S. assets, while American firms earned $12.4 billion and U.S. foreign aid contributed $2 billion more. But by this time the largest gain of all, the terms-of-trade gain, had expired.

Despite these massive transfers of foreign resources, the American economy showed the lowest ratios in the industrial world of savings and investment to national income. During 1970–73 investment averaged under 18 per cent of U.S. national income, compared to 35 per cent for Japan, 26 per cent for Germany, 24 per cent for France, 22 per cent for Canada and 19 per cent for England. This helps explain why productivity growth in the American economy has been the lowest of any Western industrial nation: the investment and financial resources were not there. During the eight-year period 1967–75, labor productivity in the United States grew by only 12 per cent, compared to 83 per cent for Japan, 46 per cent for Germany, 39 per cent for France, 30 per cent for Canada, and 26 per cent for England. Why was new investment so low in the presence of America's foreign-fed affluence? The answer is that the U.S. economy was overconsuming at home as well as internationally. Its balance-of-payments gains were being dissipated on worldwide Cold War policies, while its domestic economic surplus was being used to carry and subsidize an increasingly service-oriented postindustrial society. It was as if Americans expected all the rest of the world to perform industrial labor but themselves.

This expectation is unlikely to materialize as foreign countries break out of the U.S. economic orbit, stop financing the U.S.

federal budget deficit, stop supporting American affluence by supplying raw materials at relatively low prices, and begin regulating or purchasing for their own benefit American-owned firms abroad. They are moving to secure for themselves the benefits of their low-cost mineral production, and to use the proceeds to gain economic independence from American agricultural and arms exports—and, at a point, to compete with American exporters in foreign markets. OPEC and other raw-materials producers not only are pressing for higher commodity prices but also are purchasing majority ownership of foreign-owned firms in their minerals-export sector. Hence, these firms will no longer repatriate earnings, depreciation and depletion back to the United States and other industrial nations. Instead, these funds will be retained by the raw-materials exporters.

Raw-materials exporters hardly are interested in emulating European, Japanese and Canadian experience by relending their payments surpluses to the U.S. Treasury. They insist on being paid in real goods and services, and particularly in capital goods and related equipment with which to achieve industrial and agricultural independence from the United States. Thus, at the same time that Americans are to pay more for imports, foreign suppliers are investing their increased trade proceeds in areas that reduce their dependence on U.S. exports.

Over and above the charge suffered by the U.S. economy through loss of its foreign-fed affluence is its burden of seeking to become more independent of Third World exports by producing similar commodities at home. The Ford administration suggested that the costs of Project Independence for energy alone might amount to $100 billion through 1985. Meanwhile, America has set aside an additional 1 million acres for cotton cultivation in 1977 (from 2.9 million to 3.9 million). U.S. consumers will thus be obliged to buy high-priced domestic substitutes for commodities which they imported at relatively low prices prior to 1973. The recent surge in coffee prices is a foretaste of things to come. Furthermore, a ratchet effect seems to characterize retailers' markups of products based on imported commodities. (For instance, even though sugar prices have recently fallen back from their extremely high 1975–76 levels, the price of candy bars remains at 20 cents each.)

These developments suggest that less consumer saving will

occur as the American people seek to maintain their living standards in the face of prices increasing more rapidly than incomes. Also, internally generated profits by U.S. multinational firms are being eroded by the New International Economic Order. How then are continued federal budget deficits in the neighborhood of $50 billion per year to be financed without inflationary money creation, at a time when the American savings rate has fallen to virtually zero? How is new investment to be financed? Without a rise in the proportion of American national income which is invested, how can productivity be increased over its already slack levels? These questions suggest a vicious circle of lower investment, lower productivity and lower savings—unless the U.S. economy once again can fund its budget deficits with foreign central bank resources, and/or unless its multinational firms can recover their profit functions, and/or unless America can recover its favorable terms-of-trade vis-à-vis Third World countries so that American consumers can once again support growth in their living standards through low-priced imports. If economic recovery does occur, it will put increased pressures on world demand for Third World products and therefore create a sellers' market for these commodities.

As governments throughout the world play a more active role in their regional economies they will no doubt emulate the United States in giving preference to local suppliers. Admonitions to "Buy European" and "Buy Japanese" are emerging as a counterpart of this nation's long-standing "Buy American" campaign. The new tendency probably will begin in the arms trade and in agriculture, and extend to aircraft, capital goods, agrichemicals and related key industries in a drive to achieve general region-wide self-sufficiency.

To be sure, foreign programs to create a broad economic infrastructure will increase the market for U.S. capital-goods exports (automotives, small aircraft, electrical and industrial machinery) and even the construction of entire factories and plants (oil refineries, superports, turnkey automotive plants and steel mills). This effort necessarily will be associated with emigration of U.S. labor (engineers, managerial talent and skilled workmen) to Africa and the Near East, such as that outflow associated with American arms exports. However, the prospect of an export boom in capital goods already has led the Council of Economic

Advisers to anticipate an inflation in the price of U.S. capital goods, which may be countered by export controls similar to those levied on soybeans and other crops in 1973. The higher the rate of exports in any category, the tighter will be the domestic supply situation and the greater the domestic price pressures.

Even for areas in which America enjoys substantial export capacity such as in food and arms, foreign demand seems to have peaked as foreign economies are becoming more self-sufficient. Pressure for foreign agricultural independence was built up when the U.S. Government shifted the export market for American foodstuffs to the Soviet bloc in 1972 and then embargoed its crop exports in response to the subsequent inflation in food prices. Public pressure abroad for arms independence has been created by recent revelations about the massive foreign bribery undertaken by Lockheed and other arms manufacturers. This kind of practice may have been an accepted manner of conducting the arms business in the past, but given the new environment of public disclosure it is no longer possible, at least for American arms manufacturers. Thus, a powerful inducement to buy U.S. arms has been removed. Furthermore, America's apparent refusal to make NATO arms a two-way street when it opposed adoption of Germany's Leopard tank for NATO forces has also spurred a foreign reaction to achieve greater arms independence.

In the area of world finance the New International Economic Order implies a winding down of the U.S. Treasury-bill standard. The balance-of-payments surpluses of foreign industrial nations have been sharply eroded or reversed since the Oil War, so that their central banks have not been accumulating surplus dollars to invest in U.S. Treasury bills. OPEC countries have taken up some of the slack, but not enough to afford a major net foreign inflow. Furthermore, to the extent that the United States runs a payments deficit in today's world of floating currencies, the dollar will decline on world markets. By making imports more expensive this will aggravate domestic inflationary pressure, particularly in the event of sustained economic recovery, rising incomes, higher world demand for imported commodities and general upward pressure on world raw-materials prices. A fall in the dollar's value also would shift more American output from the domestic to foreign markets and thus cause domestic shortages.

America's relatively recent payments surpluses with Europe

have posed an altogether novel problem: these surpluses are financed by foreign central banks selling back their $90 billion in Treasury bills and other federal securities. In past years the United States paid for its imports with paper. Now it is getting paid for its exports with this same paper, redeemed in such a way as to overload its capital markets to the detriment of domestic borrowers. As foreign central banks sell Treasury bills to finance their net purchases in the United States, these sales absorb funds that otherwise would be channeled to domestic borrowers and investors. Unless America repudiates its foreign debt, or monetizes an equivalent amount of credit at home (thus paving the way for a new inflationary wave), domestic U.S. borrowers may be "crowded out." Not only must the private sector finance the federal government's new budget deficits (in the neighborhood of $50 billion per year), and also refinance the outstanding federal debt as it is rolled over (at a current annual rate of $200 billion), it also must begin to pay for the past quarter-century's string of payments deficits as foreign-owned Treasury bills are sold back at a rate of, say, $10 billion to $15 billion per year. Affluence must thus give way to financial effluence.

Meanwhile, in an attempt by all the world's regional groupings to avoid holding more than working balances of the currencies of other regions, an increasing portion of world trade may approximate barter form, such as has previously characterized East Bloc trade. The proposed U.S. grain-for-petroleum deal with Soviet Russia, and its arms-for-oil negotiations with Iran and other Middle Eastern countries are cases in point. In an inflationary world of unstable currencies there will be increasing pressure to index international trade prices. Trade flows will not be financed by international reserves to the extent that they have been in past years, and hence there will be less need for central banks to increase their foreign-exchange holdings in keeping with gross exports. Foreign central banks thus will have less desire to rebuild their holdings of U.S. Treasury bills once they let them run down.

By drying up these three major sources of international inflows —favorable terms of trade for American food and arms exports, rising earnings remitted from U.S.-owned affiliates abroad, and foreign financing of the U.S. federal debt via the Treasury-bill standard—the New International Economic Order implies a lag in America's industrial development relative to that of Europe and Asia. The nation's productivity growth already has trailed that of foreign countries for more than a decade. To increase its productivity the United States must increase its rate of investment. But in recent years the savings to finance this investment (including retained earnings by American international corporations) have come increasingly from abroad. It follows that, as the United States finds itself less able to draw upon foreign resources, it will be unable to sustain even its comparatively low rates of growth in productivity and living standards that characterized the 1960s. In the absence of these foreign inflows either consumption or investment must yield. If the domestic rate of net liquid savings is increased to finance new investment, then current living standards must be rolled back for some sectors of the American population. If an attempt is made to maintain growth in living standards, then the nation must consume its capital as it did during 1972–75. It seems likely that the economy will eliminate production of numerous types of goods and services (including some social programs and military projects) for which markets are no longer expanding or for which funds are no longer available. In any event, restoration of prosperity—if and when it comes—will have to result from domestic efforts, not foreign transfers.

Some class must have its income cut back in the face of this austere outlook, and the question is which one? As real incomes are reduced for the business sector, consumers, or the emerging nouveau-rentier class of transfer-payment recipients (of pensions, social security or welfare), these classes may seek from each other the income the economy can no longer obtain from abroad.

In this respect America's problem today may resemble the tensions that aggravated the French Revolution two centuries ago. As the American economist Simon Patten described this state of affairs, a major contributing factor to the French Revolution and subsequent Napoleonic Wars was the fact that England and not France was securing the international gains from trade:

> The great industrial inventions in England were beginning to show their effects in the growth of population and in an increased demand for food. Their larger incomes permitted her people to bid successfully

against foreign nations, and especially against France, where the in-crease of productive power was relatively slow. The food imported by England was usually in the form of wheat—the one rare thing for which there was a general demand. It thus happened that just at the time when France wanted more wheat to raise her standard of comfort, England outbid her and took the coveted grain. To say the least, England was always first supplied, and France got what was left. In bad years England took a share of the French wheat, leaving the French towns without a proper supply; and in good years, when prices were low, French country people were in distress.[2]

England obtained the economic surplus from the world econ-omy hitherto enjoyed largely by France, much as Europe and the Near East today are securing the gains from trade that previously have accrued mainly to the American economy:

The increase of [French] productive power being too slow to give the desired comfort, they were forced to grasp at the funded income of others. . . . When the French people were taking the funded surplus from their lords, better economic conditions enabled other nations to appro-priate a larger share of the international surplus to the detriment of France. The French people thus lost by the relative decline of France a large portion of the surplus taken from their leisure class. This fact and not the internal struggle brought on the real Revolution. . . . The French, failing to secure at home that net increase of income demanded by the new standard of comfort, sought to take by force the increased income that other nations, because of their improved economic conditions, were enjoying. The home struggle proved easy, but the external struggle was a failure and ended in exhausting the resources of Europe. The day had gone by when France could dominate Europe.

Not every nation could sit at Nature's first table, Patten con-cluded. "This frustrated France's cry for liberty, fraternity and equality—it could not be an international cry, but only national in scope. The productive power of Europe at that time was not great enough to make all its inhabitants comfortable, nor was its wheat crop large enough to permit all to live on bread." Today a similar set of relationships may govern America's world status. The U.S. economy faces the prospect of paying for its imports with real economic output—most particularly with capital goods —rather than with mere computer-printed central bank credits. Its foreign debts run up so cavalierly in the past are now falling due. Its response will probably be to grow increasingly national-istic.

To be sure, there are countervailing forces. As the locus of world prosperity shifts to European and Third World countries, the path will be opened for the Western defense burden to be borne more by the regions most directly concerned. American withdrawal of its NATO troops from West Germany will oblige Western Europe to divert resources from its civilian economy to sustain its own troops. And foreign prosperity will increase U.S. export prospects in specific categories, mainly heavy industrial goods rather than the so-called glamour consumer goods and electronics that sparked the economic expansion of the 1960s. Instead of continued expansion of services and consumer-goods production, America must refocus its attention on industrial growth to pay its own way domestically and internationally.

All this is occurring at a time when industrial capitalism has lost its ideology, save that of technological inertia (the "postindustrial economy" in which technology presumably will do nearly all the industrial and agricultural work, as if this somehow can be accomplished without massive new debt to finance new capital, which requires new savings, and hence forgone current consumption). Laissez faire is dead, and business interests have hesitated to create new rationales for systematic state economic intervention save that of the crudest nationalism. Pragmatic forces rather than reasoned long-range programs are responsible for today's statist policies.

Regulation of prices at the international margin soon requires domestic price and income controls. In country after country this has spurred a confrontation between federalism and antifederalism. Given today's international pressures, only the statist parties can supply an ideology fitting the new world conditions. Under conditions of declining productivity growth and living standards, and in the face of a labor force growing more rapidly than private-sector job opportunities, the government will be called upon as arbiter of relative incomes, prices, credit allocation and trade patterns. For better or worse, it will become much more active in shaping the market structure within which private enterprise operates in pursuit of profit maximization. At best—as far as traditional laissez faire ideology is concerned—it may "farm out" its decisions for private enterprise to implement. The result may give the appearance of markets operating freely, but it is a rigged game. All that remains to render "free market economics" altogether obsolete is an economic doctrine explaining how governments may create new operative functions to secure, by the visible hands of state policy, the objectives that the withered invisible hand of the marketplace can no longer provide.

CHAPTER 19

The American Response

America's strategy in the face of the New International Economic Order is to render it no more than a tentative scenario, and to reestablish the pre-1973 state of affairs wherever possible. The Treasury-bill standard is to be reinstated while gold, sterling or a Eurocurrency are rejected as viable alternatives. America's official debt to foreign central banks is to be effectively wiped off the books by "funding" it into the world monetary base and giving it to "needy"—i.e., dependent—Third World countries. American export prices are to be supported as foreign countries continue to depend on U.S. grain, arms and aircraft, in payment for which Third World countries are to compete among themselves once again to export their raw materials. Europe is to speak in world affairs with nine national voices rather than with one. In short, both the European and Third World economies are to return to their former complementarity with the American economy. U.S. economic strategy is to continue drawing upon foreign resources in order to sustain growth in its living standards and government spending.

America's interest lies in restoring those elements of the postwar economic order that obliged foreign countries to finance, through their central banks, the entire growth of America's federal debt during 1946–73; to sell their raw materials to U.S.-owned firms at prices substantially below those received by American producers for similar commodities; to permit U.S. firms to appropriate much of their export surplus; and to finance multilateral foreign-aid programs that served specific U.S. aims and helped the U.S. balance of payments while financing increased production (and hence lower export prices) of raw materials imported by the United States.

International finance remains the focal point both of the New International Economic Order and the American response. At stake is whether the United States once again will be able to run up dollar debts to foreign central banks as its trade and payments fall back into deficit. Will OPEC supplant Europe and Japan as America's major creditors, using oil earnings to buy U.S. Treasury securities and thereby fund U.S. federal budget deficits? Or will Eastern Hemisphere countries subject the United States to a gold-based system of international finance in which renewed U.S. payments deficits will connote a loss of its international financial leverage?

From the American vantage point, restoration of the Treasury-bill standard requires that the emergence of any workable alternative to the dollar be aborted. Gold must be dethroned and European monetary (hence political) integration dissipated. OPEC must be confronted with little option but to invest its surplus petrodollars in U.S. Treasury securities.

During 1973–75 these objectives appeared unattainable unless the United States maintained the balance-of-payments surplus it had enjoyed during the last nine months of 1973. America's international payments remained relatively close to equilibrium (by recent historical standards) thanks to its relative self-sufficiency in oil, its arms exports and its continued grain sales to the communist nations. Even so, its balance of payments fell into a deficit of about $1 billion per month by mid-1976. And yet OPEC, with little to-do, replaced the central banks of Europe and Japan in financing this deficit. As America spent more dollars abroad, and as these dollars found their way to the central monetary agencies of Saudi Arabia and other oil-exporting countries, they were recycled to the United States by investment in Treasury securities. (OPEC also channeled a more modest flow of bank deposits and private-sector investment to the United States, as well as buying massive amounts of arms.)

Gold was not surging in price as it had in past periods of U.S. deficits, but was stagnating at around $132 per ounce. IMF auctions of gold scheduled through 1978 and possibly augmented by U.S. Treasury sales indicated continued downward pressure on gold prices. Furthermore, the dollar was strengthening in the wake of sterling's fall from $2.40 to under $1.70. Indeed, Britain announced in December 1976 that it would phase out sterling permanently as a key currency, leaving no single national currency to compete with the dollar. European monetary union and political integration had made no progress since the Tindemans Report, while separatist pressures rent the continent from Basque Spain to Celtic Britain. The world seemed to be acquiescing to a renewed Treasury-bill standard. European diplomacy lost the single-mindedness it had achieved during the 1973–75 confrontation. World "cooperation" on U.S. terms became a distinct prospect.

In the area of world monetary reform the United States continues to pursue an alliance with those Third World countries whose balance-of-payments deficits have widened in the face of rising world food and energy prices. If they will vote to "fund" the U.S. dollar overhang—its $105 billion debt to foreign central banks—by incorporating it into world monetary reserves as a new form of irredeemable fiat money, the United States will support a similar wiping out of the Third World's foreign-aid debt. America would also support an expunging of Britain's official foreign debt (which Britain publicly called for in December 1976), as well as Europe's Inter-Ally debts dating from World War I (a claim which the U.S. Treasury still keeps on its books), in exchange for European central banks dropping their claims on the Treasury. Collectively, the world's debtor governments, including the United States, would not be obliged to redeem their official obligations to other governments. Creditor nations would convert their specific claims on the United States, Britain or Third World countries into generalized fiat assets of equivalent value. The central banks which currently hold $105 billion in claims on the United States thus would still have $105 billion to spend, but this sum would no longer be a specific liability of the U.S. Treasury. If any part of this new fiat credit were spent in the United States, the U.S. Government would come into possession of the new spendable asset (a kind of super-SDR), rather than merely reducing its liability to foreign central banks as is presently the case. Only under this new set of rules would America find its self-interest to lie in running payments surpluses once again.

The U.S. financial stance, which was developed largely by Secretary of State Kissinger and Secretary of the Treasury Simon, is akin to that taken by England with regard to its World War I debts. In 1923 England said that it would relinquish its claims on its wartime allies (mainly France and Russia) to the extent that the U.S. Government would relinquish its claims on Britain.

Today, the United States is proposing to forgive the Third World countries' foreign-aid debt if other industrial nations (plus OPEC) agree to relinquish their claims on the U.S. Treasury and the poorer debtor countries. If the U.S. plan is not accepted, the onus of collecting the world's foreign-aid debt would thus be cast onto the shoulders of other nations. America could represent itself as demanding repayment from Latin America, Asia and other debtor countries merely to pay Europe, Japan and OPEC. This posture depicts it as being passive in a triangular flow of payments from Third World countries, via the U.S. Government and World Bank, to the central banks of Europe, OPEC and Japan.

Payments-surplus nations are thus to be exploited in the same fashion that America exploited Europe and Japan prior to March 1973, and Saudi Arabia since the Oil War. Payments-deficit countries will be kept in line by America's more traditional creditor-oriented strategy exerted through the IMF, the World Bank and other world lending organizations. In particular the momentum of European economic and political integration must be slowed —for after all, how can the Middle East work closely with a European Community that is dissolving in the face of local separatist movements?

Meanwhile, American trade strategy suggests an alliance with Europe to hold down the price of world raw-materials exports, by seeking domestic self-sufficiency in raw materials while promoting export competition among Third World exporters. To be sure, domestic raw-materials prices in the industrial nations may rise as recourse is made to higher-cost local production (North Sea oil for Europe and synthetic coal liquids for the United States). But a higher degree of domestic self-sufficiency would reduce import demand, thereby putting downward pressure on world prices. The difference between relatively low import prices and high domestic production prices is to be taken, if possible, by governments in the industrial nations via tariffs levied on raw-materials imports. The industrial nations may thus obtain relatively cheap raw-materials imports as Third World exporters forgo the higher commodity prices being earned by high-cost industrial-nation producers. As compensation for this sacrifice most raw-materials exporters would enjoy increased net purchasing power through cancellation of their aid debts. (Meanwhile, the United States would price its food and arms exports as high as possible by entering into world export agreements of its own with other supplier countries, e.g., Canada for wheat and Europe for arms.)

To be effective, American strategy must accept as a *fait accompli* the irreversible changes that have occurred in the world economy since 1973. If America's pre-1973 objectives are to be maintained, their tactics must be adjusted in light of the world's new circumstances so as to separate those elements of the New International Economic Order that may be rolled back from those which may not. For one thing, the U.S. attempt to roll back world oil prices has visibly failed. A major tactic was to have been development of a higher degree of American energy self-sufficiency, stemming both from conservation and development of domestic resources. But the movement toward energy conservation hardly got off the ground as Americans quickly turned back to large-sized cars and began to speed up their driving once again. Only continued economic recession seems to be holding down America's energy demand. As for the future, the costs of developing domestic energy substitutes are turning out to be far greater than indicated by early government statements. Coal liquefaction and gasification plants will cost in the neighborhood of $1 billion each, and the coal available for these plants is located mainly in the Northwest, where the requisite water is so scarce that coal processing would entail writing off these regions for agriculture and livestock. It also would create a massive demand for specialty steel, pressing up domestic steel prices, hence industrial costs generally. Another major alternative to imported oil has seemed to be nuclear power, but existing plants lack proper safeguards for waste disposal and the Carter administration has therefore reduced funding for nuclear plants. Alaskan oil is proving to be higher in sulphur than was originally anticipated, and is posing delivery problems as California is seeking to restrict tanker transport in its coastal waters. Thus, America's leverage in holding down energy prices is not very strong.

In addition to its dual set of alliances with industrial nations and Third World countries, the United States may ally itself with the communist nations, and particularly with the Soviet Union, so as to reimpose Cold War strains that will bring external pressure to bear on both Europe and the Third World. The trick is to bring this pressure without driving America's Cold War allies together into a single mass that may withdraw as a unit from the U.S. economic orbit.

America's diplomatic alliances thus represent a triple strategy: confrontation of the industrial nations by a joint U.S.-Third World debtor block in international finance; confrontation of Third World countries by industrial nations acting to form a consumer cartel to roll back primary commodity prices; and confrontation of both Third World and industrial nations by U.S.-Soviet détente to keep the satellites of each system in their place, so that the existing state of world affairs may not be disturbed so long as it benefits both superpowers.

However, this is not the only prospective scenario. Industrial nations outside the United States may calculate that they can do better by paying higher raw-materials prices and initiating a circular flow process: OPEC and other Third World commodity producers will recycle their export earnings in the form of a demand for industrial exports and investments in Europe. They may advance the funds in the form of purchases of substantial shares in key companies, payment for turnkey projects and for industrial and agricultural capital goods. These purchases would trigger an export-based economic recovery in Europe and Japan, enabling them to retain their claims on the U.S. economy. To be sure, Europe and Japan would be construed as breaking rank with the United States if they created a geo-economic complementarity of trade and investment that excluded the United States. U.S. default on its debt to central banks in Europe and Japan would cause an even deeper break with these nations. (If such a default occurs, European governments might settle their claims on the U.S. Government by taking over ownership of U.S. affiliates abroad, extending the process of world fracture.)

The following alternatives are thus posed. Either the U.S. Government and foreign debtor governments will pay their debts or they will not. Either creditor governments will insist that their debtors pay them in the form of real goods, services and ownership and control of their industry, or they will accept conversion of their claims into generalized purchasing power such as new-SDRs. Either raw-materials export prices will remain high (with governments in the exporting countries receiving the cost differential between their own low-cost production and the relatively high-cost production costs entailed in the industrial nations) or commodity export prices will fall below production costs in the industrial nations, so that the economic rent will accrue to governments, businesses and consumers in the latter.

These sets of alternatives can all be resolved without a world economic crisis. Any crisis that occurs will stem mainly from political antagonisms. Among the emerging regional economic blocs there exists a multiplicity of possible combinations and no certainty that any given combination, once formed, will persist. Europe may integrate itself most closely with the Near East and Africa, while Japan moves toward Southeast Asia, and the United States and Canada move to integrate their economies more closely with those of Latin America. Or, Japan may remain in the dollar area. Political and economic alignments may cut across geographic and military divisions. The world has become much more complex than it was during the early division between Western and Communist countries following World War II when Washington and Moscow were the only poles of the world political economy.

America must bear major responsibility for the today's global fracture. It deranged international finance by its policy of "benign neglect" of its balance of payments, by supplanting the gold standard with the Treasury-bill standard, and by concluding that its interest lay in bringing on international financial crisis if its allies did not remain economic satellites. The United States more than any other country broke up GATT with its export embargoes of 1973 and its demand for a world system of "voluntary" quotas on foreign exports to the United States. The future of world trade, finance and investment will be determined in large part by whether foreign countries seek to avoid world trauma by succumbing to America's nationalistic economic challenge, or choose to promote their own autonomy by accepting the U.S. challenge and minimizing the resulting trauma by reaching monetary and trade agreements among themselves to bridge the transition between the old and the new international economic systems.

America enjoys a major tactical advantage in this looming confrontation between the two most probable world scenarios: it has only a single government instead of Europe's nine or OPEC's seventeen. This may enable it to outmaneuver Europe and OPEC in situations where speed of response is a decisive factor. Until Europe expresses its diplomacy through a single set of technicians representing a European Parliament with its own Ministry of Foreign Affairs it must secure the adherence of all nine member countries before acting.

The United States has shown itself remarkably flexible in responding to world developments. When it seemed so hopelessly indebted to the central banks of Europe and Japan that it had finally lost its international economic autonomy and freedom of action, it recognized that its debts had become nearly uncollectible and that foreign countries had a stake in maintaining the value of these debts by supporting the dollar, and perhaps even by transforming U.S. official debts into the foundation for world monetary reserves. By repudiating gold convertibility of the dollar, America transformed a position of seeming weakness into one of unanticipated strength, that of a debtor over its creditors. (There is a popular saying in America that if a borrower owes his bank $5 thousand that he cannot pay, then he is in trouble, but if he owes $5 million then the bank is in trouble.) America's $105 billion debt to foreign central banks holds the world credit system hostage to U.S. threats and leverage. When foreign countries sought to dispose of their surplus dollars by purchasing U.S. products, creating domestic shortages, the American government imposed export embargoes. When OPEC sought to use its surplus dollars to purchase U.S. industry the government imposed foreign investment regulations preventing foreign investors from buying more than 5 per cent of any U.S. firm without government approval. The world outside the United States thus found its dollars to be of dubious value, blocked from being spent on anything except what the United States deemed to be in surplus. Many more examples come easily to mind. Faced with the loss of viable markets for its farm exports, the United States turned quickly to Soviet Russia and China. It responded to higher world prices by selling Treasury bills and arms to the oil exporters. It responded to increased foreign competition in textiles, steel and other products by ignoring its earlier rhetoric about "free" international investment and trade, and imposing a far-reaching system of trade barriers.

So adroit were these responses that some people have actually speculated that the United States was behind the Oil War and other economic crises, on the ground that any nation that benefits from a world change must, ipso facto, have had a hand in bringing it about. And yet no government could have had the foresight to plan for all the world changes that have occurred since World War II. The truth is merely that American foreign policy has been flexible, imaginative, rapid and decisive in responding to new world developments, however unforeseen they may be. U.S. officials have calculated, apparently correctly, that in any given world crisis the American government's superior flexibility, coupled with the simple inertia of its past world power and Europe's hesitation to rock the boat, will give the United States a critical advantage. Its officials have prepared contingency plans for numerous possible future economic crises. These plans are to be presented to Europe, OPEC and Third World countries on a take-it-or-leave-it, all-or-nothing basis in an atmosphere not conducive to foreign reflection on the full consequences of these proposals. America's strategy to fund the dollar overhang by wiping out its foreign debt is one example of a plan awaiting a suitable crisis.

Through its many government agencies, assisted by an array of think tanks and private consultants, the executive branch and Congress continually question the degree to which current world economic institutions and principles serve to maximize America's national interests, and debate various ways in which these institutions can be changed. Congressional committees that include representatives of specific U.S. interests press for adjustment in world economic policies. The United States thus has moved to impose far-reaching sets of import quotas before waiting for changes in international law enabling it to do so legally. It has imposed export embargoes overriding binding commercial contracts. Congress for its part has rejected tariff agreements reached by negotiators representing the executive branch of government. In general, the U.S. Government has imposed its will on foreign countries while complaining bitterly and loudly when other countries move to protect themselves from U.S. actions.

Europe, Japan and Third World countries have tended more to work within the behavioral constraints imposed by existing world economic institutions, whereas the United States has been quite willing to unilaterally abrogate their rules. Within the United Nations and its agencies, Third World statements on the

New International Economic Order have concentrated on moral principles and on the inequities of existing world income distribution rather than translating these principles into the fine print of binding international agreements. One reason for Third World frustration is the refusal by America, West Germany, England and other industrial nations even to discuss the most vital issues at hand. The United States in particular has fully mastered the axiom that control over the agenda of meetings and conferences represents control over the substance of their outcome. Strategically, therefore, the first U.S. objective in any international agreement or organization is to secure the power to block or veto any proposal with which it disagrees. With such an advantage the nation can develop new plans on an ad hoc basis in response to new situations.

America's superior tactical position gives a somewhat tentative nature to the prospective New International Economic Order. Many scenarios still remain possible. For instance, OPEC's emergence has thrown Europe, Japan and oil-importing Third World countries into payments-deficit status, rendering them dependent either on OPEC to recycle its petrodollars, or on the United States to take the lead in creating a new form of international credit. Both the Middle East and the United States may therefore seek to draw Europe and Third World countries into their respective orbits, by specifying the terms on which international credit—hence oil and food—will be provided. OPEC may refuse to accept fiat-dollar credit or its New-SDR derivative. It may elect to keep its oil in the ground rather than to give it up for fiat-dollar credits that finance U.S. world policies rather than its own. OPEC officials may explain that existing Third World debts to the United States and other industrial nations are the legacy of projects that have had countereffective results (e.g., food aid which has led to increased agricultural dependency, or export infrastructures that have contributed to an oversupply of world raw materials, hence deteriorating terms of trade and reduced ability to repay the Third World's international debt). The benefits of Third World investments financed by this foreign-aid debt have accrued largely to the aid-lending countries themselves. Hence, OPEC may conclude that the international debt problem is one for the Third World and industrial nations to settle among themselves, and that settlement of this debt issue must be reached before new petrodollar credits can be extended under today's noncreditworthy conditions. Pending such a solution, it can do with its trade surpluses just what America did with its: extend credit conditional upon obtaining ownership over foreign resources and influence over foreign diplomacy.

The New International Economic Order thus may not emerge in the form presently envisioned either by Europe or by Third World countries. The United States may succeed in driving a wedge between Europe, the Near East and Africa, as well as between Japan and the rest of Asia. It may play off the industrial nations against the Third World generally, and within OPEC it may play off Iran against Arabia. What it cannot do is roll back the carpet of time, or the new philosophy of economic development and self-sufficiency that has now achieved a critical momentum of its own.

The Western Alliance may be breaking apart as a consequence of the new regionalist tendencies, but this seems to be a precondition for its members moving onto a higher plane of development. The postwar system of private-sector ownership of Third World resources failed to help these countries achieve a broadly based economic development. It was associated with dictatorial political forms rather than with meaningful democracy, and with growing poverty and dependency rather than an elevation in the quality of life and labor or increased economic self-sufficiency. The greater international equality that had been an ideal of classical laissez faire doctrines did not materialize in practice. Governments are therefore moving to create what was not achieved by private-sector investment and its ancilliary foreign aid system: enhancement of living standards and productive powers for 80 per cent of the world's masses. Even within the industrial nations, Europe and Japan are moving to become free from the sway of American nationalism that has drawn even more financial resources from its industrial allies than from Third World countries.

One development is certain above all others: whether led by socialist governments or monarchies, countries are regulating market forces to serve their own national or regional self-interest. To analyze this phenomenon economics must once again become political economy as it was prior to the 1870s. The interlude played by laissez faire, emanating from England at the time of its industrial revolution and influencing the course of world affairs since 1945, is ending. Its place is being taken by a kind of neomercantilism based on regional self-sufficiency in essentials, and on a highly political focus of economic life and social transformation. Economic forecasters must now look to this political social setting of world trade and investment.

Notes

CHAPTER 2. THE TREASURY-BILL STANDARD VERSUS THE GOLD
STANDARD

1. John V. Deaver, "Deficits, Dollars and Gold," *Business in Brief*, no.
   73 (April 1967). An almost identical statement appeared that same
   week by the Bank of America's Rudolph Petersen—somewhat to
   the embarrassment of the U.S. Treasury, which found such explicit
   crowing to be rubbing salt in Europe's wounds.
2. Valéry Giscard d'Estaing, "The New World Economic Order,"
   speech delivered at the École Polytechnique, October 28, 1975.

CHAPTER 3. THIRD WORLD PROBLEMS

1. Terence McCarthy, "An Age of Scarcity: Oil Is Only the Beginning," *Ramparts*, vol. 12 (May 1974), p. 28.
2. Message from President Eisenhower to Prime Minister Mossadegh,
   June 29, 1953. (Reprinted in Ralph H. Magnus, ed., *Documents on
   the Middle East* [Washington, D.C.: American Enterprise Institute
   for Public Policy Research, 1969], pp. 122–123.)
3. Allan F. Mathews, "World Economy: As the Rich Get Less Rich,"
   letter to *New York Times*, February 22, 1974.
4. Chase Manhattan Bank, *Balance of Payments of the Petroleum Industry*
   (New York: Chase Manhattan Bank, 1966).
5. "The President of Venezuela Responds to the President of the
   United States" (advertisement), *New York Times*, September 23,
   1974.
6. "The Shahanshah's Proposal for a New Oil Pricing System" (advertisement), *New York Times*, November 11, 1974.

CHAPTER 5. THE EVENTS OF 1973

1. "Text of Kissinger's Speech at A.P. Meeting Here on U.S. Relations
   with Europe," *New York Times*, April 24, 1973; "Europeans Welcome Plan for New Atlantic Charter," *New York Times*, April 25,
   1973; "Brandt Is Said to Oppose a 'New Atlantic Charter,'" *New
   York Times*, May 5, 1973.

2. United Nations General Assembly, Sixth Special Session, "Provisional Verbatim Record of the Two Thousand Two Hundred and Eighth Meeting," New York, April 10, 1974 (A/PV. 2208).
3. Terence McCarthy, "An Age of Scarcity: Oil Is Only the Beginning," *Ramparts*, vol. 12 (May 1974), p. 30.
4. "Text of the European Economic Community's Proposal on Relations with U.S.," *New York Times*, September 24, 1973; "Excerpt from Monetary Reform Draft," *New York Times*, September 26, 1973.
5. "Singapore Halts Fuel to U.S. Units. Acts After Arab Threat to Cut Off Supply to Island," *New York Times*, November 15, 1973.
6. James O. Goldsborough, "France, the European Crisis and the Alliance," *Foreign Affairs*, vol. 52 (April 1974), p. 538. "Political Sheath on the Arab Oil Weapon," *New York Times*, November 10, 1973; "French Criticize U.S. Role. Cabinet Aide Asserts 'Brutal' Mideast Crises Put Ability to Keep the Peace in Doubt," *New York Times*, November 13, 1973; "Brandt Criticizes U.S. Policy Methods," *New York Times*, November 14, 1973. See also "French Urge European Defense Step-Up," *New York Times*, November 22, 1973.
7. "Kissinger Asserts U.S.-Soviet Gains Hinge on Mideast. . . . In Year-End Appraisal, He Tells of Disappointment on Ties with Europe," *New York Times*, December 28, 1973.

CHAPTER 6. U.S. TRADE STRATEGY CULMINATES IN EXPORT EMBARGOES

1. "Soviet Purchase of Grain from U.S. May Total Billion," *New York Times*, August 10, 1972, and "Mismanagement of Wheat Sales to Soviet Found. G.A.O. Accuses Agriculture Department of Permitting Costly Export Subsidies," *New York Times*, July 9, 1973. A review of the history of the grain deal may be found in James Trager, *Amber Waves of Grain* (New York, Fields/Dutton, 1973).
2. "After the Fall. Devaluation of Dollar Seen as No Panacea; Many Problems Remain," and "Phase 3 Controls Led to Dollar Devaluation, Many Observers Say," *Wall Street Journal*, February 14, 1973. "Burns Vows End to Devaluations," *New York Times*, February 21, 1973.
3. See, for instance, "$10 Billion in Farm Exports: Reachable by 1980?" *Farm Index*, October 1972.
4. Reuters release: "Montecatini Edison Employee Says Firm in Advanced Talks on Trade Pact with USSR," February 12, 1973; "Soviet Is Seeking a Loan in Europe. Terms Asked for $1 Billion from Banks Called Barely Enough to Cover Costs," *New York Times*, June 23, 1973.
5. "Grain Surpluses Almost Sold Out. U.S. Government to Leave

Business Within 10 Weeks—Free Market Is Due. Readjustments Ahead. Situation Sparked by Sale of Wheat and Soybeans to Soviet Last Summer," *New York Times*, April 24, 1973; Terence McCarthy, "How the U.S. Went Bankrupt," *Ramparts*, June 1973; "Grain Drain: Export Rise Threatens to Empty Farm Bins, Push Food Even Higher," and "Commodities: Tighter Farm Export Reins, Output Boost Urged by Some to Curb Rising Food Prices," *Wall Street Journal*, August 6, 1973.

6. Eliot Janeway, "Utilizing U.S. Agripower," *New York Times*, Op-Ed page, July 16, 1973, as well as his unpublished speech to the New York Society of Security Analysts, September 7, 1975. Another proponent of this attitude was William Schneider, Jr.: *Can We Avert Economic Warfare in Raw Materials: U.S. Agriculture as a Blue Chip* (New York, National Strategy Information Center, 1974). Mr. Schneider envisages "the exercise of economic warfare in agricultural commodities as a routine component of U.S. diplomacy," for such ends as "to influence resource allocation within the Soviet economy" and also as a means of "improving [the U.S.] bargaining position vis-à-vis raw materials suppliers," "extracting military basing rights from otherwise reluctant nations," and "inhibiting alliances hostile to the interests of the United States." (Pp. 34, 37, 39, 43.)

7. "Soybeans and Cottonseed Under Export Embargo," *New York Times*, June 28, 1973; "Impact of Mark Move Weighed. Revaluation of German Mark Seen a Blow for Products Here," *New York Times*, June 30, 1973. "Scrap-Metal Export Controls Imposed; Limited Soybean Shipments Resumed," *New York Times*, July 3, 1973.

8. "Japanese Upset by U.S. Soybean Curbs," *New York Times*, July 7, 1973; "Japan May Back Europe on Trade. Opposition to Liberalizing Terms at GATT Talks Is Hinted by Tokyo Aide," and "From Europe's Viewpoint, Soybean Crisis Has Ended. Commodity Available After 2 Months of Shortages, But Confidence in U.S. as Reliable, Cheap Supplier Is Lacking," *New York Times*, September 4, 1973.

9. "Canceled Orders Vex Grain Trade. Exporters Expressing Fear over Validity of Sales Contracts Overseas," *New York Times*, May 19, 1975.

10. "World Reserve of Grain Is Urged," *New York Times*, September 22, 1974. "International Grain Reserve Aim of U.S. Proposal," *Journal of Commerce*, August 25, 1975.

11. "Butz Says Soviet Grain Ban Will Stay, Despite Crop Report," *Journal of Commerce*, September 5, 1975. "The Smoke from Tulse Hill," *Journal of Commerce*, August 26, 1975; "Judge Rules Grain

Boycott Is Not Protected by the Constitution," *New York Times,* August 28, 1975.

12. "Meany Details Pact on Sales to Russia," *New York Times,* September 11, 1975; "Boycott Seen Changing U.S. Trade Policy," *Journal of Commerce,* September 11, 1975.

13. "Bergland's Plan—A Wheat Cartel?" *New York Times,* February 28, 1977.

14. "U.S. Envoys in Moscow. Grain Purchase Pact Sought with USSR," *Journal of Commerce,* September 11, 1975; "Gatt and the Carriers," *Journal of Commerce,* September 3, 1975; "Tentative US-Soviet Grain Ship Rate Set," *Journal of Commerce,* September 18, 1975.

15. "A Particular Thorn," *Journal of Commerce,* September 18, 1975.

CHAPTER 7. THE OIL WAR TRANSFORMS WORLD DIPLOMACY

1. "Kissinger Asserts U.S.-Soviet Gains Hinge on Mideast. . . . In Year-End Appraisal, He Tells of Disappointment on Ties with Europe," *New York Times,* December 28, 1973.

2. "4 Arab Ministers Confront Common Market Meeting," *New York Times,* December 15, 1973; "Closer U.S.-Allied Consultation Urged by British U.N. Delegate," *New York Times,* January 24, 1974; "French Mission to Arabs Begins," *ibid.*

3. "France Offering Kuwait Arms and Plants for Oil," *New York Times,* January 29, 1974; "Jobert Hints Gain on Saudi Oil Pact," *New York Times,* January 31, 1974.

4. "Oil Parley to Open Today; Limited Results Expected. U.S. Hope for a Code Governing Private Deals Now Thought Unlikely to Come from 2-Day Meeting in Washington," *New York Times,* February 11, 1974.

5. "France Is Joining Oil Talks Warily, Affirms Opposition to U.S. Plan as the Washington Parley Approaches," *New York Times,* February 7, 1974.

6. "Europeans, Setting Stance for Oil Talks, Rebuff U.S.," *New York Times,* February 6, 1974; "France Is Joining Oil Talks Warily," *op.cit.*

7. "French Moves May Spur Tough Response by U.S.," and "French Dispute Criticism by U.S.," *New York Times,* March 7, 1974; "French Question Oil Policy of the Arabs," and "Bonn Plan for Allies to Consult Stirs Little Enthusiasm," *New York Times,* March 23, 1974.

8. "U.S. Cancels Meeting with Europeans," *New York Times,* March 9, 1974; "President Warns European Allies Rift Can Cause U.S. Troop Cut," *New York Times,* March 16, 1974.

9. "U.S.-Bonn Accord on Troops Signed. West Germany Will Pay $2.2 Billion of Costs," *New York Times,* April 26, 1974; "Bonn Bids Europe Give U.S. Access to Policy-Making. Americans Would Be

Asked to Meet Group Preparing Bloc's Decision Papers," *New York Times*, March 21, 1974; "New British Government Pledges Closer U.S. Ties," *New York Times*, March 20, 1974; "Britain Presses Market; Warns of Vote on Quitting," *New York Times*, April 2, 1974; and "French Again Block Plan for Consulting,' *New York Times*, April 3, 1974.

10. "Common Market Seeks U.N. Voice," *New York Times*, June 25, 1974.

11. Geoffrey Barraclough, "Wealth and Power: The Politics of Food and Oil," *New York Review of Books*, vol. 22, no. 13, August 7, 1975.

12. "Kissinger's Talk of Force over Oil Worries Germans," and "Military Men Challenge Mideast 'Force' Strategy," *New York Times*, January 6, 1975. See also "U.S. Avoiding Retraction of Threat of Force," *New York Times*, January 20, 1975.

13. "Peddling Arms in a Persian Market," *Manchester Guardian and Le Monde*, January 19, 1974; "U.S. Role Grows in Arming Saudis," *New York Times*, September 11, 1974; "French Sell Saudi Arabia $800 Million in Weapons," *New York Times*, December 5, 1974; "West Relying More on Weapons Sales to Mideast," *Journal of Commerce*, September 5, 1975; "U.S. Sells Saudis 60 Jet Fighters for $750 Million. Contract on F-5's Includes Pilot Training and Parts—Transfer Prohibited," *New York Times*, January 10, 1975.

14. "Sadat Says Arab Oil Countries Would Ruin Wells If Invaded," and "Shah and Sadat Open Mideast Talks," *New York Times*, January 10, 1975. See also *Oil Fields as Military Objectives: A Feasibility Study*, Committee on Foreign Affairs (House of Representatives), 94th Cong., 1st Sess. (August 21, 1975).

15. Barraclough, *op. cit.*

16. Valéry Giscard d'Estaing, interview in *Le Figaro*, November 12, 1975.

17. "Kissinger Warns West on Its Reds," *New York Times*, April 14, 1976; "Summary of Kissinger Speech to U.S. Ambassadors" [December 1975], *New York Times*, April 7, 1976; "State Dept. Summary of Remarks by Sonnenfeldt" [also in December 1975], *New York Times*, April 6, 1976.

18. "European Socialists Rebuff U.S. on Ties with Reds," *New York Times*, February 5, 1976; "France's Reds Cultivate an Image of Independence from Soviet," *New York Times*, February 10, 1976; "Western Europe Forging a Multinational Politics. Parties Increasingly Cooperate Across the Frontiers, Without Nationalistic Complaints of Foreign Meddling," *New York Times*, February 9, 1976; and "Socialist Support of Israel Waning," *New York Times*, January 27, 1976.

19. "Tindemans Puts the Case for Closer Union," *Manchester Guardian and Le Monde,* January 18, 1976; "U.S. Sees No Place for Communists in West European Governments," *ibid.*

CHAPTER 8. AMERICA'S NEW FINANCIAL STRATEGY

1. Valéry Giscard d'Estaing, address to the Conference on International Economic Cooperation, Paris, December 16, 1975.
2. Alfred Hayes, "The International Monetary System: Retrospect and Prospect," Federal Reserve Bank of New York, *Monthly Review,* December 1974, p. 289. See also the statements of IMF head Mr. Witteveen quoted in "IMF Head Finds a Monetary 'Gap.' Says Ease of Global Credit Brings Inflation Threat," *New York Times,* May 15, 1974.
3. "Excerpt from Monetary Reform Draft," *New York Times,* September 26, 1973. See also "Text of the European Economic Community's Proposal on Relations with U.S.," *New York Times,* September 24, 1973.
4. "Oil Fund Backed at Bank Parley," *New York Times,* November 23, 1974; "U.S. Opposes Renewal of Special Facility for IMF Oil Loans, Treasury Aide Says," *Wall Street Journal,* January 7, 1975; and "UK Official Says Enlarged Oil Facility Under IMF 'Urgent,' " *Journal of Commerce,* January 14, 1975. See also "Europeans Agree on a Plan to Invest Surplus Oil Funds," *New York Times,* January 8, 1975.
5. Hayes, *op. cit.,* p. 289.
6. "Petrodollar Pile-Up, and How to Invest It," *New York Times,* November 11, 1974. A good review of such proposals can be found in Geoffrey Barraclough,"Wealth and Power: The Politics of Food and Oil," *New York Review of Books,* vol. 22, no. 13, August 7, 1975, p. 27 (quoting George Ball's speech before the Trilateral Commission, The Metropolitan Club, Washington, D.C., December 8, 1974, pp. 8-9, and also American Enterprise Institute, *Dialogue on World Oil* [1975], p. 88).
7. Jacques Kosciusko–Morizet, French Ambassador to the United States, address before the Los Angeles World Affairs Council, March 11, 1975.
8. "Conflict over Gold, and How to Resolve It," *New York Times,* June 8, 1974. An early proposal along these lines was made in a 1972 report by Dr. Danielian for the International Economic Policy Association entitled *The United States Balance of Payments: From Crisis to Controversy* (Washington, D.C. 1972), defended by Secretary Shultz at the September 1972 IMF meeting, and by the 1973 *Economic Report of the President* (pp. 124–25).
9. National Advisory Council on International Monetary and Finan-

cial Policies, *Annual Report to the President and to Congress, July 1, 1973–June 30, 1974* (Washington, D.C., 1975), p. 40.

10. "Accord Set on Use of Monetary Gold. 'Group of 10' to Allow Pledging Holdings at Negotiated Price as Loan Collateral," *New York Times,* June 13, 1974.

11. "Treasury Gold Sale Termed a Success," *Journal of Commerce,* July 2, 1975.

12. "Agreement on Gold Is Reached," *New York Times,* September 1, 1975.

13. "Monetary Accord Seen as Unlikely,' *New York Times,* May 24, 1975.

14. "Slow-to-Emerge U.S. Oil Plan, Shaped by Kissinger, Gathers Force," *New York Times,* November 20, 1974; "Treasury Weighs Saudi Investing. Talks with Nation Cited on Possible Purchases of Special Issues," *New York Times,* June 19, 1974; "Saudi Reply to Simon Likely Soon," *Journal of Commerce,* July 31, 1974; "Simon Urges Arab Switch to Longer-Term Holdings," *New York Times,* June 20, 1974; "International Banks Shun Oil Dollars," *Journal of Commerce,* September 12, 1974.

15. M. T. Mehdi, "Of Oil and Food, of Goose and Gander,' *New York Times,* October 4, 1974. (Mr. Mehdi is Secretary General of the Action Committee on American–Arab Relations.)

CHAPTER 9. CLOSING THE OPEN DOOR TO WORLD INVESTMENT

1. "Saudi Says Oil-Price Cut Must Be a Joint Arab Step," *New York Times,* January 29, 1974; "Saudi Arabia Sets 5–Year Plan with Investment of $140 Billion," *New York Times,* May 19, 1975.

2. "Refining the Cruder Facts of Life" [interview with the Shah of Iran], *Manchester Guardian and Le Monde,* January 19, 1974; "France, Iran Enter Agreements Valued at $6 Billion," *Journal of Commerce,* December 24, 1974.

3. "Should U.S. Curb Investing by Foreigners?" *New York Times,* April 7, 1975; "France Gives Iran Stake in Uranium," *New York Times,* January 4, 1975.

4. Gerald A. Pollack, "The Economic Consequences of the Energy Crisis," *Foreign Affairs,* vol. 52 (April 1974), pp. 461–462; Geoffrey Barraclough, "Wealth and Power: The Politics of Food and Oil," *New York Review of Books,* vol. 22, no. 13, August 7, 1975, p. 27.

5. Khodadad Farmanfarmaian, Chairman of the Development Industrial Bank of Iran; Armin Gutowski, Professor at the University of Frankfurt am Main and an adviser to the West German Economic Ministry; Saburo Okita, President of the Overseas Economic Cooperation Fund and Chairman of the Japan Economic Research Center, Tokyo; Robert Roosa, former Under Secretary of the Treasury

for Monetary Affairs; and Carroll L. Wilson, M.I.T. professor, 'How Can the World Afford OPEC Oil?" *Foreign Affairs,* vol. 53 (January 1975), pp. 203, 217–219, 221.

6. William Safire, "Oil Doves and Hawks," *New York Times,* January 6, 1975.

7. Anatol Balbach, "Foreign Investment in the United States—A Danger to Our Welfare and Sovereignty?" in Federal Reserve Bank of St. Louis, *Review,* vol. 55 (October 1973), p. 11; "Concern on Oil-Money Flow Causes Scrutiny of Controls. Buffers Sought for Sensitive Industries," *New York Times,* December 26, 1974; "Oil Dollar Curbs Opposed. Arab State in the U.S. Seen Deterring Oil Ban," *Journal of Commerce,* January 14, 1975; "Should U.S. Curb Investing by Foreigners?" *New York Times,* April 7, 1975.

8. "Camel Money," Washington *Post,* Janaury 21, 1974; "McCloy Testifies He Took the Oil Companies' Case on International Talks to President Kennedy," *New York Times,* February 7, 1974.

9. "Oil Dollar Curbs Opposed. Arab Stake in the U.S. Seen Deterring Oil Ban," *Journal of Commerce,* January 14, 1975; "Petroleum Price Rises Mean All Bets Are Off on Economies of the West," *Wall Street Journal,* January 9, 1974; "Late Ticker," New York *Post,* February 21, 1975; "Some of Arab Oil Wealth Is Flowing West, But Only a Limited Amount Has Surfaced as Investments," *New York Times,* April 25, 1974; "U.S. Companies Oppose Restrictions on Investments by Foreigners," *New York Times,* March 6, 1975; "U.S. Warned on Buying Costly Oil," *Journal of Commerce,* January 21, 1975.

10. "Before Making Big Investments, Oil Nation Investors Seen Agreeing to Consult U.S.," *Journal of Commerce,* March 19, 1975; "Office to Monitor Investors Planned," *Journal of Commerce,* March 10, 1975.

11. "Treasury Official Says No Arab Takeovers of U.S. Firms Likely," *Journal of Commerce,* January 22, 1975.

12. Eliot Janeway, "Globaloney in a New Key," *Saturday Review,* February 8, 1975.

13. "Multinational Firms, Under Fire All Over, Face a Changed Future," *Wall Street Journal,* December 3, 1975.

CHAPTER 10. THE ENDING OF U.S. FOREIGN AID

1. National Advisory Council on International Monetary and Financial Policies, *Annual Report to the President and to the Congress,* July 1, 1972–June 30, 1973 (Washington, D.C., 1974), p. 15.

2. *Ibid.,* pp 18–19.

3. *Ibid.,* p. 16, and "U.S. Seen Lagging in Asian Bank Aid," *New York*

Times, October 28, 1974; "New Aid Measure Killed in House," *New York Times,* January 25, 1975.

4. "Low-Cost Loans to Poor Lands Backed," *New York Times,* September 26, 1973. See also "Shultz Scores S.D.R. Tie to Poor-Land Aid. Treasury Secretary Confronts Developing Nations Head-on," *New York Times,* September 28, 1973.

5. "Petrodollar Pile-Up, and How to Invest It," *New York Times,* November 11, 1974.

6. "A Case Study in Disillusion: U.S. Aid Effort in India," *New York Times,* June 25, 1974. "New Delhi Is Blamed for the Worsening Food Crisis," *New York Times,* September 13, 1974; Increases in Aid to India in Doubt. Western Diplomats There See Atom Test Raising Questions for Future," *New York Times,* May 21, 1975.

7. The National Advisory Council on International Monetary and Financial Policies, *Annual Report to the President and to the Congress: July 1, 1974–June 30, 1975.* (Washington, D.C., 1975), p. 29.

8. "Turkish Aides Dismayed by House Vote to Halt Aid," *New York Times,* September 26, 1974; "U.S. Threat of Military Aid Cutoff to Turkey May Undermine NATO," *Journal of Commerce,* September 26, 1974.

9. "U.S. Blocks Rights Data on Nations Getting Arms," *New York Times,* November 19, 1975.

10. "Kissinger at U.N. Tells Poor Lands to Avoid Threats. Also Advises Producers Not to Join Together on Model of the Oil Countries," *New York Times,* April 16, 1974; "Now It's 'Food for Politics,' " *New York Times,* November 12, 1974; "Ford Seeks Israel Link to Viet Aid," *New York Post,* January 30, 1975; "Details on Saigon's Status Delaying Food Aid Decision," *New York Times,* January 21, 1975; "Hatfield Says Food Aid Should Be Humanitarian, Not Political," *New York Times,* February 19, 1975.

11. "U.S. to Boycott U.N. Fund to Aid Countries in Crisis. Decision Is Expected to Be Regarded as Retaliation for Controversial Majority Actions Taken at Assembly Session," *New York Times,* December 18, 1974.

Chapter 11. America's Steel Quotas Herald a New
Protectionism

1. National Advisory Council on International Monetary and Financial Policies, *Annual Report to the President and to the Congress: July 1, 1974–June 30, 1975.* (Washington, D.C., 1975), p. 49.

2. "Steel Quota Plan of U.S. Under Fire," *Journal of Commerce,* April 19, 1976; "E.C. Will Not Limit Steel Exports to U.S., Despite Quotas

Threat," *Journal of Commerce,* May 19, 1976; "Ford Steel Plan Barred by E.E.C.," *New York Times,* May 19, 1976; "World Trade: Isn't Any Action Now to Control Imports of Specialty Steel Just a Little Late?" *Journal of Commerce,* May 20, 1976; "Steel Firms' Operations Near Capacity," *Journal of Commerce,* May 24, 1976; "Specialty Quotas Hotly Disputed," "Japanese May Limit Special Steel Exports," and "Japan to Hold Talks on Trade with U.S., E.C.," *Journal of Commerce,* June 7, 1976; "U.S., Japan Seeking Steel Trade Accord," *Journal of Commerce,* June 8, 1976; "Specialty Steels Will Face Quotas, *New York Times,* June 8, 1976; "Specialty-Steel Import Quotas Cleared by Ford," *Wall Street Journal,* June 8, 1976; "US-Japan Special Steel Pact Seen," *Journal of Commerce,* June 9, 1976; "US-Japan Steel Trade Accord Set," *Journal of Commerce,* June 10, 1976; "Import Quotas Put on Specialty Steels," and "Steel Price Rises Upheld by Inflation Council Study," *New York Times,* June 12, 1976; "Article XIX: Scattering the Shots," editorial, *Journal of Commerce,* October 21, 1976; and "International Steel Code?" *Journal of Commerce,* November 30, 1976.

3. Eleanor M. Hadley, "Specialty Steel Agreement," letter to the *New York Times,* August 11, 1976.

4. "E.C. Warns Japan on Trade Gap," *Journal of Commerce,* July 15, 1976.

5. "French-Belgian Steel Link Is Set to Counter Germans," *New York Times,* July 24, 1976.

6. "Japanese Will Notify E.C. Today of Decision to Cut Steel Exports," *Journal of Commerce,* November 25, 1976; "Japan Calls E.C.'s Bluff on Demands," *Journal of Commerce,* November 29, 1976; "International Steel Code?" *Journal of Commerce,* November 30, 1976; "Ford Urged to End European-Japanese Steel Pact," *New York Times,* December 10, 1976.

7. "Japan Firms Won't Curtail U.S. TV Sales," *Journal of Commerce,* September 29, 1976.

CHAPTER 12. THE ENDING OF LAISSEZ FAIRE

1. Alvin H. Hansen, *America's Role in the World Economy* (New York, Norton, 1946), pp. 99–100.

2. "U.S. Briefs the Latins on Trade Bill," *New York Times,* January 15, 1975.

3. "U.S. Firms Protest New Trade Preferences," *Journal of Commerce,* March 5, 1976.

4. "U.S. to Urge Bank for Poor Nations. International Agency Would Attract Private Funds to Produce Raw Materials," *New York Times,* April 16, 1976; "Excerpts from Kissinger Address to U.S. Conference on Trade and Development," *New York Times,* May 1976;

"Kissinger Offers Plan to Fight World Poverty," and "Under Kissinger Plan, Resources Bank Would Act as Insurance Pool," *Journal of Commerce*, May 7, 1976. See also "Dialogue's Future Tied to Nairobi," *Journal of Commerce*, May 6, 1976.

5. "Bonn Modifies Position on 3rd World Demands," *Journal of Commerce*, May 26, 1976; "Bonn Shifts on Third-World Pricing Aid," *New York Times*, May 26, 1976; "Poor Nations United, Rich at Odds at Trade Conference," Washington *Post*, March 28, 1976; "Rich Lands Split at Africa Talks," *New York Times*, May 28, 1976; "Nations to Seek to Iron Out Differences," *Journal of Commerce*, May 28, 1976; and "UNCTAD IV: Substance or Symbol?" *The Economist*, May 29, 1976; "3d World Accepts Compromise on Trade; U.S. Plan Is Rejected," *New York Times*, June 1, 1976; "Basic Disagreement at UNCTAD Meeting Last Month Came as No Surprise," *Journal of Commerce*, June 3, 1976.

6. "More Than He Can Chew?" *Journal of Commerce* editorial, May 30, 1976.

7. "Zaire to Mexico," *Journal of Commerce* editorial, March 2, 1977.

8. "Carter Rejects Shoe Tariff Rises; Asks Taiwan, South Korea Pacts," *New York Times*, April 2, 1977.

9. "Japan May Control Color TV Exports," *New York Times*, April 8, 1977.

10. "Court Orders Duties on Electronic Goods Coming from Japan," *New York Times*, April 13, 1977, and "Added Duties on Japanese Goods Set," *Journal of Commerce*, April 13, 1977.

11. "Foreign Car Tax Rebate: New Problem," *Journal of Commerce*, April 25, 1977, "Auto Rebate Plan Faces Big Hurdles. Will It Violate Rules of Gatt?" *Journal of Commerce*, April 27, 1977, "U.S. Dilemma: Rebates for Fuel-Saving Foreign Cars," *New York Times*, April 30, 1977, and Evans and Novak, "Detroit in the Scales," New York *Post*, April 30, 1977.

12. "Italy Moves to Protect Montedison," *Journal of Commerce*, April 25, 1977.

CHAPTER 13. BASIC OBJECTIVES

1. Valéry Giscard d'Estaing, "A New International Economic Order." address in N'sele, Zaire, August 8, 1975.

CHAPTER 14. WORLD FINANCIAL REFORM

1. Terence McCarthy, "An Age of Scarcity: Oil Is Only the Beginning," *Ramparts*, vol. 12 (May 1974), pp. 29–30, quoting H. Robert Heller, *International Trade* (Englewood Cliffs, N.J., Prentice-Hall, 1971), p. 5.

2. "Currency of Iran Linked to S.D.R.'s Instead of Dollar," *New York Times*, February 13, 1975; "OPEC to Restudy Prices If Dollar Sags," *New York Times*, March 8, 1975; "Saudis End Link to Dollar; Oil Price Rise May Result," *New York Times*, March 15, 1975; "Mideast Ties to S.D.R. Could Raise Oil Prices," *New York Times*, March 25, 1975; "OPEC Maps End to Dollar Link with Oil Prices," *Journal of Commerce*, May 23, 1975; "OPEC Continues Freeze on Oil Prices," *New York Times*, June 13, 1975; and "Oil Nations to Hike Prices Again Oct. 1. Switch to SDR Link Proposed," *Journal of Commerce*, June 12, 1975.

3. "Officials Weigh Future of EEC Unit of Account," *Journal of Commerce*, February 26, 1975.

4. "The Retreat from the Dollar," *Journal of Commerce*, May 23, 1975.

5. "The Shahanshah's Proposal for a New Oil Pricing System" (advertisement), *New York Times*, November 11, 1974; and "No Economic Basis Foreseen for Oil Price Boosts by OPEC," *Journal of Commerce*, May 23, 1975.

6. Jean-Pierre Fourcade, interview in *Les Echos*, January 28, 1975.

7. "Poor Lands Seen Swamped by Debt," *New York Times*, December 18, 1975; United Nations General Assembly, Sixth Special Session, "Provisional Verbatim Record of the Two Thousand Two Hundred and Eighth Meeting," New York, April 10, 1974 (A/PV. 2208), p. 41.

CHAPTER 15. NEW AIMS OF WORLD TRADE

1. Valéry Giscard d'Estaing, interview in *Le Figaro*, November 12, 1975.

2. Mahbub ul Haq, Opening Statement to the Third World Forum in Karachi, Pakistan, January 5, 1975. Reprinted from Society for International Development, *International Development Review*, 1975 (no. 1), p. 8, and "The Shahanshah's Proposal for a New Oil Pricing System" (advertisement), *New York Times*, November 11, 1974.

3. René Servoise, "New Third World Strategy: Solidarity, Not Charity," *Manchester Guardian and Le Monde*, May 23, 1976.

4. Council of Economic Advisers, *Economic Report of the President, transmitted to the Congress: January 1976* (Washington, D.C., 1976), pp. 151–152.

5. "U.S. Firms Protest New Trade Preferences," *Journal of Commerce*, March 5, 1976.

6. Michel Jobert, speech before the Sixth Special Session of the U.N. General Assembly, April 10, 1974.

7. Jean-Pierre Fourcade, address to the IMF and World Bank meetings, September 2, 1975.

8. Jacques Kosciusko-Morizet, address before the Los Angeles World Affairs Council, March 11, 1975; Valéry Giscard d'Estaing, "A New International Economic Order," address in N'sele, Zaire, August 8, 1975.

9. "Copper Exporting Group Is to Convene to Emulate the Oil Producers on Prices," *New York Times*, April 22, 1974.

CHAPTER 16. GOVERNMENT REGULATION OF INTERNATIONAL INVESTMENT

1. "Mideast Nation, Thought to Be Kuwait, Buying Stock in Japan's Nippon Steel," *New York Times*, March 6, 1975.

2. Maurice J. Williams, "The Aid Programs of the OPEC Countries," *Foreign Affairs*, vol. 54 (January 1976), pp. 308–324; "$1 Billion for Poor Lands Is Pledged by Shah of Iran," *New York Times*, February 22, 1974; and "Kuwait to Invest Riches in Arab Channels," *New York Times*, March 7, 1974.

3. "Arabs Vow Money for New Aid Fund," *New York Times*, November 18, 1974; "World Bank to Get $750 Million Loan from Saudi Arabia," *New York Times*, December 18, 1974; "Oil Lands Aid Poor Ones; $5 Billion Allotted in '74," *New York Times*, January 18, 1975; 'Arab Oil Nations Will Aid Others. $80 Million in Compensation for Price Rises Is Set—Service Company Planned," *New York Times*, May 5, 1975; and Richard A. Debs, "Petro-Dollars, LDCs, and International Banks," Federal Reserve Bank of New York, *Monthly Review*, January 1976, quoting an UNCTAD report of October 29, 1975 on "Financial Cooperation Between OPEC and Other Developing Countries."

4. "France Is Seeking Wide Africa Bloc. Former Portuguese Lands May Join Present Group," *New York Times*, March 10, 1975.

5. Valéry Giscard d'Estaing, "A New International Economic Order," address in N'sele, Zaire, August 8, 1975.

6. "French Minister, in Cairo Visit, Stresses Recognition of Israel," and "France in $6 Billion Iran Pacts," *New York Times*, December 24, 1974; Jacques Kosciusko-Morizet, address before the Los Angeles World Affairs Council, March 11, 1975.

7. Peter Seidlitz, "Sudan: Breadbasket for the Arab World?" *Swiss Review of World Affairs*, December 1975; The Economic Intelligence Unit, *Quarterly Economic Review: Sudan*, 1975, passim; Bundesstelle für Aussenhandelsinformation, Market Information: *Sudan—Wirtschaftsstruktur* (BfA No. A/211, July 1974); Karl Lavrencio, "Survey Could Reveal New Fertile Area," *The Times* [London], March 25, 1975.

CHAPTER 17. THE FUTURE OF WAR

1. "Iran Plans Military Cuts Despite Record Budget," *New York Times,*
   February 21, 1977.
2. *Journal of Commerce,* various dates in December 1976.
3. "Canadians Warned on Following U.S. Pattern on Fleet Subsidies,"
   Journal of Commerce, September 10, 1975.
4. "NATO Tank Trap," editorial in *New York Times,* April 9, 1976.
   "Britain Going Ahead with Its Radar Plan. Decide Against Waiting
   for System U.S. Is Planning for NATO," *New York Times,* April 1,
   1977. See also "U.S. and Bonn Gaining on Tank Components,"
   New York Times, March 17, 1977.
5. "Swiss Upset by Loss of Electric Pump Order," *Journal of Commerce,*
   May 14, 1976; and "U.S. Compensation Part of Swiss Deal Un-
   clear," *Journal of Commerce,* June 4, 1976.
6. "Arms Sale to China Opposed," *Journal of Commerce,* April 27, 1976.

CHAPTER 18. SOME IMPLICATIONS OF THE NEW INTERNATIONAL
ECONOMIC ORDER

1. Simon Patten, *The Development of English Thought: A Study in the Economic Interpretation of History* (New York, 1899 [Garland, 1974]), p.
   283.
2. John A. Hobson, *Imperialism: A Study* [1902] (Ann Arbor, University
   of Michigan Press, 1965), pp. 145–149.

Index

NOTE: The following abbreviations are used:
EEC   European Economic Community
Eur   Europe
IMF   International Monetary Fund
NIEO   New International Economic Order
OPEC   Organization of Petroleum-Exporting Countries
Th.W.   Third World countries
Tr-bill std. Treasury-bill standard
WB   World Bank

283

Diplomacy *(cont'd)*
3–4, 7–8; transformation of, 236–41; united Europe, 91
Dollar, alternative to, 1, 67, 178; creation of, 14, 26, 250; decline, 238, 251; devaluations, 50, 53, 59–60, 63, 94; and gold, 11–16, 73, 101–3, 264; grain exports, 71, 73; as key currency, 21–22; "overhang" problem, 100–103, 107, 182, 264–65; regional consolidation, 168, 171; restoration of, 257–59, 264; and SDRs, 179–80; surpluses, 94–97; and Vietnam war cost, 219
Dunlop, John, 75

Eastern Europe, 51, 168
Eastern Hemisphere, 166, 197, 215, 225; break with US, 210; and gold standard, 258;
Echeverría Alvarez, Luis, 201
Ecuador, 148
Egypt, 64, 78, 87; and Eur trade, 80; and foreign political aid, 132; and French projects, 213
Eisenhower, Dwight David, 43–44, 127
Embargoes, 263, 265; agricultural, 59, 62, 72–74; oil, 59, 64–65; raw materials, 221; threat of, 237, 239
Emigration and immigration, 171; of labor, 30, 160, 173, 250
Employment and unemployment; and exports, 237; in Europe, 140; and protectionism, 154–57, 159; in US, 8–9, 15–16, 136–37; and war effect on, 219–20, 235; in world, 134
Energy; Carter program, 156–58; conservation, 88, 97–98; consumption, 46, 88; crisis and Eur/US reaction, 79–84, 86–88, 261; crisis link to financial disorder, 100–101; and Eur dependence, 65;-intensive industry development, 207; oil substitutes, 200; US independence in, 66, 88, 174, 192
England, 19, 39, 114, 157, 174, 188, 232, 248. *See also* Europe; European Economic Community
airborne radar system, 230; air route agreements, 227–29; Callaghan on US policy, 85–86; foreign debt, 182, 259; free trade movement, 34–35, 239–41, 267–68; and monetary reform, 258–59; and North Sea oil, 152, 201; oil industry, 41–43; and oil-loan facility, 99; postwar economics, 8–12, 15, 61; and pound sterling, 21–22, 59–60, 176, 238, 258; Sudan investment, 213; UNCTAD conference, 145, 148, 151, 198–99; WWI debt, 102
Equilibrium; and export prices, 183, 185–86; government imposition of, 202; of international payments, 226; and laissez faire, 185, 187; NIEO definition, 1–2, 169; and Tr-bill std., 26, 31
Eurodollar, 49, 71, 168, 171, 177–78
Europe, 37, 39, 47, 247, 254. *See also* European Economic Community; European Snake; NATO
antagonism toward US policies, 50–54, 61–68, 73, 90, 262; arms production, 230–32; bank development, 18–22; commodity agreements and UNCTAD, 144–47; and communist parties, 90–91, 245–46; defense structure, 55–56, 225; foreign investment controls, 208, 238; gold sale, 105–6; Mediterranean region, 167–68, 221, 223, 244; monetary reform, 60, 62, 177–81, 258–59; in NIEO, 173–74; North Sea oil, 88–89; and oil industry, 44, 46; oil-loan facility, 97–100; Oil War, 59, 63–65; OPEC alliance, 112–13, 118, 232–33; political integration, 61–64, 91–92, 259, 264; postwar economic system, 7–16, 48; protectionism, 157–59, 188; response to Kissinger doctrine, 61–65, 87, 91–92; single voice advantage, 62, 263–64; Th.W. relations, 65–68, 78–87, 221, 223, 239, 244; Tr-bill std., 94–97, 100–110, 249, 258; US current strategy and, 257–58, 260–65; US import quotas, 156–57; US military occupation of, 52–54, 80, 85, 87, 255; and US/Soviet détente, 55–56, 62–63, 81, 89; war debt, 216–19
European Economic Community (EEC), 212, 245. *See also* Europe
currency fluctuations and monetary policy, 60, 63–64, 67, 95–96, 177, 179, 258–59; foreign policy, 62–64, 66, 91–92; formation of, 51–52; grain markets, 73; Japanese exports to, 140–42; Mideast economic alliance, 66–67, 82–84; New

European Economic Community
(*cont'd*)
Atlantic Charter rejected, 61–62;
political union, 61–64, 66,
91–92, 259, 264; Th.W. trade
and aid, 67–68, 80–81, 212–13;
US energy proposal opposed,
80–83; and US import quotas,
138–40; US strategy re, 257,
260; at UNCTAD conference,
150–51; and VAT, 155
European Selling Price, 157
European Snake, 60, 67, 79, 92, 106,
168, 171; EEC unit of account,
179–81; threat to, 95–96; tied to
gold, 166, 173
Executive branch, 240–41; and
Cabinet importance, 241–42
Exploitation, economic; North-South
potential for, 168–69; of Th.W.,
40–47, 204; by US, 171, 246–47
Export-Import Bank, 71, 212
Exports. *See also* Protectionism;
Tariffs; World trade
commercial vs. government, 123;
commodity agreements, 143–44;
and dollar oversupply, 94–95;
Eur/OPEC trade, 66–68; floating
currency effect on, 60–61;
foreign aid credits, 121–22; and
oil prices, 88–89; postwar
markets, 8–9, 11–16, 22–25, 237;
Th.W. emphasis, 36–38, 46–47,
242–43; Th.W. independence,
166, 209–10; US contract
abrogation, 73–74, 77; US
embargoes, 62, 135, 237; US
future, 226–35, 237; US grain,
70–76; US quotas, 135, 154–57
Expropriation, 118–19

Faisal, King of Saudi Arabia, 82
Federal Reserve System, 20, 22, 116;
and gold removal, 25; international
credit, 152–53
Fiat Motor Company, 208
Finance, international. *See also*
Monetary system; Treasury-bill
standard
instability, 94–97; in NIEO,
251–52, 257–60, 263; post-Oil
War, 97–100; reform, 171, 174,
176–84; US domination of,
152–53, 167, 243
Finland, 134
Fiscal policy, 25
Floating currency system, 59–61,
95–96, 176, 178, 251
Food and Agriculture Organization
(FAO), 214

Food resources and production. *See
also* Grain trade and production;
United States, agricultural policies
aid to India, 129–30; IMF loan
fund, 99–100; regional
consolidation and, 167; Russian
grain deal, 70–72, 75; in Sudan,
213–15; Th.W. lack of, 36,
39–40, 47, 63; US embargoes,
59, 62, 72–74; US exports, 50,
62, 69–70, 121–23, 135; US
foreign aid, 130, 133, 135; wheat
agreement, 76–77
Ford, Gerald, 75, 193
Ford administration, 132–33, 135–36,
139–41; energy independence cost,
249; trade legislation against
OPEC, 145, 148
Foreign Assistance Act, 131–32
Foreign debt. *See* Debt payments,
international
Foreign Investment Study Act, 116
Foreign ownership. *See also*
Multinational firms
in Eur, 52; by OPEC, 113–18,
207–8, 238, 264; in Th.W.,
46–49, 246–47
Foreign policy, 240–42, 245; EEC,
62–64, 66, 91–92, US, 265
Fourcade, Jean-Pierre, 180, 196
France, 19, 52, 174, 185, 221, 232,
248, 259. *See also* Europe;
European Economic Community
call for Eurocurrency, 180–81;
communist party of, 91, 93, 233;
and Eur autonomy, 84–86,
89–90; gold revaluation, 104;
and NATO, 52, 85; and NIEO,
166; nuclear exports, 233; oil
cartel, 41–42; OPEC alliance, 80,
82–84, 86, 109, 111, 113, 195,
212–13; postwar economic
system, 8, 10–11; stable
exchange rates, 106; steel cartel,
140; at UNCTAD conference,
151, 199; US finance attacked,
100–101; and US import quotas,
157; and world minerals
agreements, 202; WWI debt, 102
Franco, Francisco, 92
Free market mechanisms, 153, 170,
188; end of, 255–56
Free trade principle, 9–10, 12, 34,
245. *See also* Laissez faire
economics
history of, 230–43; pressures
against, 134–42; US postwar
policies, 14, 69; and US
protectionism, 154–59, 210;
Vietnam war effect on, 50

Third World *(cont'd)*
206–15, 238, 249; domestic
policies, 242–43; Eur alliance,
3–4, 65–68, 78, 89–92; EEC
compensatory financing, 196;
foreign debt, 153, 165, 182–83,
195, 259, 266; inflation and, 63;
intergovernmental agreements,
199–202; and IMF, 107; and
IRB, 149–50; and multinationals,
120, 127, 204–6; and NIEO, 1–3,
165–66, 174, 265–67; and oil
price, 97, 100, 109; OPEC aid,
128–29, 197, 210–15; and
postindustrial society, 187–88;
postwar economics, 14–15, 134;
regional consolidation, 167–68,
195–98; replacement cost of
resources, 190–92; and statism,
242–45; terms of trade, 1–2,
54–55, improved, 1, 167,
185–91, 196–97, 248–50; and
Tr-bill std., 22, 32;
underdevelopment causes,
34–47, 242–43; UNCTAD
conference, 143–53; US foreign
aid, 103, 122–23, 130–33, 135;
US military involvement, 225;
US and monetary reform,
259–60; US trade policies,
48–49, 56, 73, 135, 257, 260–65;
US-Soviet détente and, 62–63
Tin, 197, 200
Tindemans report, 62, 91–92, 259
Trade Act of 1974, 135–36, 138,
154–55, 157
Trade Policy Review Group, 148
Treasury-bill standard, 17. *See also*
Gold
and balance of payments, 3,
30–32, 109, 236–37;
depreciation, 237; effect of Cold
War on, 53–55; emergence of,
22–25; Eur break from, 78–79;
foreign acceptance of, 25–33;
foreign aid and, 127; foreign
debt, 20n, tables, 26–28; vs. gold
standard, 17, 31, 258, 263;
independence from, 166, 174,
251–52; and OPEC, 98, 108–9,
238, 249; problems and
maintenance of, 94–95, 100–103,
237; replacement of, 176, 178,
254; restoration of, 257–59; and
WB, 128
Trudeau, Pierre, 76
Tucker, Robert, 87
Turkey, 30, 74, 92, 95, 223; military
aid to, 121, 130–31

United Arab Emirates, 111, 206, 226
United Kingdom. *See* England
United Nations, 63, 82, 132, 265–66;
EEC and, 86; "good conduct"
code, 204; impotence of, 107; and
intergovernmental trade
agreements, 195–96, 198; Middle
East debate, 91; Relief and
Rehabilitation Admin., 13; Th.W.
dominance of, 133; Trade and
Development conference, 145–53,
204
United States. *See also* Multinational
firms; US-Soviet détente
agricultural trade policy, 8, 12;
abrogation of contracts, 73–74,
77, 135; embargoes, 59, 62,
72–74, 77; vis-à-vis EEC, 52,
135; food price rise, 70–72,
75–76; price supports and
protectionism, 14, 69; with
Soviets, 55, 62, 60–78, 237, 251;
surpluses, 50, 69–70, 123,
135
Agriculture Department, 71, 74
air route agreements, 227–29
arms industry, 222, 226–27;
aircraft production, 227, 230–31,
233, 250; economic implications
of, 232–235, 238; NATO
competition, 230–31
balance of payments; and arms
sales, 226, 233–34; deficits,
14–17, 22–34, 48–50, 52–54,
251; and dollar devaluation,
59–61; EEC monetary reform,
64; and foreign aid, 123–25,
247; and inflation, 134–35; and
IDLIs, 125–28; multilateral
loans, 123–29; and OPEC, 251,
258; Soviet grain deal and,
70–72; surpluses, 22, 95, 98,
176, 251–52; WB contribution
to, 126
capital markets, 95, 127
Cold War, 22, 49–51, 53–54, 123,
219, 248, 261–62
Commerce Department, 116
and communism, 48, 50–51, 145
Congress, 13, 224, 230; foreign aid
opposition, 122, 129–33; and
gold sale, 104; ITO rejected,
143–44, 151; and Johnson
admin., 53; military
involvements, 224, 226, 242; and
NATO support, 85; OPEC
ownership of US firms, 116–17;
protectionism, 14, 50; quotas
and controls, 135, 156, 265; and
Turkey, 92, 131; Senate: